A DETAILED GUIDE TO
SELF-PUBLISHING
with
AMAZON
AND OTHER ONLINE BOOKSELLERS

VOL **1**

Chris McMullen

COPYRIGHT

A Detailed Guide to Self-Publishing with Amazon and Other Online Booksellers, Vol. 1
How to Print-on-Demand with CreateSpace & Make eBooks for Kindle & Other eReaders

Chris McMullen
Cover design by Melissa Stevens: theillustratedauthor.net

Sixth edition published in May, 2014 (for new cover and minor updates)
Fifth edition published in November, 2013 (to add **index** and minor updates)
Fourth edition published in May, 2013 (minor updates)
Third edition published in March, 2013 (to include references to material in Volume 2)
Second edition published in February, 2013 (regarding the discontinued 4-for-3 program)
First edition published in November, 2012
First printing in November, 2012

Books > Education & Reference > Publishing & Books > Authorship
Books > Education & Reference > Writing

ISBN-10: 1480250201
EAN-13: 978-1480250208

CONTENTS

Introduction iv
1 Choosing a Publishing Service
    Print-On-Demand Paperbacks with CreateSpace 6
    eBook Publishing Services and Online eReaders 16
2 Formatting Your Book Interior
    Using Microsoft Word to Make a Paperback Interior 21
    Revising Your Manuscript to Create an eBook 47
3 Creating a Book Cover
    Using Microsoft Word to Make a Paperback Cover 67
    Converting Your Cover into an eBook Thumbnail Image 127
4 Self-Publishing Your Book
    Publishing Your Paperback Book with CreateSpace 132
    Publishing Your eBook Online 180
Resources 209
The Author 212
Catalog 213
Index 219

Volume 2 Contents

5 Editing Your Proof
    Proofing Your Paperback   Proofing Your eBook
6 Creating Author Pages
    Creating an Author Page at Amazon   Creating Your Own Websites
7 Useful Tips about Amazon and Other Booksellers
    Understanding Amazon's Website   Exploring Other Online Booksellers
8 Marketing Strategies
    Low-Cost Marketing Ideas   Other Marketing Options

INTRODUCTION

I have written and self-published over a dozen books with CreateSpace, which is an Amazon company. I write non-fiction books in areas that interest me. Most of my books are math workbooks, as I am very passionate about helping people improve their fluency in fundamental math skills, like arithmetic and algebra. It all started after I had written a pair of volumes on the fourth dimension – another of my passions, and also the topic of several papers that I have written in the field of collider physics – when I discovered, in my search for a publisher, that Amazon had a self-publishing company.

Writing, formatting, and publishing books – the technique of trying to turn ideas into a printed work of art – has evolved into a hobby for me. I wrote this book with the aim of helping many other writers who, like myself, were not entirely satisfied with the traditional publishing industry and were considering the prospects of print-on-demand self-publishing. I have also published some puzzle books, golf books, chess books, and science books. I have learned much about the self-publishing process – many ideas that I wish I had known when I started out. While I can't pass this wisdom onto my former self, I can try to share it with other writers, such as you. This is the spirit with which I have written this book. I sincerely hope that you find much of the information helpful, and I wish you the best of luck with your books! ☺

One of my main goals in writing this book was to provide a wealth of practical information, and also to state the information concisely. I expect that you want to spend more time writing your own book, and less time listening to some other author drone on along some tangent. Thus, I have tried to stick to the point, and I have deleted several paragraphs which didn't actually provide any valuable information. I hope that you appreciate this. Also, I have tried to adopt a friendly, conversational tone, so that, hopefully, you will feel that someone (but not me – that would be creepy) is right there speaking with you, helping you publish your book with confidence.

I have tried to write this book in such a way that it reads well if you read it straight through, yet is also organized so that you can easily find the information that you're looking for if you consult the book as you need it: For example, you will probably want to have this book handy while you are applying any of the step-by-step techniques – like how to submit your book to the publisher or how to modify the content of your manuscript in order to format it as an eBook. The new 18-page index should also come in handy.

Chapter 1

Choosing a Publishing Service

Chapter Overview

1.1 Print-On-Demand Paperbacks with CreateSpace
1.2 eBook Publishing Services and Online eReaders

This chapter answers questions about the following topics, and more:

- ☑ Reasons that millions of paperback books and eBooks are now self-published, and how print-on-demand services and eReaders have revolutionized the publishing industry.
- ☑ The advantages of self-publishing print-on-demand paperbacks with CreateSpace,[1] which is part of the Amazon[1] group of companies.
- ☑ A survey of some self-publishing options – such as color versus black-and-white, binding options, and book sizes.[2]
- ☑ The prospects for getting physical copies of your book to appear on bookshelves in bookstores across America.
- ☑ Popular eReaders – including Kindle, Nook, and Sony – and self-publishing services where you can make an eBook available for them.[3]

---

[1] CreateSpace and Amazon are trademarks of Amazon.com, Inc. These trademarks and brands are the property of their respective owners.
[2] We will explore self-publishing options in much more detail in Chapter 4.
[3] Kindle is a trademark of Amazon.com, Inc. Nook and Barnes & Noble are trademarks of Barnes & Noble Inc. Sony is a registered trademark of Sony Corporation. These trademarks and brands are the property of their respective owners.

1.1 Print-On-Demand Paperbacks with CreateSpace

1.1.1 A Revolutionary Self-Publishing Concept

mazon has made it possible for anyone to self-publish a book and make it available for sale directly from Amazon's website either as a paperback or as an eBook. The paperback option is made possible by CreateSpace, which is part of the Amazon group of companies.[1] CreateSpace is not only an affordable, simple, and high-paying means of selling physical copies of a book on Amazon, but CreateSpace also offers distribution to bookstores, other online booksellers, educators, and libraries. The eBook option at Amazon is made possible by Kindle.[3] Paperback self-publishing is introduced in Sec. 1.1, while eBook self-publishing is introduced in Sec. 1.2.

Each chapter of this book separately addresses the issue of publishing paperback books and eBooks. For paperback publishing, we will focus almost exclusively on CreateSpace, since they offer quick and easy publishing on Amazon and very high royalties, with the option of publishing your book without any fees. For the eBook option, we will often refer to Kindle, but we will also discuss publishing eBooks through other eBook publishing services – such as making your eBook available on the Barnes & Noble Nook and the Sony Reader.[3] Much of the information that is relevant for publishing paperbacks through CreateSpace or eBooks through Kindle would also relate to publishing print-on-demand paperbacks or eBooks with other publishing services.

CreateSpace is a print-on-demand self-publishing service. Whereas a traditional publisher spends months producing and distributing thousands of books and then hopes to sell all of them, CreateSpace manufactures and distributes books as they are sold. If a book published with CreateSpace is purchased at Amazon, the book is manufactured and sent to the customer without any noticeable delay – just as if the book had been sitting on a shelf in Amazon's warehouse.

1.1.2 Advantages of Print-On-Demand and eBook Self-Publishing

The print-on-demand and eBook concepts have revolutionized the self-publishing industry. Following are some reasons that self-publishing has recently become very common:

- ☺ You can publish an eBook for free with Amazon, Barnes & Noble, and other popular online booksellers. You can also self-publish a paperback with CreateSpace for free. Prior to the print-on-demand revolution, a self-published author had to pay for hundreds of books to be manufactured up front, and also pay to distribute them to bookstores. Take a moment to appreciate the benefits of this new technology.

☺ Both self-published print-on-demand paperback books and self-published eBooks can now reach a very wide audience. Since self-published books – both paperbacks and eBooks – can be made available for sale directly on Amazon's and Barnes & Noble's websites, these books are available to millions of customers throughout the world on the most popular online bookstores. CreateSpace also has distribution options for physical bookstores, other online bookstores, educators, and libraries. Prior to Create-Space, it was very challenging for a writer to self-publish a book and persuade major booksellers to purchase their self-published books.

☺ A print-on-demand book reaches the market almost immediately, whereas it takes six months to a year, on average, for a traditionally published book to reach the market; eBooks reach the market in a matter of hours. Print-on-demand paperbacks and eBooks are the quickest ways to publish time-sensitive material, such as a book that relates to current events or ways to deal with the present state of the economy.

☺ It is difficult and time-consuming to get a book published with traditional publishers, but it is very easy to publish a book with CreateSpace or to publish an eBook with a variety of eReaders. Traditional publishing requires purchasing the current copy of *Writer's Market*, writing query letters, sending self-addressed stamped envelopes to several publishers and/or agents, and waiting months to hear a response, which often includes many rejection letters even if the book does get published. More and more authors are choosing to save the hassle, headache, rejection, and lengthy waiting period of the traditional publishing process by instead self-publishing with a print-on-demand publisher and/or publishing an eBook.

☺ You can earn a larger royalty for your book using CreateSpace for paperbacks, and publishing eBooks with Amazon, Barnes & Noble, etc. (see Sec.'s 4.1.4-5 and 4.2.5).

☺ It's possible to self-publish your book using a company that you trust: CreateSpace is an Amazon company, Kindle and Nook are Amazon and Barnes & Noble eReaders.

☺ You can promote your book as little or as much as you would like. You don't have to commit to a great deal of book promotion in order to persuade an editor to publish your book.

☺ Print-on-demand books are available indefinitely. Millions of traditionally published books are available for a couple of years and then become unavailable. This is because thousands of books were manufactured up front, and once those copies were sold, the publisher determined that there was not demand to publish thousands more. A print-on-demand book can be available for sale for decades, earning royalties for a lifetime.

☺ You can self-publish your book just the way you like it. No editor will modify your book. No publisher will require you to make conceptual or physical changes to your book, simply because the publisher feels that those changes would earn the publisher more profit (or worse, if it is just to cater to the whims of an editor). You are in full control of the content and appearance of a self-published book.

☺ It's easy to make revisions, even after your book is published. If you want to make a change to your book, you don't have to create a new edition. Your revisions reach the market very quickly, since your book is printed on demand.

☺ You can skip the struggle of breaking through the publishing industry as a first-time author. If your self-published book is successful, it could help you to publish a second book through a traditional publisher.

☺ If you change your mind, your self-published book can be retired. You are still free to pursue traditional publishing.[4]

☺ Some publishers are actually using CreateSpace and similar print-on-demand services, and are also publishing eBooks. That's right: Publishers are realizing the many benefits of print-on-demand and eBook technology, and are using it themselves. Some publishers actually publish print-on-demand paperbacks and eBooks the same way that you can do it yourself! You can skip the middleman, publish print-on-demand paperbacks and eBooks directly yourself, and thereby earn a larger royalty.

1.1.3 Disadvantages of Print-On-Demand and eBook Self-Publishing

To be fair, there are some disadvantages of self-publishing to consider:

☹ Self-published authors do not receive an advance on their royalties. It's possible to earn thousands of dollars up front if you can get a book published with a traditional publisher. Celebrities and well-known writers can earn huge advances, like a hundred thousand dollars, but that's not typical. A modest advance of five to ten thousand dollars is more likely, yet still challenging to come by for a first-time author. The publisher must really believe in your book to be willing to invest in a large advance.

> ☺ Although you are likely to earn much more money in the near future if your book is traditionally published, print-on-demand and eBook self-publishing can accrue a significant amount of money over the long term. If you could receive a $10,000 advance, but then after one year your book is retired and that's the only money you ever receive, or if you could receive $2,000 a year on average over the course of three decades – which would you prefer? When you self-publish a book, you can potentially continue earning royalties on it for the rest of your life.

☹ Your book is much more likely to appear on the bookshelves at Barnes & Noble and other bookstores if your book is traditionally published. Top bookstores are much more likely to order physical copies of books from established publishers, where books have passed a review process.

---

[4] If you used a free ISBN from CreateSpace, a traditional publisher won't be able to use this same ISBN. Other details relating to the ISBN are discussed in Sec. 4.1.6.

- ☺ You can make your book available to bookstores on CreateSpace's catalog and their website for direct orders from bookstores and online booksellers. Your book may appear on Barnes & Noble's website this way,[5] but it's much more unlikely that physical copies of your book will appear on their bookshelves if you self-publish your book.
- ☹ If you're a celebrity or if you have expertise in the area in which you are writing, this increases your chances of getting published traditionally, along with a healthy advance.
  - ☺ On the other hand, this would also help your self-published book have success. Celebrities already have an audience; and expertise is an asset in nonfiction.
- ☹ Having an editor review your book and accept it for publication may provide a sense of satisfaction or may serve as a status symbol. Anybody can self-publish a book, but only a select group of books are accepted for publication.
- ☹ If you get published traditionally, it may open many wonderful opportunities. If your book is successful, it may make it much easier to get a second book published.
  - ☺ If your self-published book is successful, you will also establish a fan-base, many of whom will be looking for more books. On the other side, if you traditionally publish a book, many fans may buy your second book even if it's self-published. If Stephen King self-published a novel, don't you think it would still be a bestseller?
- ☹ Some features of a physical book are not currently available through CreateSpace. For example, CreateSpace specializes in softcover books. A variety of other options, such as spiral bound books, are readily available through various traditional publishing houses.
- ☹ You need to create your own PDF files for the interior and cover of your book if you self-publish. You can't just send a hard copy to the publisher.
  - ☺ Fortunately, once your book is typed, it's very easy to convert the interior to a PDF file, and it's not so painful to make a nice cover – as explained in Chapters 2-3. Also, if you absolutely don't want to do this yourself, CreateSpace does offer some paid services that can help you out.
- ☹ You have to promote your own work when you self-publish.
  - ☺ However, most publishers also expect authors to promote their own books. You pretty much have to promote your own work no matter what. One difference is that when you self-publish, you don't have to make promises to the editor in an effort to get your book published.

---

[5] If you search for my name at Barnes & Noble's website, you will see that books that were self-published with CreateSpace have, in fact, become available for sale there. But you probably won't find my books in their stores.

1.1.4 Choosing a Print-On-Demand Self-Publishing Service

If you decide to self-publish your book, you must choose your publishing service(s). There are actually many self-publishing options. Self-publishing services usually specialize either in paperback books or eBooks. There are also a few that provide other options, such as hardcover books.

I recommend self-publishing your book both in print and as an eBook. This way, you reach the largest possible audience (and you'll be eligible for **Kindle MatchBook** – see Sec. 4.2.7). There are millions of people who buy physical books, and there are also millions of people who buy eBooks. If you only publish one way or the other, you are missing out on a potentially large market. You will probably earn a much larger royalty on eBooks, percentage-wise, which allows you to price your book lower to, hopefully, sell more copies. Again, we will discuss paperback self-publishing services throughout Sec. 1.1, and return to eBook self-publishing services in Sec. 1.2.

CreateSpace is a very popular self-publishing service for softcover books. I have used CreateSpace for all of my self-published paperbacks (over a dozen titles), and continue to trust them and consider them to be the best self-publishing service. Therefore, in this book I will focus on CreateSpace for softcover self-publishing. In a moment, I will discuss how to find a few alternatives, but first I will list many reasons that I prefer CreateSpace over other services:

- ✓ A book can be self-published with CreateSpace for <u>free</u>. It's reasonable to invest about $35 to self-publish your book with CreateSpace. This is a very low-cost service. (At the same time, CreateSpace also offers a variety of paid services, in case you feel that you really need help with some aspect of the publishing process.)
- ✓ Once your book is self-published with CreateSpace, you can make it available for sale at Amazon for free. In this way, your book reaches a huge market very easily.
- ✓ Since CreateSpace is a print-on-demand publisher, your book is always in stock. Your book shows as 'In Stock' on Amazon's website. Your book is manufactured and shipped whenever it sells. It will still be available for purchase several years from now.
- ✓ CreateSpace is an Amazon company. I first signed up with CreateSpace because I love Amazon, and have been a long-time loyal customer. My trust of Amazon was extended to CreateSpace, and it turned out to be a good decision for me.
- ✓ The royalties are very good. Percentage-wise, it is much higher than traditional publishers pay even well-known, established authors (unless you choose to price your self-published paperback very low).
- ✓ It is very easy to self-publish a book with CreateSpace. You will be guided through the process in Chapters 2-5.
- ✓ Expanded distribution options are available, allowing your book to potentially reach physical bookshelves, sell on other websites, and even sell to libraries.[6]

---

[6] Royalties are somewhat lower for expanded distribution options, as we will see in Sec.'s 4.1.4-5.

- ✓ CreateSpace specializes in quality trade paperback books, with high-quality 60# paper and laminated full-color covers.[7]
- ✓ Authors can buy copies of their own books for very cheap – as little as about $2 per book (see Sec. 4.1.4) for a black-and-white interior, depending on the number of pages.
- ✓ You set the list price of your book. In this way, you actually control the sales price[8] of your book and control your own royalty. We will explore this more in Sec.'s 4.1.4-5.
- ✓ You can choose between white or cream pages and black-and-white or full-color interior. There are numerous trim sizes to choose from. They offer four ISBN options.
- ✓ As an author, you get detailed sales reports. Sales post on your CreateSpace sales report in as little as a few hours after books are purchased on Amazon. You can see which book (if you have multiple titles) sold when, and exactly what your current total of royalties is for the month. There are numerous ways to filter and search through your sales reports, too. I like CreateSpace's sales reports much better than Kindle's.
- ✓ Help is available when you self-publish with CreateSpace. There are many useful help pages on their website, you can ask questions in the CreateSpace community – where other self-published authors can share their experience – and you can even talk directly with a sales representative by email or telephone. They also offer a variety of professional publishing services, if you are willing to pay for it, such as designing a cover, editing a manuscript, or marketing your book.

Even though I'm a big fan of CreateSpace,[9] I still encourage you to explore your publishing options to see which option is the best fit for you. If you want to explore the traditional publishing route, you need to find a copy of the current *Writer's Market*,[10] read a few books on writing book proposals and query letters, and consider finding a literary agent.

---

[7] In the past, I have been told that it's possible to order your book in hardcover, too. However, hardcover books require a hefty up-front fee (couple hundred dollars), cost more to order, and won't be available at Amazon.

[8] The actual selling price of your book may vary. Amazon or another bookseller may choose to offer a discount, and some other booksellers may actually charge more than the list price that you set. Amazon will show the price that you set as the list price, and if they choose to sell it for less it will show that your book is on sale.

[9] Yes, I do love CreateSpace. It worked out very well for me. I'm not sure if I would have published any books, let alone 60 paperback titles, if not for them. Remember, I was not paid or even encouraged by Amazon or CreateSpace in any way to write this book. When I wrote this book, these companies had no idea that I was writing such statements. This is not a sales pitch nor an advertisement – just a simple recommendation from a satisfied customer. I encourage you to explore all of your publishing options.

[10] *Writer's Market* comes out with a new edition every year, and also has different books for different genres (like poetry). You can save a bundle of money if your local library has a copy to borrow. You might also explore free information about query letters, book proposals, and finding publishers and literary agents – using your favorite search engine. Many publishers' websites have information about their manuscript submission policies – many big publishers don't accept unsolicited materials and require you to have an agent, but there are some that welcome proposals straight from the author and have detailed advice about how to prepare the proposal.

However, if you wish to self-publish, you can skip all of that and focus more time on writing your own books.

CreateSpace's major competition is Ingram Spark, which launched in the middle of 2013. Ingram is a major distributor to bookstores. When a self-publisher uses CreateSpace's Expanded Distribution option, one result is that the book is listed in Ingram's catalog. Ingram Spark is the self-publishing version of Lightning Source, which is a major print-on-demand service used by many small publishing companies. You can learn more about Ingram Spark from their website, www.ingramspark.com. One possible advantage is a discount for book-stores, although getting your print-on-demand book in any bookstore is a challenge, and works best when you show up and deliver your books in person (for which this discount option doesn't matter); having a bookstore find your book in the Ingram catalog and stock it is very unlikely. Personally, I remain loyal to Amazon and use CreateSpace because I love the opportunities that Amazon has created for authors. I also like the easy access to Amazon offered by CreateSpace, with a book that's always in stock through print-on-demand. However, Ingram Spark looks like an excellent company comparable to CreateSpace. You should check them both out and decide for yourself. (A third option is Lulu.)

Beware of publishing services (like vanity presses) that require you to invest hundreds, or even thousands, of dollars to publish your book. Some of these are scams intended just to get your money. Others are legitimate – i.e. they will actually publish your book – but probably will not sell enough copies for you to break even. A traditional publisher won't charge you any fee to publish your book, and will sell many, many more copies of your book than those publishing services that demand a large payment. I strongly recommend using either a self-publishing or traditional publishing option that is FREE.

There are self-publishing services that charge you only for the cost of printing your books, and allow you to buy as few books as you would like to have printed. (In the previous paragraph, I was talking about publishing services that require you to pay a few hundred to thousands of dollars, and publish your book for you – i.e. you are paying for the privilege of having your book published. Since it's so easy to do this for free, it's not a privilege that you should have to pay for.) In this case, if the service is legitimate, you will at least have hundreds or thousands of copies of your book to sell to show for your self-publishing investment. However, you then have to distribute and sell your own books. This is the way self-publishing was a couple of decades ago. These days, you can use a print-on-demand self-publishing service and skip the hassle of having to distribute or sell your own books. I highly recommend using a free print-on-demand self-publishing service, and not paying money to have hundreds of copies of your book shipped to your home.

Another option is through R.R. Bowker. This is a major company that sells ISBN numbers and compiles lists of published books. If you want to be your own publisher or if you want to self-publish, you could purchase an ISBN directly through R.R. Bowker. (CreateSpace offers a free ISBN option, yet still allows you to purchase your own ISBN.) R.R. Bowker also allows you to pay a fee to make your manuscript visible to publishers. I don't recommend paying a fee to get your book published, and publishers are so overwhelmed with manuscript proposals that I can't imagine too many editors finding a gem this way and then contacting the author about publishing his/her book. If anything, it seems that a small or unheard-of publisher is more likely to contact you through this method. If you want a publisher to notice you, you need to do the hunting (or get an agent to do it) – the big publishers are not hunting for you unless you happen to be a celebrity or a popular, established author.

If you explore other self-publishing options, I recommend the following:

⊗ Don't pay a fee – since you can get the same (or better) quality and service for free.

⊗ Only send your manuscript to a reputable, established company.

⊗ Independently (i.e. don't trust their own testimonials) verify that many other authors have achieved some measure of success with that publishing service.

For the remainder of this book, I will focus specifically on CreateSpace features when I describe how to self-publish a softcover book. I will also describe a variety of eBook publishing services, such as how to publish on Amazon's Kindle and Barnes & Noble's Nook, when I describe how to self-publish an eBook.

1.1.5 Self-Publishing Options

Let us now discuss some self-publishing options, since knowing what options are available may impact your choice of publishing service. Each of these options will be considered again in more detail in a subsequent chapter. Here is a sample of which options are available with CreateSpace:

✓ CreateSpace specializes in softcover books with glossy or matte covers (the matte finish is a new feature). They also offer both free and paid Kindle conversion services to convert your softcover book into Kindle format (but, as this book will explain, it's fairly simple to do this on your own). In the past, CreateSpace representatives have informed me that hardcover is possible, but there is a significant one-time fee for hardcover books, and you have to distribute and sell your own hardcover books – they won't be printed on demand and sold by Amazon directly like the softcover books. There are no binding options – e.g. you can't have your book spiral bound through CreateSpace. If you are specifically looking for hardcover books, board books, or spiral-bound books, for example, you should explore other publishing services.

✓ The cover will be printed in full color, but you must choose between a black-and-white interior and a full-color interior. Black-and-white costs much less than full-color, which means you make a much greater royalty for the same list price (or you can sell a black-and-white book for less than a full-color book and make the same royalty).

Unfortunately, if your book has 300 pages, and only 1 page needs to be in color, you still have to choose the full-color interior option as if your entire book were in color – i.e. you don't save anything by printing fewer pages in color.

✓ There are 15 trim sizes to choose from, 12 of which are industry-standard trim sizes. The smallest is about the size of a mass market paperback – 5" by 8" – and the largest is the size of a standard sheet of paper – 8.5" by 11".

✓ Black-and-white books can be printed on white or cream paper.

✓ The covers are not only full-color, but are laminated – this makes the book more durable. The books are high-quality, and the printing and binding are professional. The interior is printed on 60# paper, which is thick and sturdy. Many other publishers print paperback books on cheaper paper, which is more likely to tear – this is especially true of puzzle books, workbooks, mass market paperbacks, and international editions. The cheaper paper helps other publishers sell books at very low prices, while the high-quality paper that CreateSpace uses will help your book stand out in quality.

✓ Your book must have a minimum of 24 pages. The maximum varies, depending upon whether you choose black-and-white or full-color, the trim size, and whether the paper is white or cream. A black-and-white book can have as many as 828 pages, and a full-color book can have as many as 500 pages – depending on the trim size.

✓ If your book has at least 100 pages, you can include spine text – which makes your book's title visible on a bookshelf. If your book has less than 130 pages, but more than 100 pages, the spine text has to be very narrow – the publisher requires you to leave room on both sides to allow for printing variations, so that the spine text doesn't wrap around to the front or the back of the cover.

✓ Unfortunately, you can't print on the inside of the front or back cover. You can't put a design there or put useful reference information there, for example. The inside of the front and back cover will just be white. One or more pages will be added to the end of your book: The last page will have a bar code at the bottom (which has an important number if you want to report a manufacturing defect to CreateSpace) and state when and where the book was manufactured; the rest of this page will also be plain white.

✓ You are in complete control of your own manuscript when you self-publish with CreateSpace. No editor will suggest any content changes and nobody will check your spelling or grammar (unless you want to pay for these optional services). They just check that you followed the manuscript submission guidelines. So you are solely responsible for any typos, mistakes, formatting issues, etc.

✓ When you self-publish with CreateSpace, you just need to check a box in order to have your book made available for sale at Amazon (it's free!). You can also have your book made available for purchase through other Expanded Distribution channels (now free – it used to be $25), which allows other booksellers, libraries, and schools to purchase your book directly through the publisher.

✓ You need to make a PDF file for the interior and cover of your book (described in detail in Chapters 2-5). It's very easy to do, but for those who absolutely want to avoid doing this, CreateSpace also offers this as an optional paid service.

✓ CreateSpace offers a variety of paid services to help with manuscript preparation, editing, formatting, and some marketing. There are also free webinars, free marketing ideas, tips and suggestions, and a CreateSpace Community where you can ask experienced authors for help or advice.

1.1.6 Prospects for Getting Your Book in Bookstores

Before we get into eBooks in Sec. 1.2, let's address one more issue that may be on your mind: What are the prospects for getting physical copies of your book to appear on bookshelves in bookstores across America?

CreateSpace is part of the Amazon group of companies, and makes it very easy to make your book available for sale on Amazon's website, but Amazon doesn't have bookstores across the United States like Barnes & Noble or Books-A-Million. However, CreateSpace does offer an Expanded Distribution option (it's now free – it used to be $25). The Expanded Distribution channel allows online booksellers, libraries, schools, and even traditional in-store booksellers to purchase your book directly from the publisher (you also make less royalty through the Expanded Distribution channel than if your book sells directly through Amazon). If you select the Expanded Distribution channel, your title will be included with the catalog that CreateSpace provides to bookstores, libraries, and schools. So it is possible for your book to magically appear on a bookshelf in a bookstore, but it is very unlikely that it will just show up there all by itself.

If you select the Expanded Distribution channel, here is what will likely occur. First, some online booksellers will sell copies of your book on your Amazon listing where customers can purchase New or Used books from other sellers. On the one hand, you make a higher royalty when customers buy your book directly from Amazon than through one of these other sellers. However, customers tend to prefer purchasing directly through Amazon – for one, they are eligible for Super Saver shipping (and any special offers, if there are any) when they buy your book directly from Amazon. Also, when potential buyers see that your book is not only sold by Amazon, but also by other booksellers selling books on Amazon, it makes your book seem more widely distributed – it gives your self-published book more credibility.

Secondly, you may be able to find your book for sale on other websites. For example, there is a very good chance that your book will become available at Barnes & Noble's and Books-A-Million's websites (through Expanded Distribution). You can find most of my titles on these and other websites, and all of my titles have been self-published through CreateSpace. If nothing else, the Expanded Distribution channel will greatly enhance your online reach.

If you would like to see physical copies of your books on bookshelves somewhere, you probably need to take the initiative and visit your local bookstores. Start out with small local bookstores, as they often like to support local authors – their friends, family, and acquaintances are likely to give them a little extra business. Show the owner or manager a copy of your book – or if you have multiple titles, spend some time preparing an appealing catalog of your books on your computer, and print it out – and inquire about the prospects of having your hard work show up on their bookshelves. Booksellers can go to CreateSpace's website (they have a special website for bookstores) and purchase your book directly from the publisher. You can also purchase books at a discount from CreateSpace and try to sell them directly. It is reasonable to get your books to appear on some bookshelves with one of these methods. If you want your books to be distributed to larger bookstores, go to their websites and read the guidelines for publisher submissions. Barnes & Noble, for example, has a detailed set of guidelines for what you need to do in order to have them consider selling your book in their bookstores (online is much easier, in-store is much more challenging). It's probably very unlikely for your self-published book to show up in Barnes & Noble bookstores, but it is reasonable to get your book in smaller bookstores. See Sec. 4.1.7 and Chapter 8 for more information about this. If you really want to see your book sitting in Barnes & Noble, maybe you should give traditional publishing a shot (or become a publisher yourself).

1.2 eBook Publishing Services and Online eReaders

1.2.1 A Brief Introduction to the eBook Concept

There are many different kinds of eReaders. Amazon has the Kindle, Barnes & Noble has Nook, Sony has the Reader, and so on.[11] Each brand of eReader also comes in a variety of models, varying in the size of the screen and whether or not the images are in black-and-white or color. For example, the Kindle Fire is Amazon's color eReader.[12] Even cell phones, tablets, and laptops can serve as eReaders.

There are a few incentives for publishing exclusively on the Kindle, but there is a wider market available if you publish your eBook on a variety of eReaders.[12] Authors and publishers who make their books available for Amazon's Kindle may choose to include their titles with Kindle Select. Inclusion with Kindle Select requires publishing exclusively with Amazon, so if you choose this feature, you can't also publish the same (or similar) eBook with any other

---

[11] Kindle, Kindle Fire, and Amazon are trademarks of Amazon.com, Inc. Nook and Barnes & Noble are trademarks of Barnes & Noble, Inc. Sony is a registered trademark of Sony Corporation. These trademarks and brands are the property of their respective owners.
[12] We will address the choice of where to publish your eBook in Sec. 4.2.1.

eBook services. Two benefits of Kindle Select are: (1) Amazon Prime members may borrow up to one eBook per month for free, and if they borrow your Kindle Select title for free, Amazon pays you a royalty for this; and (2) you may make your eBook available for free (this time, without earning royalties) to all buyers for as many as five days in a three-month period, which can be a useful tool for promoting your book. The main disadvantage of going with Kindle Select is that your book will be available to a wider audience if you publish your eBook on a variety of eReaders. We will return to Kindle Select features, including the pros and cons, in Sec. 4.2.7.

Like print-on-demand self-publishing, the eReaders are revolutionizing the publishing industry. Amazon, Barnes & Noble, Sony, and other eBook publishing companies have successfully marketed their eReaders such that millions of customers now own eReaders, and therefore millions of people are purchasing eBooks for their eReaders. In addition, it is fairly easy for anyone to publish an eBook – you don't have to be a publisher or even a traditionally published author. As a result, millions of eBooks are now being published, including numerous self-published eBooks by first-time authors.

The technology of the eReaders has brought many new possibilities for buying and reading books. If you suddenly want a book now, and you have an eReader, you can literally start reading the book in a few moments. You no longer have to wait until the bookstore opens, and you don't have to wait weeks for a book that was out of stock. Once you get hooked with an eReader, you won't ever buy another bookmark: eReaders automatically mark your place. You can also highlight the eBook, and quickly check the definition of a word without getting up from your chair to get a dictionary. The eReaders have many other features of convenience. Unlike paper, the technology of eReaders encourages books to be written in color: Whereas the cost of printing in color is often prohibitive of publishing a book in color, this is not the case with eBooks (however, pictures add to memory, which is an issue). Another interesting feature of eBooks is that they can also be interactive – like games.

Since no money is spent on paper or print cartridges, eBooks can be potentially be published with a lower list price than a paperback or hardcover book, and the royalties paid to authors are often much higher. Authors who publish their own eBooks can make royalties of up to 70%, whereas the standard royalty for traditionally-published books is about 15%. If you publish a paperback book for $7.99, the same book could be easily sold as an eBook for $2.99, yet the author might easily draw a larger royalty from the lower-priced eBook. Just imagine selling more copies because the cost of the book is less, while also making more money for each book that you sell. This is why millions of eBooks are being published. Similarly, since many eBooks have a list price between 99 cents and $2.99, millions of eBooks are being purchased: For $20, you can buy 7 eBooks or 3 paperbacks – which is the better deal?

Unfortunately, not all eBooks have a low list price. Some traditional publishers have made bestselling books into eBooks, but have held out at the higher price. Some books that have sold millions of copies for $9.99 in the bookstore are also selling for $9.99 as eBooks.

These publishers are drawing a royalty of up to 70% for their eBooks – while they make much less profit if they sell the paperback book for the same price – and choosing not to share one penny with the reader of the eBook edition by reducing its cost. I've been disappointed with the eBooks by a few of my favorite authors – that the publisher didn't choose to discount the eBook compared to the price of the paperback (and, usually, the big-name publisher's eBook has many formatting errors, which the paperback lacks). When the publisher doesn't discount the eBook, I buy the paperback book instead.

However, there are thousands of good, low-priced eBooks. Most authors and publishers do pass the savings onto the readers, and they probably sell many more eBooks by doing so. Those few publishers who don't discount their eBooks hopefully don't sell as many eBooks (they certainly don't deserve it – I suggest not supporting this practice).

In general, traditionally published books that are offered as eBooks don't sell for $3.99 or less; they are usually $5.99 and up. Even if the eBook list price is less than the paperback list price, traditional publishers usually don't publish their eBooks too cheap. Many self-published eBooks, on the other hand, sell for 99 cents or $2.99. Many buyers are willing to take a chance on a self-published eBook that interests them simply because the eBook is so affordable. The higher prices of the traditional publishers' eBooks are good for self-published authors. (These are the main trends, presently. There are a few exceptions, both ways – i.e. self-published books with a high list price, and inexpensive eBooks by bestselling authors.)

There is one more important advantage that an eBook offers over a paperback book: Once you sell enough paperback books, some of them will be resold as used books. Authors don't receive royalties for books that are resold. However, when an eBook sells, it won't be resold, cutting into the author's royalties.

1.2.2 A Note on eBook Formatting

The main issue with publishing an eBook is formatting the eBook. If your manuscript consists only of plain text, the formatting will be very, very easy. If you have a lot of rich text formatting – like fancy fonts, headers, footnotes, bullets (•), tabs, WordArt, text effects, textboxes, etc. – in your manuscript, you will have to do some editing in order to make your book format nicely as an eBook. If you have numerous pictures or equations, these will also add to the work that you must do to format your eBook.

Some formatting features that are possible with paperback books are not possible with eBooks. The reason behind this is to give the reader control of things like font style, font color, and font size. The editor of a paperback book decides how large the font will be and which font will be used, whereas the reader of an eBook is given control over these things. Another difference is that there is no such thing as a 'page' in an eBook. Therefore, an eBook does not have a table of contents with page numbers. Instead, a table of contents in an eBook consists of a set of links to click on that take the reader directly to the beginning of each chapter (this is called an active table of contents).

Since the reader may change the font size, the publisher has virtually no control over how much text will appear on the screen at any time. If you're publishing a novel, this isn't as important, but if you're publishing a children's picture book, a puzzle book, or a math workbook, for example, the formatting of the eBook becomes somewhat more complicated. We will discuss how to format your manuscript into a quality eBook in Sec. 2.2.

Another issue with the formatting has to do with the variety of eReaders available. Some customers will have color eReaders, many will have black-and-white eReaders. Some eReaders have a large screen, many have a small screen. You must consider these different options if you want your eBook to appear well for all of your buyers. Additionally, there are a few subtle differences in the way that an eBook will appear on eReaders sold by different companies. Your eBook may look a little different on Kindle than on Nook, for example. If you're publishing flash cards, with the question on one picture and the answer on the next picture, your eBook won't work very well if customers see both pictures on the screen at the same time, for example. Thus, it's important for you to learn what your eBook looks like in every form in which it is available. We will consider these differences in Chapters 2 and 4.

Chapter 2

Formatting Your Book Interior

Chapter Overview

2.1 Using Microsoft Word to Make a Paperback Interior
2.2 Revising Your Manuscript to Create an eBook

This chapter answers questions about the following topics, and more:

- ☑ If you are planning to sell your book as an eBook as well as a paperback book, there are several points that you will want to consider when you format your manuscript.
- ☑ The advantages of using Microsoft Word to format your book interior.
- ☑ Important differences in recent versions of Microsoft Word.
- ☑ Formatting tips, such as page size, font selection, linespacing, headers, page borders, page numbering, margins, footnotes, citations, columns, tables, pictures, equations, and more.
- ☑ Front and back matter, including the title page, copyright page, contents, acknowledgments, introduction, foreword, references, index, biography, and more.
- ☑ How to convert your Microsoft Word document into a PDF file.
- ☑ Why the file for your eBook will be considerably different from the file for your paperback book interior.
- ☑ How to revise the file for your paperback book interior to create an eBook.
- ☑ Formatting pictures and equations for your eBook.
- ☑ How to create an active table of contents using hyperlink bookmarks.

2.1 Using Microsoft Word to Make a Paperback Interior

2.1.1 Advantages of Using Microsoft Word

If you haven't already typed most of your book, I highly recommend using Microsoft Word to prepare your manuscript for convenience and ease of use (Adobe InDesign and Serif Page Plus are professional alternatives). Even if you have already typed much of your manuscript with a different word processor, you can still save it with a .doc extension and then open it with Microsoft Word (or copy and paste the contents into a blank Word document). Advantages of using Microsoft Word to format your book interior include:

- ✓ The more recent editions of Microsoft Word (starting in 2007) have a built-in feature (or a link that will take you to Microsoft Word's website to add the feature for free) to convert your finished manuscript from a Word document to a PDF file. This will be very convenient, since you must first convert your manuscript files – one for the interior and one for the cover – into PDF files in order to self-publish with CreateSpace.
- ✓ Microsoft Word is also highly compatible for making eBooks. Many companies who sell eReaders, such as Amazon, provide many useful tips for publishing your eBook specifically with Microsoft Word. You can also easily convert your Microsoft Word document into HTML or other formats, which may be better-suited for your eBook.
- ✓ This and the next chapter will specifically describe how to use a variety of features of Microsoft Word to format the interior and cover of your book and eBook.
- ✓ Other software that you may use, such as clipart or a more professional PDF conversion program, is very likely to be compatible with Microsoft Word.
- ✓ Microsoft Word has numerous features to help you make a very professional looking book, as will be described in this and the next chapter.

2.1.2 Differences in Recent Versions of Microsoft Word

You will want to note that there are some important differences in the recent versions of Microsoft Word, some of which are described below. I will describe the specifics for how to use Microsoft Word 2010 in this book. Many features are implemented much differently in Microsoft Word 2003, while most features are the same or similar in Microsoft Word 2007.

- ❖ Microsoft Office introduced new file extensions in 2007. The default format for Word documents now includes a .docx extension, which does not work in editions of Microsoft Office from 2003 and earlier. The newer editions of Word (2007 and 2010) can read both types of documents, but the older editions (2003 and earlier) can't open a file with a .docx extension. This is important if you intend to use more than one computer as you type your book, or if you collaborate with a coauthor. If you start writing your book in Word 2007 or 2010 and then try to open your file in Word 2003 on another computer, you won't be able to do it unless you first save it with a .doc extension (by changing the "Save As Type" option to a Word 1997-2003 Document). If your manuscript includes many formatting features that are only available in the 2007 and 2010 editions, it may look considerably different when saved in the old format.

❖ Word 2007 and 2010 include an option to save your file as a PDF file. The first time that you choose this option, Windows may open your internet browser (it will probably ask for your permission first) and take you to Microsoft's website in order to download this free feature. This is very convenient because most self-publishing services, including CreateSpace, require you to submit your manuscript files in PDF format. Earlier editions of Microsoft Word did not have this file conversion option.

❖ Numerous features available with Microsoft Word changed location between 2003 and 2007. There are now several tabs that appear at the top of the program – including File, Home, Insert, Page Layout, Mailings, Review, View, and others (like Format) that are not always present. If you are accustomed to using Word 2003 and suddenly change to Word 2007 or 2010, you will notice this abrupt change, and will need to relearn how to use various features. It's also an issue if someone is helping you use a feature on Microsoft Word (or if you are searching for help online): Make sure that you are getting advice for your version of Word; otherwise, the instructions may not be helpful. **Little has changed from 2010 to 2013.**

❖ There have been numerous changes in the options for drawing and formatting pictures between Word 2003, 2007, and 2010. For example, in Word 2003 you had freedom in the size of the gridlines and could place an object virtually anywhere on the page; in 2007, the grid was simply on or off and just one size; but in 2010, some of the flexibility has been revived. For the most part, the picture formatting options improved a little from 2007 to 2010. However, one noticeable change is the selection pane. In previous versions of Word, you could draw a rectangle with the cursor to select multiple drawing objects, but in Word 2010 you have to instead go into the selection pane and choose them one by one within the pane. The selection pane makes it easier to grab objects that are hiding behind other objects, but also makes it more difficult to grab several objects at once (I wish the old method would work, too).

❖ The equation editor received a major overhaul in 2007. This is important if you plan to type equations or formulas in your book. If so, and you plan to publish your book as an eBook, you should read Sec.'s 2.2.6-7 about formatting equations for an eBook before you spend much time typing them. If you go back and forth between Word 2003 and the newer versions, your equations will get converted going between .doc and .docx formats. In Word 2007, the equations sometimes didn't format properly when converting to PDF, but I haven't observed this problem with Word 2010.

2.1.3 Briefly Explore the Features of Your Version of Microsoft Word

Check out the features of your Word edition. At a minimum, I recommend that you check your file saving options as follows. Open a blank document in Microsoft Word and find where to Save As. If you have 2007 or 2010, you will click on a File tab at the top left of the screen, then select Save As. After selecting Save As, see if Word Document, Word 97-2007 Document, and PDF are three of the many options in the window that pops up. In 2007 and 2010, click the bar next to Save As Type in order to find these options.

It is worth browsing the tabs that appear at the top of the screen in Word 2007 or 2010. This will help you see where most of the formatting options are found, and you might see something of interest when you do this. When you have a Word document open, at the top of the screen you should see a variety of tabs: From left to right, if you have Word 2007 or 2010, you should see File, Home, Insert, Page Layout, References, Mailings, Review, and View (it could be a little different, as some tabs depend upon what features you may have already installed and others only appear when you've selected a relevant item in your document, such as a picture, table, or equation). Click on each tab and take a few moments to browse through the variety of formatting options at your disposal. We will explore many of these features of Word as we describe them in this book. As we describe a feature, I recommend that you open Microsoft Word and try it out.

2.1.4 Choosing the Trim Size

We will focus on how to use Word to format a paperback book throughout Sec. 2.1, then turn our attention to the eBook format in Sec. 2.2. Even if you only plan to make an eBook edition, you will still want to read this section (i.e. Sec. 2.1) first, as many of the features of Word will be described in Sec. 2.1 (and not be repeated in Sec. 2.2). If you do plan to publish an eBook edition, you may find it useful to read both Sec.'s 2.1 and 2.2 before you finish writing your book. In Sec. 2.2, when we consider how to convert the paperback manuscript into an eBook, we will see that a few features of Word – like bullets and page headers – will not be in your eBook edition, and a few features – like equations, textboxes, and pictures – complicate the conversion process. You may wish to be aware of these eBook-conversion issues (again, discussed in Sec. 2.2) before you type your manuscript.

We will now discuss how to format your manuscript in Microsoft Word 2010 with a paperback version of your book in mind. The first thing that you should do is select the page size. I recommend browsing Amazon for other books similar to the one that you are writing to see what size paperbacks are common for that type of book. Mass market paperbacks common with popular fiction, for example, have a small size (like 5.5" x 8.5"). Keep in mind that most self-published authors will not compete well with titles that have been mass produced. So if you are writing fiction, you might prefer trade paperback size, which is a little larger. A workbook or textbook tends to be fairly large (like 8.5" x 11"). One nice thing about a smaller book is that it is more portable. If you don't mind doing extra formatting work, you could potentially offer two editions of your book in different sizes. For comparison, the paperback edition of this book is 8" x 10".

There is also a financial factor to consider in choosing your book size. If you publish with CreateSpace, the factor is indirect, since CreateSpace pays the same royalties regardless of the page size. Your book's royalty does depend on the page count, however. If you have a smaller book, you will probably have more pages. The first 108 pages of a black-and-white paperback and the first 40 pages of a color paperback are free. If your book is longer than this, each extra page costs you 1.2 cents for black-and-white and 7 cents for color. So if you have a black-and-white paperback that would be 200 pages with a 7" x 10" size, but 250 pages with a 5" x 8" size, for example, you would draw 60 cents more royalty per book with the 7" x 10" size than the 5" x 8" size.[13] Remember, the page count only matters if you have more than 108 pages for black-and-white and 40 pages for color. There are also benefits of having more pages, even though each page costs you a little in royalties. Your spine label can be larger, and therefore be easier to read, if you have a higher page count, for example. Also, some customers may look at the page count when considering whether or not your book is a good value.

There are several page sizes to choose from if you publish with CreateSpace. The following trim sizes accommodate 24-828 white pages (black-and-white print), 24-740 cream pages (black-and-white), and 24-480 white pages (color): 5" x 8", 5.06" x 7.81", 5.25" x 8", 5.5" x 8.5", 6" x 9", 6.14" x 9.21", 6.69" x 9.61", 7" x 10", 7.44" x 9.69", and 7.5" x 9.25". An 8" x 10" option only accommodates 24-440 white pages (black-and-white), 24-400 cream pages (black-and-white), and 24-480 white pages (color), and 8.5" x 11" accommodates 24-630 white pages (black-and-white), 24-570 cream pages (black-and-white), and 24-480 white pages (color). Finally, there are a few non-standard trim sizes: 8.25" x 6" and 8.25" x 8.25" each accommodate 24-220 white pages (black-and-white), 24-200 cream pages (black-and-white), and 24-212 white pages (color), and 8.5" x 8.5" accommodates 24-630 white pages (black-and-white), 24-570 cream pages (black-and-white), and 24-480 white pages (color). Be sure not to exceed the maximum page count for the trim size that you select (also noting whether your book will be in black-and-white or in color, and, if in black-and-white, whether or not it will be on white or cream paper).

Some of these trim sizes are industry-standard, others are custom trim sizes. If you hope to sell your book through bookstores or online retailers, you definitely need to choose an industry-standard trim size. If you print in black-and-white on white paper, the following trim sizes are industry-standard: 5" x 8", 5.06" x 7.81", 5.25" x 8", 5.5" x 8.5", 6" x 9", 6.14" x

---

[13] It might not be a 50-page difference for your book. It depends on your margins, font size, etc. When your book is completed, you can try changing the page size and see how this impacts your page count.

9.21", 6.69" x 9.61", 7" x 10", 7.44" x 9.69", 7.5" x 9.25", 8" x 10", and 8.5" x 11". (So 8.25" x 6", 8.25" x 8.25", and 8.5" x 8.5" are custom trim sizes.) If you print in black-and-white on cream paper, you only have four industry-standard choices: 5" x 8", 5.25" x 8", 5.5" x 8.5", and 6" x 9". If you print in color (white paper is then the only option), the following are industry-standard trim sizes: 5.5" x 8.5", 6" x 9", 6.14" x 9.21", 7" x 10", 8" x 10", 8.5" x 8.5", and 8.5" x 11".[14] It is possible to enter your own dimensions for the trim size – up to 8.5" x 11.69" – but with limited distribution options (see Sec.'s 4.1.7 and 4.1.9).

2.1.5 Setting the Page Size

To adjust the page size and margins of your Word 2010 document, follow these steps:

1. Click the Page Layout tab (all of the tabs appear at the top of the screen), and then (instead of clicking Size) click the tiny arrow (that looks like ) in the bottom right corner of the Page Setup group (the group appears toward the top of the screen when you are in the Page Layout tab).
2. A popup window with the Page Setup options will open when you do this. First, find where it says Apply To (near the bottom of the window) and change This Section to Whole Document – since you want to change the page size and adjust the margins for the entire document, and not just a few of the pages (that's why it's better to open the Page Setup window than to choose the Margins or Size options directly).
3. You should see three tabs in this popup window: Margins, Paper, and Layout. In Layout, you can check a box if you would like different options for the first page, and another box will allow the odd-numbered pages to be different from the even-numbered pages. The odd pages appear on the right and the even pages appear on the left (open a book and look at the page numbers on the right and left sides). You might want different headers on odd and even pages, or you might want to place page numbers on the outside of each page (which will be the right side of odd pages and the left side of even pages), for example. I recommend checking both boxes.
4. If you would like any page to be centered vertically (top is better for most), change the Vertical Alignment from Top to Center in the Layout tab (and change Apply To).

[14] This information was current, according to CreateSpaces's website, as of the publication of this book. You can visit www.createspace.com to view the current options: Click Books, click Publish a Trade Paperback, and click Printing Options. On this table, it looks like there are several industry-standard cream trim sizes, but if you click Distribution and Royalties then scroll down and click Expanded Distribution, you will see a footnote below a table that lists only four cream trim sizes. (It's possible that CreateSpace's website or options will have changed since this note was written.) It's strange that both cream paper with black-and-white and white paper with color both have limited options, yet the options are different. If you really want to check on the latest options, you can email or call a representative at CreateSpace (first login to your account, then click the Contact Support bar at the left of your Member Dashboard).

5. Now go into the Paper tab (still in the Page Setup popup window) and select your page size. Unfortunately, some industry-standard trim sizes are not default page sizes in Microsoft Word.[15] However, you can still type in the width and height of the page manually.

6. Close the Page Setup popup window and reopen it to see if the width and height are the same: In some editions of Word and various PDF converters, like Adobe, I have had issues with the program changing the page size to different values if the values that I entered were close to one of the default page sizes. If it does change slightly, the main thing to know is that each page of your file will be centered on the printed pages. If you need to, you can go with a page size that's a little larger than what you want, and increase the margins to compensate for the difference.

Note that you will need to increase the page size a little bit if your book will have images near the edge that need to bleed. When an image is designed to extend to the very edge of the page, we say that the image bleeds to the edge. An artistic page border or a page background, for example, might be intended to bleed to the edge of the page. If you have any images that need to bleed, you must add .125" to the outside margins – including the top and bottom. Therefore, you must also add .125" to the width and .25" to the height of your book. When your book is printed, each page will be cut – cutting .125" off of each outer edge of your file's page size in order to meet the specified trim size. Any images that bleed must extend this extra .125" beyond the pages final (i.e. after it is cut) trim size. This provides a little tolerance in the cutting so that you don't get a narrow white strip between the image and the page edge. For example, if you have an 8" x 10" book, and you have at least one image that needs to bleed, you should make the page size 8.125" x 10.25" and also adjust the margins to account for the extra .125" in width (add 0.125" to the left and right margins, but subtract .125" from the gutter) and 0.25" in height (add 0.125" to both the top and bottom margins). You must also ensure that any images that need to bleed extend to the edge of the page (completely across the margin) on the screen after doing this.

Images that do not bleed are considered to be live elements, and must be at least 0.25" from the final (after it is cut) page edges – so if your file allows for bleed, any live element must be 0.375" from the page edge on your screen. When you click the View tab in Word, you can check the Ruler box in order to help measure distances; the numbers are in inches, and the dots between them are in 1/8" (0.125") increments. All text, including textboxes, must also be a minimum of 0.25" from the (final) page edges.

In the Page Setup tab, set the Orientation as Portrait – not Landscape. If, for example, you select 6" x 9" as your trim size, you <u>can't</u> make a 9" x 6" book simply by choosing Landscape. If you would like the width to be longer than the height, your only option is the custom trim size of 8.25" x 6", and still you must use Portrait – not Landscape. The spine will

---

[15] Maybe this would change in the future if enough people politely asked Microsoft to add them as defaults…

always be on the left side, which is always the longer dimension (except for 8.25" x 6"). (Note: You could take a screenshot of each page in Landscape, paste the image into a document in Portrait, and rotate the image. But when you look at the final product it will seem like the spine is in the wrong place, and Amazon's Search Inside feature will probably be rotated, too. Therefore, I don't recommend trying this.)

CreateSpace has Word template files (see Chapter 5 for common formatting issues).

2.1.6 Setting the Page Margins, Including the Gutter

Follow these steps to set the page margins, including the gutter:
1. Click the Page Layout tab and then click the tiny arrow in the bottom right corner of the Page Setup group.
2. With the Page Setup popup window still open, click the Margins tab.
3. Be sure to set the margins for the Gutter, too, and place the gutter on the Left; also, check the box for different odd and even pages (see Sec. 2.1.5, Step 3). With Gutter set to Left, the gutter appears on the left of odd pages and the right of even pages.

The gutter is in addition to the side margin. For example, if your gutter is 0.5" and your left/right margins are 0.75", your overall inside margin will be 1.25" (at the left of odd pages and the right of even pages), while your outside margin will be 0.75" (at the right of odd pages and the left of even pages). Your inside margin needs to be at least 0.375" for 24-150 pages, 0.75" for 151-400 pages, 0.875" for 401-600 pages, and 1" for more than 600 pages. The minimum required outside margin (including top and bottom margins) is 0.25", but at least 0.5" is recommended.

I recommend the following margins for most books, unless you add page borders: 0.5" top, 0.5" bottom, 0.5" left, 0.5" right, and 0.5" gutter. This will make your inside margin 1" and your outside margin 0.5". If you have page borders, you might want to add a little more room for them: 0.6" top, 0.6" bottom, 0.6" left, 0.6" right, and 0.4" gutter. These were the margins for the book that you're holding (unless you're reading the eBook), so you can see for yourself whether you would prefer larger or smaller margins. If you add headers and page numbers, Word will not place them in the margins – instead, the number of text lines that you have on each page will decrease a little bit in order to make room for the header and page number. Therefore, you want to add the header and page number (we will describe how shortly) before you start making sure that each page looks perfect – since adding these features to a book that was typed without them will suddenly reposition lines throughout your file. You might want larger margins, for example, if you anticipate that your reader would like plenty of room for annotation. If you write a puzzle book or a study guide, for example, the reader may wish to make several notes on the side of the page.

2.1.7 Choose Color or Black-and-White, and Why You Need to Decide Now

Decide whether your book's interior will be in black-and-white or in full-color. Even if you just want one picture on one page to be in color, in order to do this you have to choose the full-color option. Unfortunately, you must pay the full price for color even if your book only uses color sparingly. Color is more expensive than black-and-white, especially if your book is much longer than a typical children's book. We will explore pricing and royalties in detail in Sec.'s 4.1.4-5, but for now let's talk about the difference between black-and-white and color pricing, since you should have this in mind as you format your book (as we will soon explain).

A black-and-white book (but the cover will be in color) costs $2.15 plus 1.2 center per page over 108 pages, whereas a color book costs $3.65 plus 7 cents per page over 40 pages. For a book that sells directly from Amazon's website, your royalty will be 60% minus the cost of your book. If your book is 40 pages or less, you will lose $1.50 from your royalty by choosing color instead of black-and-white. If your book is longer than 40 pages, you will also lose about 6 to 7 cents per page beyond 40 pages, in addition to the $1.50.

Here are a couple of examples. Suppose you have a 130-page book. Your book would cost $2.41 in black-and-white ($2.15 + 22 x $0.012) and $9.95 in color ($3.65 + 90 x $0.07).[16] If you priced the book at $9.99, you would receive a royalty of $3.58 (0.6 x $9.99 – $2.41) for a black-and-white book; if the book is in color, you can't even price it at $9.99 (since the book's cost would exceed 60% of the list price). If you priced the book at $19.99, you would receive a royalty of $9.58 (0.6 x $19.99 – $2.41) for black-and-white, but merely $2.04 (0.6 x $19.99 – $9.95) for color. A color book with many pages is very expensive, and requires a high list price; a black-and-white book has a relatively low cost even with a high page count, and can be priced reasonably and still draw a good royalty. Your book must have much visual appeal, or instructive use of color, for example, in order to warrant a large difference in royalty that comes from publishing a book with a high page count (compared to 40 pages) in color.

Let's look at another example that's not so extreme. Suppose you wish to publish a 40-page children's book. The book would cost $2.15 for black-and-white and $3.65 for color. If you priced the book at $9.99, your royalty would be $3.84 (0.6 x $9.99 – $2.15) for black-and-white and $2.34 (0.6 x $9.99 – $3.65) for color. A children's book with many pictures will look much more appealing in color, so if the page count is not too high, it is probably much better to publish the book in color.

Why is the decision between color and black-and-white important when you are formatting your book? The answer is that it will affect how your book looks in print. If you have text or figures that are in color, but choose to print your book in black-and-white, there may be a significant change in appearance between the colorful image (or text) that you see

---

[16] CreateSpace has a handy royalty calculator so that you can play with possible scenarios when deciding how to publish and price your book: From www.createspace.com, click the Books tab, select Publish a Trade Paperback, choose Distribution and Royalties, and scroll down toward the bottom of the page.

on your screen and the grayscale image that you see on paper. You can get a preview of this change by converting your file to PDF (described in Sec.'s 2.1.16 and 4.1.8) and printing it out in grayscale – though it could still be somewhat different than the printed page of your actual book. Text that is in bold red has an eye-catching appearance, but in grayscale it comes out as a soft gray that has much the opposite effect, for example. In such cases, your black-and-white book may look better if you change all of your text to black. Similarly, you might want to consider drawing images in Word in black, white, and gray instead of color if you will be publishing your book in black-and-white (but also make a set in color for an eBook edition).

If you are publishing your book in color, you will want to note that the colors that you see on the screen are not exactly the same as the colors that you will see on the printed page. Thus, if you plan to publish your book in color, you might like to be aware of this while you are writing or formatting your book, rather than find out for the first time when your proof arrives in the mail. We will discuss this issue in Sec. 3.1.4, as it will also affect the colors of your book's cover regardless of whether your interior is black-and-white or color.

If your book will have figures, note that we will describe some color-shifting and formatting issues regarding figures in Sec. 3.1.4. We will also discuss the formatting of pictures and how to draw images in the following chapter. So if you would like to learn how to draw pictures or insert photos into your manuscript, just wait until we get to Chapter 3.

2.1.8 Page Borders and Shading, Columns, and Page Layout Options

Microsoft Word also has some features to help decorate your pages. For example, you can find watermarks, change the page color, and insert page borders in the Page Layout tab. If you use these features, you might want to test it out and see if it will show up in a PDF (as described in Sec. 4.1.8). Some of the fill effects (like patterns and gradients) available in Page Color look much different in print than on the screen – the scale may change between your file and the actual book. Also, these page layout features will not show up in an eBook edition. Your interior can really stand out if you include these fancy page borders, but the design could also be a distraction for readers. The paperback edition of this book has a page border to help you judge the effect. Here is how you can browse through the available page borders, and – if you find one that you want to use – how to add it to your book:

1. Go the Page Layout tab, click on Page Borders, and choose the Page Border tab in the popup window.
2. Browse through Art to find several decorative borders. Once you select one border, you can simply use the up (↑) and down (↓) arrows on your keyboard to scroll through the entire list (and see a preview of each in the upper right corner of the popup window). The first several are in color, while the rest are in black-and-white.

3. If you use a page border, be sure to go into Options in the popup window and change Measure From to Text (otherwise there will be a glaring gap between the page gutter and the text margin near the gutter).

4. The Options window also allows you to change the distance between the border and the text. For this book, I used the following distances between the text and page border: 10 pts top, 0 pts bottom, 10 pts left, and 10 pts right. The discrepancy between the top and bottom reflects that the header is thicker than the footer (there is just a page number in the footer).

5. I also went into the Page Layout tab, clicked the little arrow in the bottom right corner of the Page Setup group, selected the Layout tab in the popup window, switched to Whole Document in Apply To, and set Header to 0.6" and Footer to 0.5". This was needed to create even space between the border and page edge as well as between the text and border. Depending upon the thickness of your page border and how the size of your header compares to your footer, you might need to use different values from these. Play with the options and see how it look (go to the View tab and select One Page).

6. In the Preview area of the popup window, you can remove any of the four sides of the page border, in case you want your page border just to be on the top or left of the page, for example, instead of all the way around.

You can manually force a page break by going into the Insert tab and clicking Page Break. I recommend not forcing page breaks until your book is complete. Otherwise, any revisions that you make to your book can easily change the place where you want to insert your page break. For example, if you add or delete a sentence to a paragraph, this changes the number of lines on a page. When you proofread your manuscript, pay careful attention to the page breaks, as this is a common place to find extreme formatting problems. If you use the Page Break button (instead of using the Enter key) to force a page break, this will help you if you want to convert your manuscript to an eBook file later. **Tip**: Click Page Layout, choose Breaks, then Next Page (under Section Breaks) instead of Page Break (see Chapter 5).

Most books are written in a single column. Newspapers and magazines often appear in double columns. Answer keys may appear in multiple columns. If you want to make columns, go to the Page Layout tab and select Columns. If you choose More Columns (at the bottom), you will find several column options, like changing the spacing between columns or adding lines between them.

Sometimes, you may want to insert a column break instead of a page break, in order to force text to the top of the next column. Do this by going to the Page Layout tab and finding Breaks and then choosing Column from the list.

2.1.9 Headers, Footers, and Page Numbers

Most books have a page header. A page header includes text (sometimes with some artistic design, too) that appears at the top of every page. You can have an odd-page header, an even-page header, and a first-page header that are all different (but only if you select the corresponding options in Step 3 in Sec. 2.1.5). Many traditional books have the title on the odd page header and the author's name on the even page header, for example. A famous author has some name recognition; it might not have the same effect for a self-published author to include his or her name on half of the pages through a header. You could place the title on the odd page header and subtitle, if you have one, on the even-page header, for example, or you could be creative and use the headers decoratively. You could do without a header if you want to, but your book may look more professionally formatted if you use headers. The paperback edition of this book has the title on odd-numbered pages and the chapter name on even-numbered pages (if instead you have the eBook edition, if there is any header it is probably the title and/or author and was placed there by your eReader, not by the author or publisher); **Sec. 5.1.4 shows how to make different headers for each chapter.**

To add a header, a footer, and/or page numbers, follow these steps:

1. Click on the Insert tab and look for the Header & Footer group, which includes Header, Footer, and Page Number. **See Sec. 5.1.4 regarding Roman and Arabic numerals.**
2. There are several default options to choose from (find more by using the scroll bar).
3. After you add a header or footer, you can edit the header/footer area by going to the same place and selecting Edit Header or Footer down at the bottom of the list – or you can simply double click with your cursor in the header's (or footer's) location.
4. Type the text of your header in this area, and add any decorations that you might want. In this book, I added a long line beneath the header by choosing the border options in the Paragraph group of the Home tab (while I was in the header area). If you choose Borders and Shading at the bottom of the border options, a popup window will allow you to change Apply To from Text to Paragraph.
5. Exit the header or footer area by double-clicking with your cursor somewhere in the body of your manuscript. **See Sec. 5.1.4 about different headers for each chapter.**

In the Insert tab, in the Header & Footer group there are also several page number options. You can change the style of your page numbers and the number of the first page by selecting the Format Page Numbers option. You can edit the design by double-clicking a page number – add characters around your page number, or decorate your footer, for example, the same way that you edit the header (double-click anywhere in the body of your text to exit the footer). If you place the page number on the right side of odd pages, you will probably want to place the page number on the left side of even pages (in order for this distinction to be possible, you must have checked the box for different odd and even pages in the Page Layout tab after clicking the icon at the bottom right of the Page Setup group).

2.1.10 Tabs, Justified Text, Bullets, and Paragraph Styles

You can indent a paragraph simply by pressing the tab key. With the Ruler checked in the View tab, you will see little gray triangular markers on the ruler showing you where the tab is. You can move these markers to increase or decrease a tab. The top triangle usually appears at the half-inch mark, and the bottom triangle usually appears at the left edge of the line. The bottom marker controls the indent of the subsequent lines of the paragraph, while the top marker controls the indent for the first line of the paragraph. If you will be making an eBook, tabs present a formatting issue, which we will discuss in Sec. 2.2.4 – in that case, I highly recommend using the method of Sec 2.2.4 instead. You can find more paragraph options by clicking the little icon in the bottom right corner of the Paragraph group in the Home tab.

Another important feature is the justification of your text. You can find the icons for left, center, right, and full justification in the Paragraph group of the Home tab (these icons are composed of little horizontal lines). The body text of almost all books is justified full, <u>not</u> left. This book is justified full: See how the text is even on the right side and the left side?

See the examples of left, right, centered, and fully justified text blow. The first paragraph has a jagged right edge, while both edges of the last paragraph are even. Microsoft Word automatically adds blank space between each word when you click the full justify icon in order to make every line exactly the same length. Your book will look much more professional in appearance if you justify full instead of justifying left.

> This paragraph is justified left. This paragraph is justified left. This paragraph is justified left. This paragraph is justified left. This paragraph is justified left. This paragraph is justified left. This paragraph is justified left. This paragraph is justified left. This paragraph is justified left.
>
> This paragraph is justified right. This paragraph is justified right. This paragraph is justified right. This paragraph is justified right. This paragraph is justified right. This paragraph is justified right. This paragraph is justified right. This paragraph is justified right. This paragraph is justified right.
>
> This paragraph is centered. This paragraph is centered. This paragraph is centered. This paragraph is centered. This paragraph is centered. This paragraph is centered. This paragraph is centered.
>
> This paragraph is justified full. This paragraph is justified full. This paragraph is justified full. This paragraph is justified full. This paragraph is justified full. This paragraph is justified full. This paragraph is justified full. This paragraph is justified full. This paragraph is justified full.

When you open a new document in Word, you will need to change the defaults. By default, new documents are justified left; you will need to change this to full for most of your manuscript, and many headings will need to be centered. Also, Word's default is to add space after every line. This paragraph has Word's default line spacing. See how it looks different than every other paragraph in this book. Click the little icon in the bottom right corner of the Paragraph group in the Home tab. Change the Spacing After from 10 pt to 0 pt and change the Line Spacing from 1.15 to 1 to correct the defaults. If you had already typed some or all of your manuscript, you will need to select all of it before readjusting the defaults (find the Select tool on the far right of the Home tab to Select All).

In the home tab, you can find paragraph borders and shading. This allows you to shade an entire paragraph or to add a border around a paragraph. At the bottom of the list of the Borders and Shading icon (click the arrow just to the right of the icon to find this list), select Borders and Shading to find all of the possibilities. If you select some text, you can also choose to place a border just around the text instead of the whole paragraph (but you will find that some options that apply to paragraphs don't apply to selected text). Some samples of what you can do with borders and shading are shown here in this paragraph. Beware that a few of the fancy Styles may not print quite the same in your paperback book as they look on the screen.

If you are typing a list, you might want to use bullets; but keep in mind that bullets won't appear in an eBook (but see Sec. 2.2.3 for a way to achieve the bullet effect in an eBook). In the Home tab, you can find three different bullet icons in the Paragraph group:

- The left bullet icon allows you to use symbols for your bullets.
- ☺ You can change the symbol to a checkmark or a smiley face.
- ☺ All of the bullets in the list will be the same if you use symbols. I made different bullets here, however, by starting brand new bullets. These two smiley face bullets are part of the same bullet list, while the others are separate bullet lists. At the beginning of the line, press Backspace (maybe twice) as one way to remove the bullet.
- 🌲 You can even use a picture as the symbol for a bullet. Choose define new bullet (first click the arrow next to the bullet icon), then Picture, and then Import to browse for your picture.
1) Here we have numbered bullets.
2) They automatically increase when you press the Enter key.
3) This numbered list has three bullets.
1. The rightmost bullet icon is outline format – for creating a multi-level list.
   a. This "a." appeared when I pressed the Tab key.
   b. The "b." appeared when I pressed Enter.
      i. I hit Tab again to create a new sublevel.

2.1.11 Drop Caps, Font Sizes and Styles, Headings, Symbols, and Text Formatting

M ost traditionally published books use a drop cap for the first letter of each chapter. As an example, one was used to begin this paragraph. You can easily do this in your own book using Microsoft Word, following these steps:

1. First, go to the Insert tab and choose Drop Cap.
2. Select your drop cap, return to the Insert tab, click Drop Cap again, and explore the Drop Cap Options.
3. If you place your cursor in the drop cap, you can change the font size and other font options as usual (using the Font group in the Home tab).
4. Place your cursor in the drop cap, then select the dashed blue rectangle that appears, and you will see 8 little blue rectangles at the corners and midpoint of each side: You can resize your drop cap by grabbing one of these 8 little blue rectangles and moving your cursor.
5. If you want the letter of the drop cap to be flush against the left side, place your cursor to the left of the letter in the drop cap, and hit the backspace key.

You can find most of the text options in the Home tab. This is where you can select a font and change the font size. You'll want to ensure that the font is easy for the reader to see and understand; some fonts are harder on the eyes. This book was written with Calibri size 12 font. (If you wish to make a large print edition of your book it needs to have a font size of 16 or larger.) A smaller font size can allow you to have fewer pages, which increases your royalty if you have over 108 pages black-and-white or over 40 pages color; but you don't want readers to complain that the book was difficult to read because the font was too small. If you have a library of fonts to choose from, beware that many specialized fonts do not allow free commercial use. Since your book will be available for sale, you are using the font for commercial use. Check with the company that distributed the font to see whether or not they permit commercial use of the font. Some companies allow commercial use with your purchase, some require a fee or purchase of a more expensive edition of the software, and others prohibit commercial use all together. Much clipart and many pictures have similar copyright restrictions, so you should inquire about commercial use restrictions before using any fonts, clipart, or other images. Even Office comes in personal and professional versions.

If you want to explore fonts quickly, type one sentence in a document, highlight the sentence, and browse through the fonts. You will see the sentence change into each font as your cursor is placed over the font. Alternatively, after highlighting the sentence, click the little icon in the bottom right corner of the Font group in the Home tab, and click on a font.

Note: Published books use **one** space after a period, not two. There is a compelling article on this that you can find on this by searching for "Space Invaders" by Farhad Manjoo.

Boldface and italics (these and other font options are available in the Home tab) are common ways to make print words stand out. **Boldface** is common in headings. *Italics* are used to give stress to a word or for book titles. There is a school of thought that you should avoid the use of <u>underlining</u> when typing. When you would underline the title of a book when writing by hand, you instead italicize the title when typing. <u>I guess it just looks funny to some people to see a phrase or sentence underlined.</u> There, you can judge for yourself. Underlining a single word could be effective: Personally, I like to use it with the word 'not,' as in, "Use italics, <u>not</u> underlining." If you want that 'not' to stand out, it seems to do the job. Well, it would stand out better if there weren't any other underlining on this page; the less underlining you have, the more effective it will be. The ab (but <u>not</u> abc – look carefully) icon in the Font group of the Home tab can be used for highlighting (gray would be the logical choice if your book is black-and-white). If you choose black highlighting, you need a light font (use white if your book is black-and-white), and white may read better if you make it boldface: Compare normal to **bold**. A couple of fancy options in body text (as opposed to WordArt, which we will discuss in Sec. 3.1.6) include the A icon, which might be useful in a heading, as in HEADING, and the abc icon, which is for strikethrough. After using the outline option (highlight your text and then click the A icon), there are four options at the bottom – Outline, Shadow, Reflection, and Glow – that can help you perfect it. You can find a few more font

options by clicking the little icon in the bottom right corner of the Font group in the Home tab, including the Advanced tab that you will see in the popup window and the Text Effects option at the bottom. CAPS are common in HEADINGS. It's considered rude to type sentences in CAPS – people think of this as yelling. However, if you're writing fiction, you may use CAPS for a quote from a character who is, in fact, yelling.

You may want to do something special with headings (not to be confused with a header). Headings include the titles and subtitles of a chapter, the titles of front and back matter (like a table of contents or an appendix), and any other groups of word that you would see above the body of your text. It is common to write headings with a larger font, as in Chapter 2. Headings usually stand on their own line, with one or two linespaces below them. Some headings are centered, others are justified left.

Bold Heading

The heading above is centered, boldface, large, and has two linespaces (blank lines) below it (hit the Enter key twice or add space after paragraph). Main headings may even include some symbols or artistic design to help them stand out and add decoration to your book. The following examples were made using the A icon (for Text Effects in the Home tab):

EXAMPLE EXAMPLE EXAMPLE EXAMPLE EXAMPLE.

EXAMPLE

WordArt

You can also make a heading using _WordArt_ , as we will learn how to do in Sec. 3.1.6. In this case, I highly recommend going into the Format tab (which appears only after you select the WordArt), and change Wrap Text to In Line With Text.

The default Styles that you see in more than half of the Home tab allow you to quickly format text. These can be really handy to make an eBook format from your paperback format, or vice-versa. If you want to use them, first modify the Styles (see Sec. 2.2.4).

If you use the $_{subscript}$ and ^{superscript} icons in the Font group in the Home tab, this might be lost if you convert your book to an eBook – but feel free to use them for your paperback. You can make the same effect by inserting an equation (to be described in Sec. 2.1.13), but this will also cause some formatting issues in the eBook edition. We will explore this in Sec. 2.2.

If you are looking for special symbols, you can find most of them by going to the Insert tab, clicking Symbol, and selecting More Symbols. Many standard symbols are in "(normal text)" besides Font in the window that pops up, but you can find some more by changing "(normal text)" to one of the other fonts. (The organization of those symbols could probably be improved...) MS Gothic, for example, has many symbols to choose from (it even includes Chinese and Hindi language symbols, for example). Way at the bottom of the list, you can find some common icons in Webdings and Wingdings 1-3. If you are looking for mathematical symbols, also explore inserting an equation (we will discuss equations in Sec. 2.1.13). Following is a brief sample of symbols that you might find to be useful:

© ® é Ω ⅝ ™ ❶ ÷ æ ∞ ☺ ✋ ✂ ✏ → ↑ ✎ ♦ ☂ ☎ 蜷

2.1.12 Footnotes, Citations, Cross-References, and Plagiarism

If you want to add a note without interrupting the flow of the text, you might do it with a footnote, like the one you see at the bottom of this page.[17] In the References tab, choose Insert Footnote. You can find the footnote options by clicking the little icon in the bottom right corner of the Footnotes group. For example, you can number your footnotes with Roman numerals (I, II, III, IV, etc.) or symbols (*, †, #, etc.). You can also link to longer notes placed at the end of your book using endnotes instead of footnotes. Endnotes are appropriate for a bibliography – a list of citations or references. Use Cross-reference to refer to figures, chapters, sections, tables, and pages. For example, instead of typing "as described on page 42," you could use a cross-reference so that you only have to type the text, "as described on

---

[17] This is the 17th footnote of this book.

page," and the number 42 will appear automatically (and will automatically change if the referenced text happens to change page – which may happen if you add, remove, or modify any part of the document that precedes the referenced text). Add the cross-reference to the text or item on that page (page 42 in this example) that you are referring to. That way, after some editing if the item happens to move to page 43, the page number will automatically update. However, this won't apply to the eBook edition of your book (see Sec. 2.2.3), so if you use cross-references, you'll have to change them for the eBook.

Be sure to avoid plagiarism, which is defined in the following note. If you copy one or more sentences – or even just a phrase – from any other source, enclose the sentence(s) in quotation marks and cite the source (using a style of citation appropriate for your genre). For example, suppose that I included the quote, "I do things like get in a taxi and say, 'The library, and step on it,'" [24], the [24] would refer to the 24th reference of my bibliography, where I would cite my source. The 24th reference of my bibliography would then list the author of the quote, David Foster Wallace, and the title of the novel where the quote was taken from, *Infinite Jest*. Styles for how to cite the reference differ. Instead of numbering the references in a bibliography, the references may be alphabetized. In that case, instead of writing [24] to indicate which reference the quote is attributed to, you might include the last name and year, as in [Wallace, 1996]. Find the style appropriate to your genre – and just choose one if there doesn't seem to be a standard in your genre. You can learn about a variety of citation styles by searching for "citing references" with your favorite internet search engine, for example (and sorting through the search results to determine which sources are most reliable).

> **Plagiarism**: Copying the work of another – even as little as a single phrase – and passing it off as your own is called plagiarism. Failure to cite your source – even if you paraphrase instead of quote – is an instance of plagiarism.

Don't overdo the length of the quote or the frequency of quotations from the same source. Provided that you properly cite (i.e. acknowledge) the source of your quote, you can quote with "fair use." If you feel the need to quote excessively, you must first obtain written permission from the author. Consult an attorney if you would like legal advice.

You still need to cite your reference if you paraphrase instead of quote. If you find written information and rewrite it in your own words, even though you didn't copy the exact same words, you must still acknowledge the source of your information. For example, Mark Twain once said, "'Classic' – a book which people praise and don't read." If I want to write the following, I still need to cite my source: A classic is a book which people praise without ever having read [Twain]. You don't use quotes when you paraphrase, but you must still cite the reference with brackets [] or a footnote. Place the brackets (with either the reference number or name, according to the citation style that you follow) or footnote at the end of the paraphrase, and write the complete source of the information (which usually consists of author and title) in the corresponding bibliography (or, in the case of a footnote, it will appear at the bottom of the page).

Failure to use quotation marks for direct quotes or to indicate the source of your quote or paraphrase is a serious problem that can come with serious legal repercussions.

Even quotes may carry legal repercussions. You're not allowed to quote lyrics from a song or poem (unless it's in the public domain). For other material, quotes may be used only in "fair use." Research **fair use** online or contact an attorney to learn more about this.

2.1.13 Using Microsoft Word's Equation Editor

The best way to format a formula is to insert an equation. If you save your document as a Word Document, you will be able to use the new equation editor; if you save your document as a Word 97-2003 Document, only the old equation editor will work. In the latter case (or if you have an old edition of Word), go to the Insert tab, select Object, and choose Microsoft Equation 3.0. If you convert your Word Document to a Word 97-2003 Document (which may be useful for making an eBook, as we will discuss in Sec.'s 2.2.6-7), any equations that you have will be converted to the old format. Since I have been describing how to use Word 2010 (which also applies to Word 2007 in most cases), I'm going to describe how to use the new equation editor (the old one is also pretty intuitive).

Go to the Insert tab and select Equation. Click on the top half of the Equation icon to type your own equation (as the list of default equations is very limited). Much of the equation can simply be typed, as in $y = mx + b$. Notice that letters are automatically italicized. The convention is to italicize symbols, but not units. For example, in $t = 3$ s, the t is the symbol for time, while the s is the unit seconds. You can un-italicize a letter by highlighting it and then selecting Normal Text in the Design tab, or you can go to the Home tab and hit the italics icon. Note that the Design tab only appears when you are in the equation.

If you want to make a fraction, you can type a / and then a space when you finish (of course, you must first insert the equation and then type this in the equation), as in $\frac{x}{y}$, or you can go to the Design tab (after first inserting an equation and then placing your cursor in that equation), select a Fraction, and then type the numerator and denominator into it. Exponents can be made by typing a caret (^) between the base and exponent and then hitting space, as in a^b, or by choosing Script in the Design tab. The Radical option in the Design tab is used to make squareroots like $\sqrt{7}$. You can find many other equation features, like integrals, sums, trig functions, and brackets on the right side of the Design tab. For example, the following was made by selecting Matrix:

$$\begin{pmatrix} 2 & 3 \\ 5 & -1 \end{pmatrix}$$

If you type formulas, you will want to go to the Design tab (you must place your cursor in the equation first) and click the little icon in the bottom right corner where you see the table of symbols (it looks like a triangle with a short line above it). Next, click the triangle next to Basic Math. This is where you can find many mathematical symbols, including Greek letters and arrows. If you can't find the symbol here, you can also try inserting a symbol from the Insert tab (rather than the Design tab). If you need a rare symbol that you just can't find anywhere, you could always draw your own picture, resize it, and insert it wherever you like (see Sec.'s 3.1.8-9 to learn how to draw a picture). Following is a brief sample of common math symbols: $\pm\ \infty\ \times \approx\ \in \theta\ \hbar\ \geq \Leftrightarrow \perp$. If you would like to add an accent to a symbol in an equation, choose Accents from the Design tab. That's how I made $\vec{A}$ and $\overline{12}$, for example.

Equations may look different if they are in line with the text versus being completely alone on their own line. Compare the equation $\sin\theta = \frac{\sigma}{\hbar}$ with the same equation that appears by itself below. One equation is a copy and paste of the other – it automatically changed when it appeared on its own line (if you add anything else next to it, it will change format – looking smaller, like the one above, to fit on the line of text).

$$\sin\theta = \frac{\sigma}{\hbar}$$

2.1.14 Inserting and Formatting Tables and Adding Captions to Figures/Tables

You can make a table by selecting Table from the Insert tab. If you select Insert Table, you can choose exactly the number of rows and columns that you want. If you place the cursor in the table or highlight cells in the table, you will see Design and Layout tabs appear. Click these tabs to find the table formatting options. In the Layout tab, use Properties to position the table in the center, and to find some options for cells, rows, and columns. In the Properties window that pops up, click Options to change the cell margins or to wrap or fit the text in the cell. You can add or remove rows or columns and split or merge cells in the Layout tab. You can easily change row or column widths and heights by changing the measurements that you see in the Layout tab (first highlight the row or column that you wish to modify). There are 9 icons in the Layout tab that let you position the text in any part of the cell (choose the central one if you want to center your text both horizontally and vertically). The Distribute Rows and Columns icons let you even the widths of rows and heights of columns. If you don't want your text to read left to right, try using the Cell Direction icon.

	Column 1	Column 2	Column 3
Row 1	16	32	64
Row 2	8	4	2

Use the Design tab (which appears when you have the cursor in the table) in order to change the colors, shading, and borders. There are some default shading/border schemes to choose from. To make manual adjustments (or to make changes after selecting one of the default schemes), click Borders and Shading. I made the diagonal split above using an option in Borders. Grab the line to choose a different line style (like a dashed line). Grab the ½ pt pen size to change the line thickness to some other value. After applying a line style, click somewhere above or below the table in order to get the cursor to function normally again.

Type numbered captions below all figures and tables. Start with, "Fig. 3" or "Table 2," for example. This makes it easy to refer to figures and tables throughout the text – e.g. you might write in the body of your text, "as you can see in Fig. 4." After numbering the figure or table, write a complete sentence with proper punctuation that describes the figure or table. You might want to use a narrower margin for figures and captions in order to make it clearly separate from the main text. You can do this by clicking the icon in the bottom-right corner of the Paragraph group in the Home tab and typing 0.5" (or another value) for both Left and Right. See the example of a caption below.

Fig. 7. This is an example of what a caption looks like. This would be the 7th figure of the book. The margins of the caption are narrower than the body text so that it is not confused with the main text.

A Note for Novices: Many of the "how-to" instructions will probably seem abstract if you simply read through them. If you really want to learn how to use Microsoft Word, turn on your computer, open Microsoft Word, sit down at your computer, and try the instructions out as you read this book. The instructions will make much more sense if you try to find the things that the book is describing.

If you are new to Microsoft Word and have trouble understanding something, first try pressing the F1 key or clicking the circled question mark ( ) in the upper right corner of the screen, which will take you to Microsoft Word Help. If that doesn't help, try asking a friend for help; there are also numerous help forums online where you can swiftly seek help with common computer issues. Once you get a few things clarified, you might find that other instructions begin to make more sense. As you understand the organization of Word a little better and how it works, and as you gain confidence that you can figure it out, you will probably find that things are much simpler than they may have first seemed.

As a teacher, I find that the greatest obstacle is often <u>confidence</u>. When you have doubts, you give up before you solve the problem. When you have enough confidence that you can figure it out yourself if you only just persist, you are usually able to solve the problem.

2.1.15 Copy/Paste, Undo/Redo, and Zoom Options

On the left side of the Home tab, you can find Cut, Copy, and Paste options. It may be more efficient to hold down the Ctrl button on the keyboard and press X for cut, Ctrl + C for copy, and Ctrl + V for paste. It is sometimes helpful to click the little arrow under Paste instead of just pasting. For example, if you copy/paste your ISBN from CreateSpace into your book, you can save a little time by choosing the Keep Text Only icon (otherwise, it tries to do a complicated paste of formatting styles, which takes longer). After you paste something into your Word document, you will see an icon near the end of it, which allows you to adjust the formatting (to match the source or destination, for example, or just to keep the text only). When you proofread your book, the Find and Replace options at the far right of the Home tab should be useful. For example, if you find that sometimes you write Chapter 3 and other times Ch. 3 when referring to a chapter, you can use Replace to make all of them the same.

Note the undo and redo buttons at the very top of the screen (near the save icon). You can also undo by pressing Ctrl + Z and redo with Ctrl + Y. If you make a mistake, correct it by hitting the undo button or pressing Ctrl + Z. If you want to undo the last several things you've done, hit the undo button repeatedly. If you change your mind, hit the redo button or Ctrl + Y. These buttons are precious! But beware: If you press undo several times and then make a change to your document, the redo won't work.

In the View tab, you can zoom in just as much as you want. I like to use the Page Width option when I'm typing and One Page or Two Pages to check the formatting of each page of the document. Use the Zoom button for more options. I also like to check the Ruler box, which serves as a useful measuring tool.

2.1.16 Saving Your File, Backups, and PDF Conversion

I have some advice regarding saving your file that could potentially save you a lot of headaches and frustration. First, save different versions of your file. For example, suppose you named the file for your manuscript as MyBook. After you type a chapter or so, go to the File tab and choose Save As (not Save). Now call your file MyBook2. A chapter or so later, call it MyBook3. Every once in a while, a file becomes corrupt – it won't open no matter what you do. If you save different versions every chapter or so and your file does become corrupt, a previous version will probably still work. This way, you might lose just one chapter instead of the entire manuscript. Save your file frequently – every few minutes (but only change the version every chapter or section). If you sit down and type five pages, you will be frustrated if the power goes out, or if your computer simply decides to freeze on you, just before you click Save. You can't save your file too often, but you might (and probably will) become very frustrated if you don't save it frequently enough.

The default save option is Microsoft Word format with a .docx extension. I recommend saving your Word documents this way (except where I have noted otherwise in this book in the context of publishing eBooks). If you are working on multiple computers, where one computer has Word 2003 (or earlier), you will need to choose Save As (in the File tab) and change Save As Type from Word Document to Word 97-2003 Document. This will save your file with the older extension – i.e. it will be .doc instead of .docx.

Don't save your file in only one place. You can save it to your hard drive, save another copy to a jump drive, email a copy to yourself, etc. Computers have frequent problems. If you write several books, you will almost certainly have problems with some of the files. If you save different versions and store multiple copies of your book in multiple places, you protect yourself from losing a great deal of work. Remember which one is the most recent version!

You can convert your document to PDF using the Save As option from the File tab. The first time that you do this, you may be taken to the internet to Microsoft Office to download this free feature. We will discuss the conversion to PDF further in Sec. 4.1.8.

2.1.17 Preventing and Dealing With Memory Problems

A richly formatted book can cause memory problems when using Microsoft Word – even if you have a new, top-of-the line computer with ample hard drive memory and RAM. The following items make your file increasingly complex:
- ☹ Pictures, clipart, line drawings, tables, textboxes, WordArt, and equations.
- ☹ Illustrations that you make in Word where you do not group the items together (we will discuss grouping in Sec. 3.1.8) and are positioned In Front Of or Behind Text add to the complexity more than grouped items that are positioned In Line With Text.
- ☹ Page borders, page colors, headers, footers, and page numbers.
- ☹ Footnotes, endnotes, and cross-references.
- ☹ Frequent rich formatting of text.
- ☹ Comments added using features in Microsoft Word's Review tab.
- ☹ Built-in table of contents or index inserted from the References tab.

Memory problems can cause the file to become corrupt and create problems trying to open, modify, and save the file. There are a couple of ways to help prevent this. One thing you can do is focus on writing plain text until your manuscript is complete, and add the above features after the text is finished. This way, you can save a simple file with all of your text. Then, in the worst-case scenario at least you won't have to retype any text.

Another thing that you can do is follow the advice in Sec. 2.1.16. By frequently saving files with different names (just add a version number when you save it), you have a previous version to fall back on if one file has issues; and by saving your file in multiple places, if you do have computer issues (like a problem with your hard drive or a virus), this increases your chances of finding some version of your file to work with.

You can also separate your book file into pieces. For example, if you have a 400-page book with several pictures, tables, and rich formatting, you could divide it up into four 100-page files. You can also make tables and line drawings in a blank file and save them by themselves, and only copying and pasting them into your main document at the end of your project.

2.1.18 Spelling, Grammar, Word Count, and Review Options

In the Review tab, you can find the spelling and grammar checkers. Spellcheck is very useful. If this is on, every word that Word's dictionary doesn't recognize will be underlined in red. When you finish typing your book, carefully browse through the file to find all of these red underlines – these are potentially misspelled words. Your book will make a poor impression if there is frequent misspelling. The spellcheck is not foolproof, but it does help you catch many potential mistakes. If you accidentally type 'the' instead of 'then,' it won't be a misspelling since 'the' is still a word. So you do need to proofread your book carefully, too.

Also use the grammar check, which also checks capitalization. You can find grammatical suggestions underlined in green. The grammar check is not perfect because the English language is highly complex, but it will help you catch sentences where you forgot to capitalize the first word, repeated words, verb tense issues, and fragments, for example.

Don't like Word's autocorrections? Click the File tab, click Help down at the bottom of the list, choose Options, and click Proofing. There are several boxes that you can check or uncheck, depending upon your preferences, and you can find more by clicking AutoCorrect Options.

If you are collaborating with another author, you can add comments in the Review tab. A comment allows you to highlight selected text and have a line connecting the selection to a note placed in the margin. This is a convenient way to add annotations without modifying the content of the document.

Near the bottom left of the screen, you can find the page count and the word count, which can be very handy. Click on the word count and it will even break it down to characters with and without spaces. This will be useful when you type your book's description, since there is a limit to how many characters you can use.

2.1.19 Figures, Pictures, Clipart, WordArt, and Textboxes

We will learn a few more things about Microsoft Word in Chapter 3, including how to draw pictures, how to import and format pictures and clipart, and how to use and format textboxes and WordArt (we will also discuss the issue of formatting pictures specifically for the eBook in Sec. 2.2.5). Remember, most clipart comes with a copyright restriction that prohibits commercial use, but some versions of clipart software do allow commercial use; you should always find out about commercial use before using clipart in your book. Just to be clear: What I'm saying is, if you want to learn how to draw figures, format pictures, insert clipart and format WordArt and textboxes, read Chapter 3.

If you insert a figure on its own line (as opposed to being positioned beside a paragraph), center the figure and add a caption beneath it as described in Sec. 2.1.14. (We will discuss how to position figures in Sec. 3.1.8 – first find the third group of numbered steps, then find Step 10.) If you have a large figure that you would like to be on its own page, use the Page Break feature in Insert. I suggest not doing this until your file is virtually complete, otherwise any revisions to the text that previously came just before the figure might need to move to the page just after the figure. If you need to break a line up mid-sentence, so that the first part of the sentence precedes the page break and the second part of the sentence comes after the figure, press Shift + Enter at the point where you want to chop the sentence, and cut and paste (Ctrl + X then Ctrl + V) the second part of the sentence to move it. Make sure that the second part doesn't begin with a space ( ); if so, just delete the space.

2.1.20 Title Page, Copyright Page, Table of Contents, and Other Front Matter

Before we move onto the eBook, let's discuss front and back matter. These are sections that appear at the beginning and end of your book, such as a table of contents and glossary. You should have some front and back matter, but you might not want to go overboard with this. You will find several ideas here to choose from.

Your book should begin with a title page; you can find one on the first page of this book. I suggest looking at a variety of books' title pages before making your own. The title page should have the book's title and the name(s) of the author(s). If your book has a subtitle, you might want to include that, too. Textbooks often include the names of the universities where the authors teach. Traditionally published books would also include the name of the publisher; if you choose an ISBN option where you use your own imprint (see Sec. 4.1.6), you could include that on your cover. Consider using WordArt and adding pictures or artistic decorations to your title page (described in Chapter 3).

The copyright page is usually a plain text page that lists your book's title, the name(s) of the author(s), the name of the publisher, the ISBN number (you will have both ISBN-10 and EAN-13 numbers), the copyright date, edition number, and copyright notice. Some books also include the subject of the book (like nonfiction \ writing \ publishing \ self-publishing). If your main target is Amazon, you can browse the categories there and use that to designate the subject. Traditionally published books also include a series of numbers that shows which printing was used. You can get a lot of ideas by reading a variety of copyright pages. In your copyright notice, you want to make it clear that the right to reproduce any portion of the book in any form is reserved (by the author or publisher). I have a very simple copyright notice in this book; some authors have a lengthy paragraph here, getting into the specifics; and some copyright notices strive to persuade readers not to make copies of the work and distribute them (as if the people who would do that would bother to read the copyright notice, and as if the copyright notice may actually affect their actions). If you write a fictional work, include a statement that explains that all of the characters are fictional, and that any resemblance to actual people is purely coincidental. The main thing you want from your copyright notice is legal protection. If you would like legal advice, then, of course, I'm obliged to recommend that you seek legal counsel from an attorney for all of your legal questions.

Readers will find it useful if you have a table of contents (a must for nonfiction). Keep in mind that your front and back matter will be included in Amazon's Search Inside feature. The title page, copyright page, table of contents, and introduction are the first sections that a customer will see when using the Search Inside feature. Therefore, you want these sections to look professional in order to make a good impression; and if your book is lacking any of these sections, it may stand out as a glaring omission. The heading (not header) for your table of contents should be Contents or Table of Contents. One way to make the table of contents is to insert an actual table. In Sec. 2.1.14, we described how to make a table in Microsoft Word. Alternatively, you could make two columns (as described in Sec. 2.1.8). Either way, you want your first column to be very wide and the second column to be very short. The table of contents usually doesn't show gridlines, so if you insert a table, highlight all of the cells (but be careful not to highlight any area before or after the table, or you might not get the option you need), go into the Design tab, click on Borders, and remove all of the borders.

Most books have an introduction or foreword at the beginning of the book. The introduction is usually written in the third person. If you write your own introduction, this means not to use the pronouns I, me, and my, but instead to write as if you know the author and wish to describe his or her book. (However, if you read my introduction for this book, you can see that I wrote it in the first person. I opted for a personal touch with this book, so I thought that this was appropriate.) A foreword usually is written by someone else. Traditional publishers include a foreword written by a famous author in the same genre, and advertise on the front cover that the book includes a foreword by so and so. If you know anybody who has name recognition that may add to the value of your book in this way, if you can get him/her to agree to write a foreword for your book, it serves as a marketing tool.

If you would like to acknowledge anyone – such as the support of your family, appreciation for your fans, a colleague who offered valuable discussions, the advice of a friend, or grammatical corrections offered by a reader – you can include an acknowledgments section with your front matter. You can also include a dedications page if you wish to dedicate your book to someone in particular (or even to a pet!).

2.1.21 About the Author, Bibliography, Index, Glossary, Catalog, and Other Back Matter

Back matter often includes one or more of the following sections. A glossary is useful if your book includes a lot of jargon – terms that the reader probably was not familiar with before reading your book. An index is useful with nonfiction books where a reader is likely to be searching for a specific topic. Almost every textbook has an index for this reason. An index is not useful in a book that will be read once through, but is very handy when there are specific topics that a reader is likely to search for, but not otherwise find easily. Some books include an afterword. In this internet age, many younger readers will appreciate a page of useful links to related websites – but if you do this, note that your links may quickly become outdated, and you will need to frequently update your book if you want to keep the links current. Nonfiction books often have an appendix, which contains useful information that some readers may want to explore, but which didn't quite fit into the contents.

You can provide some insight into the person who wrote the book (that's you!) with an About the Author section. You should probably write the About the Author section in the third person, as if it were written by someone else who is describing you (or you can ask someone to write this section about you). Some authors include a picture here, too. Come on, don't be camera shy. Your readers want to know about you. I'm a family man, so my photo includes a picture of my daughter. Your photo can also show your passion for your hobbies or pet or the subject in which you write, if your picture is taken while you do whatever it is that you love.

You should include a References or Bibliography section if you have any works to cite. Whether to call it References or Bibliography depends on the field in which you are writing, as does which convention to follow to cite your references properly. In physics, we cite references by placing a number in brackets, like [3], following the place in the text where we paraphrased or quoted the source or where we otherwise wish to credit a prior work, and then we have a References section at the end in a numbered list with all of the works that were cited. Other conventions use letters from the last name, for example. You can find entire books devoted to the subject of properly citing references, so instead of making a long diversion on the subject of citations, I'm going to ask you to do some research and find the method of citations that applies to your work and read up on it there (also, since there are multiple conventions, this way you can seek the convention that is appropriate for your work).

Front and back matter provides an opportunity for marketing, too. Traditional publishers take full advantage of this. If you buy a fictional work by a famous author who has written dozens of books, you will find numerous quotes about how awesome the book is from several popular book reviews, you will find a sample chapter of the next book in the series, and you will find a catalog of the author's or publisher's other books. I've seen mixed feelings about whether self-published authors should do this and to what extent. I do think that a catalog of your other books is appropriate, especially since customers who like your book will probably be interested in your other works. You might want to avoid too much marketing in the front and back matter of your book, though; most people don't like advertising and sales pitches. I included a full catalog of my books at the end of this book as a sample of what a catalog might look like, not so much because I thought you would be interested in my other books (especially, since my other books are not on the subject of self-publishing like the one you are reading, but much different subjects like math, golf, chess, and science). In the catalog, you could just list your titles in bullet format, or you could copy and paste the pictures of the front covers of your other titles from CreateSpace into your book.

Keep in mind that each page of front matter and back matter costs you money – 1.2 cents black-and-white and 7 cents color (even if the page itself is black-and-white – every page counts as color if you choose a color interior) – unless your book is 108 pages or less black-and-white or 40 pages or less color.

2.1.22 Professional Formatting and Editing Services

CreateSpace and other companies do offer professional (paid) services to format and edit your book for you. I recommend doing it yourself. It is pretty easy to use Word to format your book professionally. Try all of the features that I just described and you should, I hope, feel confident that you can do it. You <u>can</u> do it. Be positive!

If your English is poor, you might consider hiring someone (such as CreateSpace's basic copyediting service) to correct spelling and grammatical mistakes. Otherwise, I suggest not spending money on professional formatting and editing services. Until you publish your book, you don't know how much royalty you might make. Unfortunately, not all self-published books are highly successful. If you publish your book for free, rather than investing money up front, you won't be starting out in the hole.

2.2 Revising Your Manuscript to Create an eBook

2.2.1 Reformatting Your Paperback Book File into an eBook

Your file for the eBook version of your book may be significantly different from the file for the paperback version of your book. One reason is that a paperback book reads differently than an eBook. A page is well-defined on a paperback book: Numbering the pages provides a handy reference, we know exactly how each page will look when we publish the book, and we can add headers and page borders to each page.

In contrast, eReaders do not at all respect the concept of a 'page.' They are designed to let the reader control such things as the font size and font style. Since the reader will set the font size to his/her liking, there is no way to control how much information appears on the screen at any given time. Additionally, eReader screens come in many different sizes. Some buyers will read the eBook on a cell phone, others on a large computer monitor.

Page numbers, page headers and footers, and page borders will <u>not</u> be part of the eBook, since pages have no meaning. Similarly, any page margins or font size that you set may not apply to your eBook. However, the font size that you select may affect the starting point for the font size that is displayed, and the reader can then increase or decrease the font size from this point – so starting with a typical font size, like 12, may be a good idea. There are a variety of eReaders out there, and then some people use their cell phones and personal computers to read eBooks, too. You want your eBook to look good on any device.

There is one page feature that <u>will</u> work with Amazon's Kindle (but not necessarily all eReaders): The page break feature can force the eBook to begin a new page at a given point on the Kindle. You can use page breaks to ensure that a new chapter always starts on a fresh screen. If you make a puzzle or flash card book, you can make sure that the answers start on a new screen – it would be silly to have the question and answer on the same screen.

There are some other common manuscript features which eReaders will also <u>not</u> accommodate: eBooks do not respect tab spacing, most special characters (symbols), 𝒻𝑜𝓃𝓉𝓈 𝓉𝒽𝒶𝓉 𝒶𝓇𝑒 𝓃𝑜𝓉 𝓋𝑒𝓇𝓎 𝒸𝑜𝓂𝓂𝑜𝓃, textboxes, and fancy text effects (like glow). Most eReaders also do not respect tables, bullets, and footnotes, but the latest version of Kindle supports basic tables, simple bullets, and endnotes (test out whether or not your table will work – go through the initial publishing steps and check the preview). You <u>may</u> use **boldface** and *italics* for a heading (not header), phrase, or a sentence; but don't use it for an entire paragraph or more. <u>Underline</u>, ~~strikethrough~~, super^{scripts}, and sub$_{scripts}$ work on most eReaders.

You see the problem: If you've already typed your book without all of this in mind, now you have to completely reformat your book to convert it to an acceptable eBook format. Be sure to save the new file with a different name so that you will still have the old pre-eBook format in addition to the new file specifically formatted for an eReader. You would hate to make all these changes and then discover that you'd lost your original. Again, save your files in two or more different places – like your hard drive, a jump drive, and by email in case something happens to one of the files (unfortunately, it is too common to have file problems).

2.2.2 Professional eBook Conversion Services

CreateSpace offers Kindle conversion, but I <u>don't</u> recommend it. First of all, they offer both free and paid Kindle conversion. If you publish a paperback book with CreateSpace, from your book's detail page you can select the Publish on Kindle option. When you click this link, they basically collect the information from your paperback book which is relevant for publishing on Kindle. There you will find the PDF file of the book that you submitted for your paperback book, but this PDF will include numerous formatting features that are not supported in eBooks. So I strongly recommend <u>not</u> uploading this PDF file to Kindle or other eBook publishers. CreateSpace also includes a note indicating that it would be better to submit your original Word document than to submit a PDF file to Kindle. Again, the original Word document submitted to CreateSpace is designed for a paperback. As explained previously, and as we will describe how to do shortly, you must reformat your Word document before publishing it as an eBook.

CreateSpace also offers conversion of your Word document to Kindle formatting as a paid service. However, they won't convert a book that has numerous figures or equations, which are the types of books where you could really use professional help. If you don't have complicated formatting issues, it should be pretty simple to do yourself – as we will describe. If you do seek professional help for eBook conversion, make sure that they will attend to all of the important details that are described here. You'll be quite frustrated if you pay money and wind up with a poorly formatted eBook. If you really want professional help with eBook file conversion, there are some companies that provide this service. For example, from Kindle's self-publishing help page, https://kdp.amazon.com/self-publishing/help, click the link that says, Use a Conversion Service.

2.2.3 Removing Headers, Footers, Page Numbers, Borders, Bullets, and Page References

The first you thing you should do is remove all headers, footers, and page numbers from your file:

1. Select all of the text (using Select at the far right of the Home tab) in your document.
2. With all of the text selected, go to the Insert tab, and find the Remove option at the bottom of Header.
3. Do the same for Footer and Page Number.

If you used page borders or shading, go to the Page Layout tab, open Page Borders, choose <u>the Page Border tab</u>, select Whole Document in Apply To, and change Setting to None. You must also remove any borders or shading that you may have applied to paragraphs or text.

You will also need to revise your index and table of contents, since they refer to page numbers which are nonexistent in an eBook. You could change the page numbers to section numbers, but you can also include links that take the reader directly to the page. We will describe how to add such links to your contents and index in Sec. 2.2.8.

Remove extra line breaks. You get a line break each time that you press Enter. You should not have two or more consecutive line breaks in your eBook (if you had several consecutive line breaks, you probably need a page break instead). You can view all of the formatting marks in your Word document by pressing the ¶ button in the Paragraph group of the Home tab. If you press this button once, it will show all of the formatting marks. Press it again if you want to hide them.

Remove any bullets (although Kindle may support very simple ones). You can click the bullet icon in the Home tab to remove it, or place your cursor at the beginning of each bullet and use the Backspace key (you might need to do it twice to get to the left margin). If you really want some mark like a bullet, you can achieve this manually. You can just type a number, like (1), manually and place it before the line. I don't recommend trying to recreate the tab (and, remember, the usual tab spacing doesn't work): Since most eReaders have a small screen, any tabs cut into the already limited text that is displayed on the screen. Many symbols are not recognized by eReaders, in case you are thinking of inserting symbols (like ☺) in place of the usual bullet. You can enter a *small* picture (you don't want a *large* picture at the beginning of the line), in principle, but that also presents a formatting issue (see the issue with formatting equations in Sec.'s 2.2.6-7). Some simple text that the eReader recognizes is best. You will be able to view a sample of the eBook before it is published, so you will know if a symbol is not recognized (we'll get to this point shortly, too).

Look for any page references. It will be very frustrating for a reader to find a reference like "see page 24" in your eBook since there aren't any page numbers in an eBook. Use Word's Find feature at the far right of the Home tab to quickly find every instance where you used the word 'page.' If you may have used any abbreviations for page – like p., pp., or pg. – you need to find those, too. (If you search for 'p,' you will pull up every word that has a 'p' in it – so search for 'p.' instead in order to limit your results.) Instead of referring to the page, refer to the chapter or section number – like "see Sec. 3.5" instead of "see page 24."

If you used Word's Cross-reference tool, you need to manually replace these with numbers. For example, if you used the Cross-reference tool in the References tab to number all of your figures, delete those and manually type the number of each figure in. The same goes for references to chapters, sections, and any other cross-references that you may have used.

2.2.4 Reformatting Text and Paragraphs, Including Textboxes and Special Symbols

If you did not use a common font, you need to change it to a font that is very likely to be recognized, such as Times New Roman, Arial, or Calibri. Remember, the font can be changed by the customer on his/her eReader. If you used multiple fonts in your original file, make sure that all of them get changed. The simplest thing is to Select All from the Home tab (on the far right) and then choose a common font.

Did you use any textboxes? Cut (select the text and hold Ctrl and press X while still holding Ctrl) and paste (using Ctrl + V) the text from the textbox into the body of the document, and then delete the empty box that remains behind (select it, then select it again at one of its edges, and press delete). However, you may be able to treat a single word or short phrase of WordArt as a picture (but perhaps not for all eReaders), but even so it will format much better as plain text than as a picture (since it may be too small to read on some eReaders, especially cell phones that have a small screen). If it doesn't format as a picture when you preview your eBook (see Sec.'s 4.2.8-11), you can copy/paste it into Paint to make it a picture – but, again, it will format best as plain text (copy/paste it into the text and delete the WordArt box), since then customers can resize the font to their liking. If you want to leave short WordArt as a picture – or at least test it out – select the WordArt, go into the Format tab, choose Wrap Text, and select In Line With Text (afterward, you may need to use copy/paste to position it exactly where you want within the body of your text).

Similarly, remove any Drop Caps that you may have used (at the beginning of a chapter, for example). If you want to achieve a similar effect, highlight the first letter and increase its font size (the eBook edition of this book does this at the start of each chapter).

Most eReaders recognize curly quotes (', ', ", and ") and dashes (– and —) provided that they are made using the Alt key (e.g. hold down Alt while typing 0150 to make –). Don't make dashes using Word's AutoFormat feature because a few Kindle devices may not recognize them when made this way. **See Sec. 5.1.4 regarding the use of special symbols with Kindle.** For a device that doesn't support curly quotes, replace these with straight quotes.

Tables are not supported by most eReaders. Kindle's new software is supposed to support tables, but I would test this out first (Sec.'s 4.2.8-11 will describe how to preview your eBook). You can take a picture of a table (with a Snipping Tool, or print it and scan it), but if the text is small it may be difficult to read on a small eReader like a cell phone. Instead, it may be better to state the same information in plain sentence form instead of a table.

Remove any use of multiple columns, since eReaders do not support them.

Most eReaders also do not support footnotes or endnotes. In this case, you will have to remove them – you can cut/paste the text within the body of the text instead, or you can insert a number in brackets, like [4], after the text, and move the footnotes to the end of the chapter or section (a simple numbered list, in plain text in the body of your text – not footnotes, not endnotes, and not bullets). However, Kindle will automatically convert your footnotes into hyperlink bookmarks (you should test this out to be sure and see how well it works). You can also create your own hyperlink bookmarks (see Sec. 2.2.8).

Use of the tab key is <u>not</u> recognized by eReaders. Also, do <u>not</u> use the spacebar to make tabs. If you used the tab key or spacebar to indent the first line of each paragraph (or anywhere else), you need to replace all of these indentations with a method of indenting that is supported by eReaders. (Kindle may automatically indent the first line of each paragraph, but, if so, it may not do so consistently and might indent shorter or longer than you would like. Many eReaders do <u>not</u> automatically indent.)

First, you must delete all instances where you pressed the tab key or pressed the spacebar successively to create tabs. Save your Word document, then resave it with a different name (so if something goes haywire, you will still have the original as back-up). Press the ¶ button in the Paragraph group of the Home tab in Microsoft Word to show codes. Next, press the Replace button (at the far right of the Home tab), then click the More button, then click the Special button, and select Tab Character (if instead you used successive spaces to create tabs, use the same number of spaces in the Find What field – instead of the Tab Character). Leave the Replace with field empty. Click the Replace All button. This will remove all of the tabs.

Now you need to indent the first line of each paragraph (and add indentations anywhere else where you once had them and would like to keep them). You can do this for the entire document (but then you'll want to undo it for paragraphs where you don't want the first line to be indented, like the title, author, copyright page, contents, headings, etc.), or you can highlight as many paragraphs as you want and do it for all of the highlighted paragraphs at once (and then repeat the process as many times as needed). In the former case, use the Select All tool to the far right of the Home tab – you can do this at the same that you implement the Normal Style (to be described a few paragraphs from now). After highlighting the paragraphs that you to automatically indent, in Word 2010, click the little arrow in the bottom right corner of the Paragraph group on the Home tab, change Special to First Line, and enter a value in inches (like 0.25"). Note that long indentations may not format well on an eReader with a small screen. Instead of using the standard 0.5" indentation, it might be better to use a value between 0.2" to 0.3". (Chances are that some of your paragraphs already had a First Line set instead of the tab, since Word automatically does this as you type – but even if that's the case, some of your paragraphs were not, especially the first paragraph of a section. You want to ensure that there are no tabs anywhere, so it's important to do this step even if you found that some paragraphs had the First Line option already set. Also, First Line was probably set to 0.5" instead of a smaller value, so it needs to be reset anyway.) Remove any blank linespaces between paragraphs (or they may not indent properly) – created by hitting the Enter key twice at the end of a paragraph (like the one after this paragraph).

All non-centered stand-alone lines (with linespace above and below), including left-aligned headings, must have First Line indent set to 0.01"; otherwise, they will automatically be indented. To not indent any other line, like the first line of a chapter, use 0.01". Don't set First Line indent to (none); otherwise it will be automatically indented. For example, if you have blank lines in your table of contents or copyright page, be sure to adjust First Line indent to 0.01" or there will be automatic indentations of these lines. If you use a Drop Cap (not recommended in the eBook as it creates formatting problems on some devices), that paragraph should also have a 0.01" indent. Do you have any other paragraphs or lines where you don't want automatic indents? (Don't use automatic indents where you do want indents, either; it's better to set First Line to 0.3", or whichever value you are using, or it might not be consistent. Also, some eReaders may not automatically indent.)

Set First Line indent to 0.01" for any line like this that you don't want indented.

When formatting your eBook, Word's AutoCorrect feature can automatically do things that affect your eBook's formatting, but which you don't see (when you read an eBook where the paragraph style – such as font style or size, or justification – changes abruptly, this is probably the cause of the problem) – even though you don't see it in Word, your readers will definitely notice it in the eBook file (so it's important to examine your eBook carefully when using the preview tool – described in Sec.'s 4.2.8-11). Turn the AutoCorrect feature off before you make any further revisions to your eBook. In Word 2010, select the Review tab, click the Spelling & Grammar icon, click the Options button, in Proofing click the AutoCorrect Options button, select the AutoFormat As You Type tab, and uncheck all of these boxes.

Make sure that your linespacing is set to single or 1.5 and that the At field is left blank. Do this using the little arrow in the bottom-right corner of the Paragraph group of the Home tab. You should Select All and change the entire document to single or 1.5 with nothing set in the At field just to be safe.

If you want to avoid abrupt changes in paragraph style – like the font size or style suddenly changing from one paragraph to the next – you need to make your entire document 'normal.' Your eBook looks like the style is the same throughout when you view it in Word, but there are probably style changes that you don't see in Word – however, if there are hidden style changes, your customer will definitely see this with the eReader. You need to eliminate these style changes that are hidden in Word, but which will be very visible on the eReader. Before you do this, save your file the way it is and resave it with a new version (as a back-up, just in case something goes wrong). The simple way to do this is to Select All and click the Normal option at the left of the Style group in the Home tab – but not yet because first you need to modify the Normal option.

Right-click the Normal option at the left of the Style group in the Home tab and choose Modify to define what you want the Normal style to be: Choose a simple font and a size around 12, but no larger than 14, then click the Format button and select Paragraph. In this Paragraph popup window, set Left and Right to 0", change Special to First Line, set By to a value between 0.2" to 0.3", change Before and After to 0 pt (not the default 10 pt), adjust Line Spacing to Single or 1.5 (but not the default 1.15), ensure that the At field is blank (no value), and adjust Alignment to Left (Kindle, for example, will automatically justify Full).

Unfortunately, implementing the Normal style change will also make some changes that you don't want: You'll just have to unchange them individually. For example, if you want your section and chapter headings to have a larger font and to be **boldfaced**, you'll have to manually redo all of this. Right click Heading 1, for example, in the Style group in the Home tab, to make a style similar to Normal, but larger and with the boldface button pressed (for example), to make a convenient heading style to apply individually to each heading. You can create multiple heading styles for different types of headings.

Any other formatting that disappears when you implement the Normal style change will have to be reformatted, too (be sure that the AutoCorrect options are completely turned off). Look for **boldface**, <u>underline</u>, centering, and changes in font size – compare your original file to the new one. Manually add these features back into your file. If you would have a ton of reformatting to do, you could try previewing what your eBook file looks like now (see Sec.'s 4.2.8-11) – if you don't see abrupt changes in style, you might be able to get away without normalizing your text (but if your end product has those changes – this method will help to remove them). **Note**: Chapter 5 (in Volume 2) discusses Styles in much further detail.

If you created any page breaks by pressing the Enter key several times, remove those blank linespaces (with the Backspace key) and use Page Layout > Breaks > Next Page instead. Don't separate sections with multiple linespaces – instead, make a line of symbols, like * * * to indicate section breaks (like the example that follows). Alternatively, you can insert a small picture or icon that relates to the theme of your eBook to separate sections.

* * *

Try to remember whether or not you inserted any special symbols in your document. Unfortunately, most special symbols are not recognized by eReaders. The way to know for sure is to view a sample of your eBook when you go to publish it (this is described in Sec.'s 4.2.8-11): Usually, you will see a ⍰ everywhere you used a symbol that the eReader does not recognize. Be sure to change all of the ⍰'s to a recognized symbol: Any ⍰ visible in your published eBook will stand out like a sore thumb. Sometimes, if you use unsupported characters, you instead find a jumble of crazy symbols like áäæéê; you definitely want to find and change those, too. **<u>Beware that Fire supports symbols that the old Kindle doesn't.</u>**

So exactly which characters <u>are</u> supported? Obviously, the list includes uppercase and lowercase unaccented letters of the English alphabet (A-Z and a-z), single Arabic digits (0-9), and most of the punctuation marks that you find on a standard keyboard. Letters with common accents (like é, á, and æ) are supported, but many accents are not. The copyright symbol (©) and registered trademark symbol (®) are supported, but the vast majority of special symbols that you find in Symbol in the Insert tab are <u>not</u> supported. You can find a picture of symbols that Kindle supports, for example, by going to Kindle's homepage, which is https://kdp.amazon.com/self-publishing/help, then clicking Formatting FAQ down near the bottom left under Frequently Asked Questions, and then clicking the second Here under the question, "What characters are supported in KDP?"

You need to find all of the unsupported special characters and change them to something else in order to prevent ⍰'s (or jumbles of characters like áäæéê) from showing up in your published eBook. In some cases, you might be satisfied with a standard symbol that looks similar. If you really want the original symbol, you could produce the same symbol as a picture (I don't mean that you have to draw it yourself – just copy and paste it into Paint and save the file as a JPEG image). Be sure that the format of the picture is In Line With Text (click the picture, go to the Format tab, and choose Wrap Text). However, this is not a perfect solution, so you don't want to do it frequently. For one, the resolution of the image may be lower than the original symbol (generally, you get a higher-resolution image by making the image larger in the original program before you copy and paste it into Paint – which suggests making the symbol with a very large font size before you copy and paste it). Another problem is that the size of the picture will be fixed: The reader may increase or decrease the font size of text to his or her liking, but your picture will not change size. So the picture of your symbol could be very small or very large compared to the text – and it might be smaller than the text for one customer, but larger than the text for another customer. You want your picture to be about the average size of text (around 12 points), yet still have high resolution. (So if you used a very large font size to make the picture of your symbol, now you want to make sure the picture's size on the eReader is comparable to the text instead of being very large there, too. Note that the size of the picture as you see it in your Word document may not be the same as a customer sees on the eReader. When you view the sample of your eBook as you are about to publish it – Sec.'s 4.2.8-11 – you will then have some idea of how the size of your picture will compare to the text around it.) Yes, we will discuss pictures – we're getting there.

Also, look for fancy text effects (like **glow**) and any special text formatting that may not be supported (you can leave equations for now, which we will discuss shortly), as you also need to change these.

2.2.5 Formatting Pictures for an eBook

We will discuss how to format pictures in Sec. 2.2.5, and then discuss how to format equations in Sec.'s 2.2.6-7. (We will discuss how to draw and edit pictures in Chapter 3; Sec. 2.2 is on formatting for the Kindle. Also, we discussed how to make equations in Sec. 2.1.13.) If you have pictures or equations, you want them to look nice on the customer's eReader. You want to keep in mind that eReaders come in a variety of screen sizes: A cell phone screen is smaller than a typical eReader, and a PC monitor is much larger than any eReader; people read eBooks on eReaders, cell phones, and personal computers. You want your eBook to look nice on any screen. Also, keep in mind that some customers will have color eReaders, but others will have grayscale eReaders. Suppose that one of your pictures is a graph and you refer to the 'red' line: Any customer with a black-and-white screen will not know which line is red.

The first thing that you have to do with all of your pictures is to convert them to JPEG file formats. This includes any pictures that you drew yourself using Word's drawing tools, any pictures of any kind that you copied and pasted into your Word document, and any pictures that you inserted into your Word document from a file by going to the Insert tab and clicking Picture. This means just about every picture. You may be able to leave equations that you made with Microsoft Word provided that you save your document with a .doc extension instead of a .docx extension (go to the File tab, choose Save As, and select Word 97-2003 Document instead of Word Document). WordArt that is In Line With Text (click on it, go to the Format tab, and choose Wrap Text) may be okay, too (you will see for yourself when you view the sample of your eBook as you are about to publish it – see Sec.'s 4.2.8-11).

Here is a simple way to convert your picture to a JPEG file:

1. Select the image in Word, copy it (hold down Ctrl and press C while holding Ctrl down), and open Paint (you can find it in Accessories in your Start Menu if you have Windows). But don't paste the image into Paint yet.

2. When you first open Paint, you see a white rectangle (the 'canvas'). Place your cursor over the smaller white rectangle in the bottom right corner of the canvas. When you do position your cursor correctly there, it will turn into a double arrow, then you can drag the cursor (by holding down the left button of your mouse and moving the cursor). Do this to make the canvas <u>much</u> smaller.

3. Now paste your image into Paint (press Ctrl + V). If the image is smaller than the canvas, undo the paste (Ctrl + Z), make the canvas smaller, and try again until it isn't. You want the image to be larger than the canvas was before you pasted the image. When the image is larger than the canvas was, the canvas will automatically enlarge to accommodate it (that's what you want). This is important: Otherwise you get extra white space in your picture that you don't want.

4. After pasting your image into Paint, go to the View tab and Zoom In or Out as needed to get a good view of the image. Don't zoom in too far: Make sure that you can see the entire canvas (white rectangle) on the screen. Zoom in (or out) just far enough that the canvas is as large as you can make it without only seeing part of it.

5. Now return to the Home tab in Paint. If you need to crop your image, grab the Select tool, place your cursor at the upper left point where you want the cropped image to begin and drag the cursor (by holding the left button down while you move it) down to the right. As you do this, you will see a dashed black rectangle. If the black rectangle isn't positioned exactly where you want it, click somewhere outside the canvas and then try again. Once you are happy with the black rectangle's size and position, press the Crop button in the Home tab.

6. Now press the Resize button to change the size of your image. Make sure that the Maintain Aspect Ratio box is checked if you want the picture to look the same way when it is resized. In a moment, we will discuss how to choose the picture size.

7. When you are ready to save your picture, click the File icon in the top left corner of Paint, choose Save As, and select JPEG picture (or PNG if there is text or line art).

8. After you have saved the JPEG file, return to Microsoft Word.

9. Remove the old picture from your Word document (just select it and press the Delete key).
10. Insert its replacement as a JPEG file by going to the Insert tab, pressing Picture, browsing for the location of your file (where you just saved it when you were in Paint), and inserting your file into Word.

You can have an image as large as 2500 pixels on the longest size, but this is overkill: The actual eReader screen won't have more than about 1000 pixels (we will discuss the pixel size of eReaders in the next paragraph). Larger images also make your file size larger. (We will discuss file size in a few paragraphs; you probably want to consider this point before you begin resizing your images. **Also, see Sec.'s 4.2.2 and 4.2.4.**) If you have a large picture designed to fill the screen, you need a high pixel count. If you want your picture to be smaller, a lower pixel count is appropriate (but note that pixel count is <u>not</u> the same as picture size). If you are using your picture for a symbol and want it to be about the size of your text, it will be a very small picture. See how large the picture is when you first paste the JPEG file into word – this may give you a rough idea. You'll see how it will actually look on the eReader when you view the sample as you go to publish the eBook (see Sec.'s 4.2.8-11). Unfortunately, the way you best learn how to perfect the picture formatting is through a little trial and error.

Do you want to make a full-page picture that will completely fill the screen? You won't be able to do this perfectly (and keep your aspect ratio fixed), since eReader screens come in different aspect ratios. Many authors who don't realize that Kindle Fire has a different aspect ratio than the Kindle eInk, for example, become frustrated when they find that their pictures fit perfectly on one screen, but not on the other. It's not possible, though, because these screens have different aspect ratios. What you can do is design your pictures to completely fill the screen (minus minimum, automatic margins) of a particular eReader screen. For example, if you are targeting the Kindle Fire, strive to match its aspect ratio. The Kindle Fire and Nook Color have displays that are 600 pixels by 1024 pixels, while the Kindle eInk 6" and the black-and-white Nook have displays that are 600 pixels by 800 pixels. The Kindle Fire HD 7" is 800 pixels by 1280 pixels. **I recommend skipping ahead to read Sec. 4.2.2, which discusses in more precise terms how to perfect large images for a variety of eReaders.**
<u>**Insert picture, right-click the image, click Size and Position, and set Scale to 100%.**</u>
Pixel count affects the resolution of the image. Another important consideration is the size of the original image. If the image was low-resolution to begin with and you increase the pixel count, it will appear blurry. The way around this is to begin with a larger image. If you drew the picture in Microsoft Word, you can redraw it as a larger image. (You can simply lock the aspect ratio – click on the image, go to the Format tab, click the little icon in the bottom right corner of the Size group, select the Size tab, and choose Lock Aspect Ratio – and then resize the object in Word – manually enter the size in the same place where you locked the aspect ratio, or grab the bottom right rectangle of the object and drag the cursor. However,

some images will look significantly different when you do this: Lines may not meet at precisely the same place and relative thicknesses may change. So it may be better to draw a new image.) You can make the page as large as 20" by 20" in Word, so you can make a very large image if you want. If you made the original picture with a different program, you can explore that program's options to find out whether or not it is possible to make a larger image (or higher resolution image) to begin with – **but see Sec. 4.2.2 for a note about Nook**.

Cropping and resizing the image in Paint will permanently change the image. The eReaders do not respect cropping and resizing that you do in Word. So if you want to make the picture larger or smaller, you have to go back to Paint and do it there. If you simply resize the picture in Word, that won't affect how large the picture looks on the eReader.

There is a trade-off between how large and sharp a picture looks and how large the file is. So let's consider file size for a moment. Several large, high-resolution images have a significant impact on file size. If you have numerous equations or little pictures, this will really increase the size of your file, too. First of all, every eReader has a maximum file size, so if your file exceeds this threshold you won't even be able to publish your eBook with that eReader. (We will discuss ways to effectively shrink your file size in Sec. 4.2.4.) Secondly, a larger file size may cut into your royalties (as explained in Sec. 4.2.5).

For example, if you opt for the 70% royalty rate with Amazon's Kindle, a delivery fee of 15 cents per megabyte (Mb) is subtracted from from your list price before taking 70%. For example, suppose that you set your list price at $2.99 and the file size is 10 Mb. The delivery fee would be $1.50 (15 cents/Mb x 10 Mb), so you would earn 70% of $1.49, which is $1.04 (0.70 x $1.49) per sale. If you could shrink the file size down to 5 Mb, you would instead earn $1.57 per sale: The delivery fee is reduced to 75 cents ($15 cents/Mb x 5 Mb), and 0.70 x $2.24 = $1.57. The extra 5 Mb costs you 53 center per sale ($1.57 – $1.04) in this example.[18]

If your eBook contains several pictures, and you make all of your pictures 20" x 20" in Word and then save them as 2500 pixels x 2500 pixels JPEG images in Paint, you will have a very, very large file. You want to find the happy medium where you have large pictures with a good resolution, while at the same time keeping the file size down. **See Sec.'s 4.2.2 and 4.2.4.**

There are a couple of things that you can do to decrease the file size. We will explore this more fully in Sec. 4.2.4, but for now you should carry out the steps that follow. This will decrease your file size significantly if the pictures take up much of your total file size.

1. Select one of your pictures, go to the Format tab, choose Compress Pictures (near the left side of the panel, in the top right corner of the Adjust group), uncheck the box that says to Apply Only To This Picture (by unchecking this box, it will apply to every picture), check the box that says to Delete Cropped Areas of Pictures, and change the

---

[18] If you don't like math, don't sweat it. You will find a handy royalty calculator when you go to publish your eBook and/or paperback book, so you won't need to do any arithmetic to know exactly what your royalty will be. The eReader will measure your file size when you download it, and the computer will do the calculation for you. You can play around with the list price and see how it affects your royalty.

Target Outpt to Email Resolution (96 ppi). (Simply resizing a picture by dragging in a corner will <u>not</u> reduce the memory.)

2. Click on a second picture to ensure that the same settings apply to it – just to ensure that every picture did change as intended (once in a while, strangely, you have to do this to a couple of pictures in order to make it fully take effect).

Make sure that all of your figures are In Line With Text. When you insert a JPEG file using the Picture button in the Insert tab, the default is In Line With Text. If you want to check the positioning, select the picture, go to the Format tab, and press the Text Wrap button. You want In Line With Text in order to position your picture exactly where you want it. You definitely do <u>not</u> want your picture to float using In Front Of Text or Behind Text (those options position the picture at a precise point on a 'page,' but there are no 'pages' in eBooks).

Kindle users can zoom in on pictures, but the way to do this is not obvious. Since it's not easy to find the zoom option, many Kindle users aren't aware that it's possible to make the pictures larger. If you have a Kindle Fire, for example, you double-click a picture with your finger in order to zoom in on the image. Also, a picture sometimes looks larger in portrait mode than landscape mode, or vice-versa. Users toggle between modes by simply rotating their eReaders 90°, just like using most cell phones. If you have a very detailed picture, and observe when you check the sample as you are ready to publish your eBook that zoom could be of value when reading your eBook, you might consider including a note. Find the first picture of your eBook where you feel that this is important. After the figure, include a note similar to the following note. You might want to shorten such a note. Also, for many figures the landscape/portrait option doesn't actually make a difference – if that's the case with your pictures, you might just mention the zoom option.

[**Photo viewing tip**: Try rotating your eReader 90 degrees between landscape and portrait. The figures may look larger one way or the other depending on their orientation. If a figure looks small, try changing the orientation of the eReader to see if that helps. Also, many eReaders have a zoom option (that's not always easy to find, and you usually have to zoom in on each photo individually – i.e. the zoom usually doesn't "lock" in place). For example, on the Kindle Fire, double-tap your finger on a picture to zoom in on it.]

2.2.6 Formatting Stand-Alone and Mid-Sentence Equations for an eBook

If you typed any equations by going to the Insert tab and selecting Equation, your equation will have serious formatting problems unless you save your file with a .doc extension (instead of a .docx extension). In order to do this, go to the File tab, choose Save As, and change Word

Document to Word 97-2003 Document – but don't do this yet: First, turn all of your stand-alone equations into JPEG files (as described below), and then change the file format. After saving the file as a Word 97-2003 Document, you may be able to reduce your file size somewhat by saving the file back as a Word Document while also checking the box that says to Maintain Compatibility With Previous Versions Of Word (this option only come ups when resaving a .doc file with a .docx extension). I suggest waiting until the rest of your eBook is complete before resaving your file in different formats. (When you go to open a file, you can tell the difference between a .doc file and .docx file if you look carefully. If you view icons, you will notice a slight difference in the 'W.' If you place your cursor over the file and wait a moment, it will tell you if it is a Word Document or a Word 97-2003 Document.)

If you have equations that are in the body of the text (as opposed to being on their own line), you will want to format them so that they look approximately the size of the text when the customer reads the eBook on his/her eReader. When the customer adjusts the font size, all of the text will becomes larger or smaller, but equations and pictures will not. This makes the text look larger than the equations or vice-versa, and also makes the equations look like they are above or below the line (and also affects the line spacing on the screen) – because the bottom of the equation is lined up with text, but the equation has some white space underneath. The best you can do is have the equations be about the same size as the text when the customer first opens the eReader. What you see on the sample when you are about to publish it (once again, we will discuss that in Sec.'s 4.2.8-11) is where you want the text and equation size to roughly match.

Equations placed on their own line can (and probably should) be made larger than equations that are parts of sentences. You can copy and paste (with Ctrl + C and Ctrl + V) your equation into a new Word document temporarily, increase the font size to a much larger value, and copy and paste the equation into Paint (see Sec. 2.2.5) in order to make a JPEG picture out of it. Then you can insert the JPEG file for your equation into your Word document the same way that you do for all other pictures. A large, high-resolution image will enhance the appearance of your equation. If you have some equations that are mid-sentence and others that are on their own line, having the ones on their own line as a JPEG file will prevent those equations from getting resized if you follow my suggestion for how to resize the mid-sentence equations. You might consider moving mid-sentence equations to be on their own line (so you will need to adjust your original sentence, too, if you do this), since you can make a larger equation this way. Mid-sentence equations may not look as good as a large equation on its own line can (since you can make it a large picture on its own line).

It's not easy to format a book with a large number of equations. Long equations are especially difficult to format so that they are easy to read (especially, small details like exponents and subscripts) on eReaders with small screens. If you wrote a textbook or otherwise have numerous equations in your book, I suggest going through the process of trying to format just a few pages (pick those with the most challenging formatting issues) and see how it looks when you view the sample as you are about to publish it (see Sec.'s 4.2.8-11). (I'm not saying to publish a few pages of your book – I'm saying to go through the process so that you can view a sample of a few pages of your eBook, then go ahead and delete it instead of finishing the publishing process. If you have pictures, tables, or rich formatting of any kind, it would be wise to make such a sample and see how it looks before you go through a great deal of trouble to reformat your book. First, see if the trouble will be worthwhile.)

2.2.7 Resizing Mid-Sentence Equations

Note that this section applies to mid-sentence equations only. Make sure that any stand-alone equations have already be converted into JPEG images (not only that, but you must have deleted the original equation and inserted the JPEG file in its place) before you follow these instructions. **<u>Save a new version of your file in case you don't like the result.</u>**

If you made your equations with Word 2007 or 2010 using the Equation button in the Insert tab, there is a trick (for Kindle – not necessarily all eReaders) that you can apply to increase or decrease the size of mid-sentence equations relative to the text. Intuitively, you might expect that if the equations are typed with a size 12 font and that the font size of the text is also 12 pt, they should match. Unfortunately, it doesn't always turn out this way. When you view the sample of your eBook as you are almost ready to publish it, if you need to adjust the size of mid-sentence equations relative to the text, here is what you can do:

1. Go back to the Word Document with the .docx extension (don't use a Word 97-2003 Document with a .doc extension, and don't use a Word Document that was saved in such a way as to be compatible with Word 97-2003 documents).
2. Find one of your equations and make sure that you can place your cursor within the equation and format it as usual (if instead it opens in a new window with the old 2003 equation editor, you don't have your Word Document in the correct format).
3. Select all of your text (using the Select button at the far right of the Home tab), increase or decrease the font size of the document (don't worry, you will change it back in a moment) so that the font is larger if you want your equations to look larger relative to the text and the font is smaller if you want your equations to look smaller relative to the text.
4. Save your file as a Word 97-2003 Document with a .doc extension (again, using Save As).
5. Select all of your text again, and now return the font size to its original size.

This changes the size of your equations relative to the text. View a new sample where you go to publish your eBook (Sec.'s 4.2.8-11) and see if this is good enough. Unfortunately, you may need to do this a couple of times using a little trial and error if you want to perfect it.

When you are satisfied with the result, you will want to go back and increase the font size of headings and any other text that had been larger than the body text (since all of the text became the same size when you used Select All).

2.2.8 Reformatting Your Table of Contents and Index, and Adding Hyperlinks

You need to revise your table of contents and index (if you have one). Don't format your table of contents (or your index) as an actual table. Start out by just compiling a list without page numbers, placing each row of what was your table on its own line (use the Enter key to go onto the next line) in the body of your text. Be sure to keep your heading (Table of Contents) and the page break that came before the table of contents (and do the same for the index). Instead of including page numbers, you can include section numbers (like 'Sec. 3.5' instead of 'Page 53') – but you really don't even need section numbers if you use hyperlinks.

When your (single-column) list is complete, you are ready to add links to it. It's not complicated at all, and Word 2010 has a built-in tool for it. By adding links, customers will be able to click the link to Chapter 4 or your Glossary, for example, and go directly there on their eReader. This is called an Active Table of Contents, and it provides Easy Navigation for the customer (that's the jargon for it).

There are two ways to make an Active Table of Contents. One method is to use Word's built-in Table of Contents tools, which works as a cross-reference. Unfortunately, the built-in Table of Contents tool is not supported by all eReaders (such as Smashwords – Sec. 4.2.10). The second method is to use Word's bookmark tool. I recommend the bookmark method, especially if you plan to publish your eBook with a variety of eReaders.

Following are the instructions for making an Active Table of Contents using Word's built-in Table of Contents tool. Remember, this method is <u>not</u> supported by all eReaders.

1. Place your cursor on an empty line (just hit Enter to make one), go to the References tab, press Table of Contents (on the left side), and select Insert Table of Contents (near the bottom of the list).
2. In the window that pops up, uncheck the box that says to Show Page Numbers (since you don't want to have page numbers in your table of contents) and check the box that says to Use Hyperlinks Instead Of Page Numbers.
3. You will see the following message in the body of your text: "No table of contents entries found." That's okay because we will now add the entries.
4. Highlight a heading that you want to link to the table of contents, like "Introduction" or "Chapter 4" (wherever you find that heading – a separate word or phrase that precedes the text of a section of your book).
5. Go to the Home tab and select a heading style that you like (there are several headings to choose from in the Styles group on the right half) – be sure to choose a 'heading,'

not something else, and make sure that the heading stands alone by itself (as opposed to being part of a paragraph). Right-click a heading style if you want to modify it.

6. Now go to the References tab and press Update Table in the Table of Contents group (at the left).
7. If it worked, this heading will appear in your table of contents.
8. Place your cursor over the heading in the table of contents and then, while holding Ctrl, click the heading with the mouse (first press Ctrl, then click it while still holding Ctrl). This will take you directly to the page where that section begins.
9. Add other entries to your table of contents the same way.

The second method of creating an Active Table of Contents is to use bookmarks. This is the method that I recommend. Following are the instructions for making an Active Table of Contents using bookmark hyperlinks (starting with your single-column list):

1. Don't use any bookmarks that Word may have automatically generated. Instead, be sure to make your own bookmarks as described below.
2. Go to the first item that will appear in your Table of Contents – it may be Chapter 1 or the Introduction, for example. Find the actual heading in your eBook (not the words from your single-column list). Highlight the words in your section heading (Chapter 1, or Introduction, for example).
3. With the section heading highlighted, go to the Insert tab and click Bookmark.
4. Type the name of the section without spaces (e.g. Chapter1) and click Add.
5. Repeat these steps for every section heading that will be included in your Active Table of Contents.
6. Now highlight the text in the first item in the single-column list that will become your Active Table of Contents (e.g. Chapter 1 or Introduction).
7. With the text still highlighted, go to the Insert tab and click Hyperlink. Select Place In This Document, choose the corresponding bookmark, and press OK.
8. Repeat these steps for every item listed in your Table of Contents (but don't link the Table of Contents heading to itself).

When you go to publish your eBook, be sure to test out the links in your Active Table of Contents in the preview (see Sec.'s 4.2.8-11) to ensure that it works correctly and that the formatting is satisfactory. You can create active links in an index using this same method.

After you have made your Active Table of Contents, be sure to delete the list you had compiled in preparation for it. If you are reading the eBook edition of this book, you can see how this works: Go to the Active Table of Contents near the beginning of the book and click on the various links there.

At the end of each chapter (and front matter or back matter section), you may want to create a hyperlink bookmark to allow the reader to return to the table of contents. You can do this with the bookmark method described above (but, basically, in reverse).

You can add hyperlinks within the body of your text, too: You can create a bookmark hyperlink, which works like your Active Table of Contents, to take readers to another point in your eBook (e.g. if in your paperback book you said, "See Sec. 4.3," in your eBook you can turn this into a hyperlink so that if a reader clicks it, the eReader will take the reader directly to Sec. 4.3); or you can create a hyperlink for a web page, which takes readers outside of your eBook to the internet (e.g. if you want to provide the web page for NASA, you can do this as a hyperlink so that a customer who clicks on the web address in their eReader will go directly to that webpage, as in http://www.nasa.gov).

If you want to add an internal hyperlink (i.e. to direct a reader to a specific section of your eBook), do this by using Word's bookmark tool. We discussed this a few paragraphs ago – i.e. the second method of creating an Active Table of Contents. The function works the same way for all internal hyperlinks. For example, you can create a bookmark for Sec. 4.2, then add a bookmark hyperlink anywhere you would like to refer to Sec. 4.2.

You can add an external hyperlink (i.e. to a webpage) by highlighting the text, clicking Hyperlink on the Insert tab, and typing the full web address (including the http:// part) in the Address field (the Text To Display field may be different from the web address). Be sure to include the http:// in the Address field or the hyperlink will _not_ work in the converted eReader file. After inserting the hyperlink, press and hold down the Ctrl button while left-clicking on the hyperlink to test it out – if it doesn't take you to the webpage, check that you typed it correctly (better to copy/paste the rest of it into the field, then add the http:// to the beginning manually if it isn't already there – instead of 'typing' it).

To create a hyperlink to an email address, type just the email address in your text – such as nobody@nowhere.com – but add mailto: to the beginning of the email address in the Address field of the hyperlink popup window (or the hyperlink will _not_ work in the converted eReader file).

When you preview your eBook file (see Sec. 4.2), remember to test out all of the hyperlinks in your Active Table of Contents, index, and any other internal or external hyperlinks that you created. It would also be a good idea to test them out now in Word.

Do _not_ include hyperlinks to marketing pages for your affiliates. Some eReaders (if not all) do not allow this, and so this may cause your eBook not to get published (or to become unpublished later). You _may_ include a hyperlink for your author webpage (at the end of the eBook, for example) or to a webpage that lists your other eBooks, for example; the problem is linking to advertisements and affiliates' marketing pages.

Don't include too many hyperlinks. Many eReaders have a touchscreen where the reader uses his/her finger to advance the page: If there are several hyperlinks on a page, the reader may inadvertently click a hyperlink while trying to turn the page, which can be quite frustrating for the reader. Also, bear in mind that a reader who was happily enjoying your eBook and clicks on an external hyperlink in your eBook might not return to continue reading your eBook – so avoid providing distractions for the reader in the body of the text. The best place for external hyperlinks is a separate page toward the end of the eBook.

End your eBook with a brief thank you note, a list of any other books that you've written, a hyperlink to your author page, hyperlinks to your FaceBook page or blog posts, and perhaps an email address and a brief About the Author section, which could include an appropriate author photo. The last page of your eBook is a good place for brief, tasteful marketing (not advertising or links to affiliated marketing pages, but to your other works): If the reader made it to the end of your eBook, they may have enjoyed your eBook enough to be interested in more of your writing. The end of your eBook is a golden opportunity.

2.2.9 Formatting Adjustments and Community Help Forums

Although I have mostly referred to Kindle, you can use the same file for other eReaders, with few exceptions. For example, the latest version of Kindle is supposed to support tables, but most eReaders may not support them yet. You may need to make a few adjustments for rare differences between eReaders (we will discuss some of these differences in Sec. 4.2). When you view your sample for a particular eReader, you will see first-hand if you need to make any formatting adjustments. We will discuss how to publish your eBook with a variety of eReaders – not just Kindle – in Sec.'s 4.2.8-11.

If you run into specific problems and can't find the solution in this book, remember that you can discuss your publishing experiences with other self-published authors like yourself. If you encounter a problem with picture formatting with your eBook – or any other publishing problem – chances are that other authors have had the same problem and figured out a solution, and someone will likely to be happy to help you. For example, you can ask questions to be answered by other self-published authors of Kindle eBooks at the following community forum (for Nook and other eReaders, see Sec. 4.2.12):

http://forums.kindledirectpublishing.com/kdpforums/forumindex.jspa

The link to the community forum for CreateSpace is

https://www.createspace.com/en/community/index.jspa

If you type your issue into the search field of your favorite internet search engine, there is a good chance that you will find the answer there, too.

Now would be a good time to explore the links in the Resources section at the back of this book. You can find some useful publishing resources there.

Chapter 3

Creating a Book Cover

Chapter Overview

3.1 Using Microsoft Word to Make a Paperback Cover
3.2 Converting Your Cover Into an eBook Thumbnail Image

This chapter answers questions about the following topics, and more:

- ☑ How to create a single-page document that includes the front cover, back cover, spine, and allows room for slight printing variations.
- ☑ How to make spine text and center it perfectly, how to center text and images on the front and back covers, and how to know where the bar code and ISBN will appear.
- ☑ The importance of having a cover that looks nice both as a thumbnail image and as a paperback book cover, and how to preview what the thumbnail image will look like.
- ☑ How to make a cover that looks nice both as a thumbnail image and in paperback.
- ☑ What information you want to be clearly visible on your thumbnail image.
- ☑ Formatting options for textboxes and WordArt, how to draw color pictures using Word's built-in drawing tools, and how to insert pictures.
- ☑ A variety of tips for making a cover in Microsoft Word, such as how to save memory if you have several images, allowing for slight printing shifts, and preventing color variations.

3.1 Using Microsoft Word to Make a Paperback Cover

3.1.1 Finding Sample Covers

rowse through a variety of sample covers. First look at the covers of your own books at home. Then take a trip to the library or bookstore. Next, view a variety of covers by browsing through Amazon's, Barnes & Noble's, and other booksellers' websites. Look at the covers of both paperback books and eBooks. It is important to view both paperback covers and thumbnail images.

Find a book that you can hold in your hand and view online at the same time. Do this with a few books for which you really like the cover. Compare how the cover looks in person to how the thumbnail image looks. Ultimately, you want your book cover to look good both as a paperback book and as a thumbnail image.

Note some covers that you particularly liked, and also find some covers that really didn't appeal to you. Make some notes of what stood out both ways – good and bad. You definitely want to keep this in mind as you design your cover.

Looking through covers, you're not just contemplating what looks great and what looks awful. You're also getting ideas for what is possible, which colors go well together, how large the font needs to be to make key words stand out, and various ways in which a cover might grab attention, for example. Note the different items that you find on covers, like the title, subtitle, author, what goes on the spine, descriptions and quotes on the back cover, etc.

I have included samples of a variety of my books. It's not because I thought that my own covers were the best. Rather, it's that it was very easy to obtain permission to use them, and I could use my own covers for free. I did, however, make most of my covers myself, and most of the images are pictures that I made from scratch using Microsoft Word's drawing tools. (However, I have hired a cover designer for a few books, including this one.) You can also make your own cover and draw your own images with Microsoft Word – or you can take photos and use those pictures – as I describe how to do in this chapter. You will learn how to draw pictures in Microsoft Word in Sec.'s 3.1.8-9, and how to format pictures in Sec. 3.1.12.

If you are reading the paperback version of my book, you can see what the front covers of some of my books look like in color as they appear on the front and back cover. If you are reading the eBook, all of the cover images in the eBook edition are in color. I selected the samples on the cover, and in the following figures, to try to show some variety – I didn't choose which covers to place there based on how popular the books are.

In addition to the front covers, you can find samples of some of my full cover spreads on the following pages. These show you what my Word files looked like for the full cover, including the front cover, back cover, and spine. Your cover will have a similar layout to these full cover spreads. I included my full cover spreads mainly to help you understand this layout.

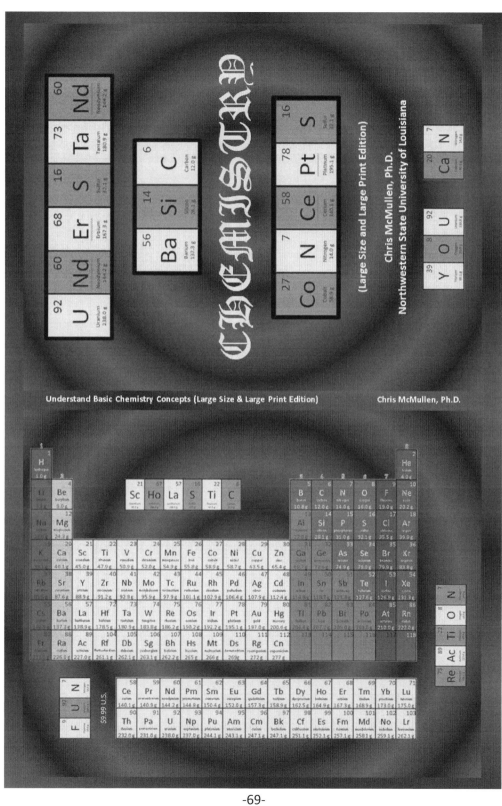

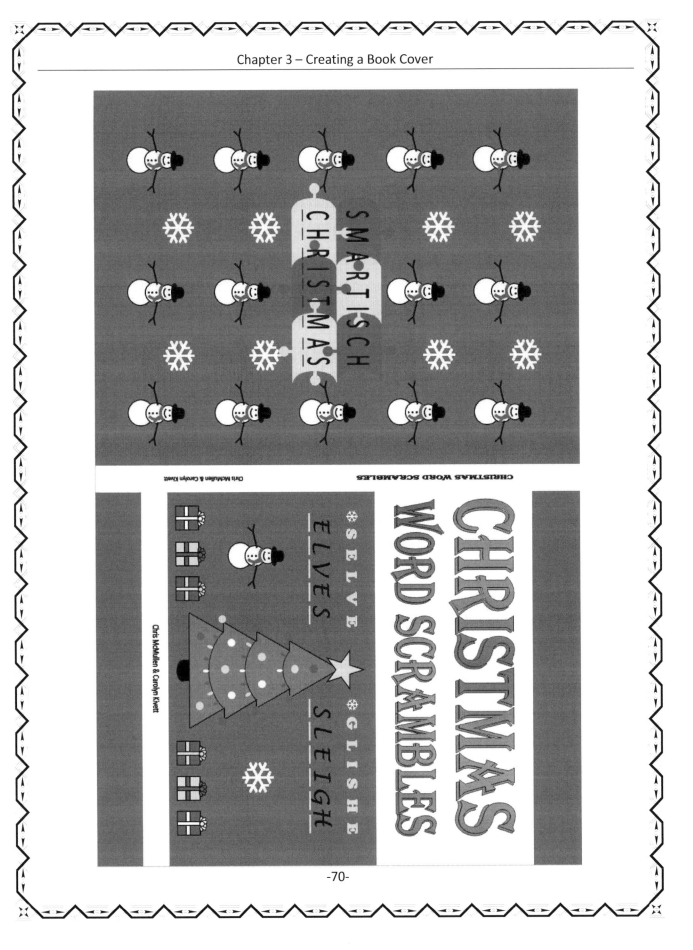

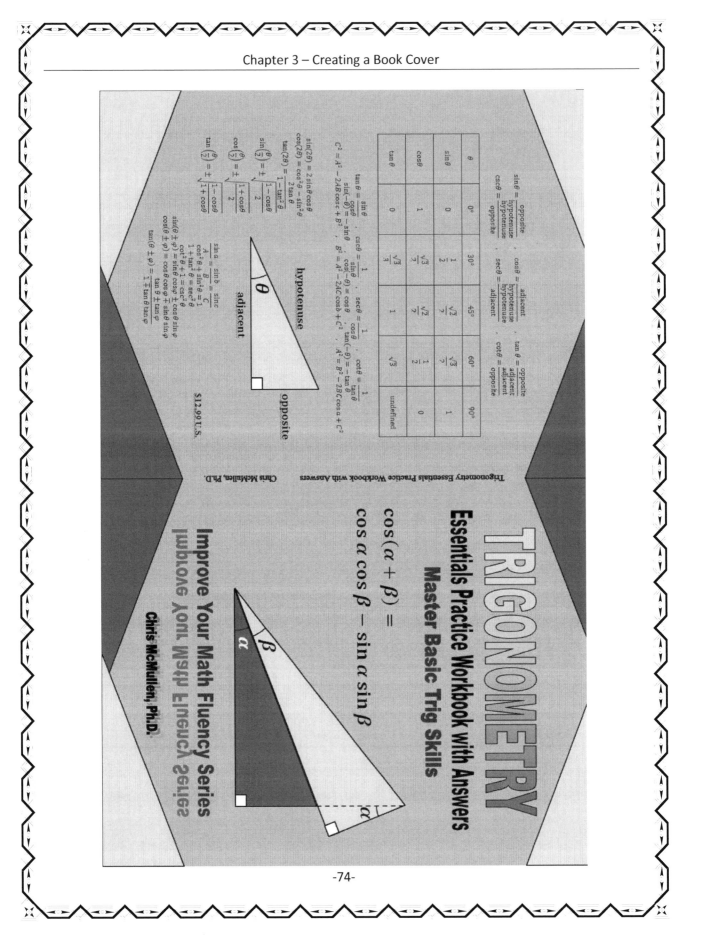

GOLF WORD SCRAMBLES

ALEGE
EAGLE

YIWARFA
FAIRWAY

YUNROCT BULC
COUNTRY CLUB

KAJC UNISLACK
JACK NICKLAUS

Chris McMullen
and
Carolyn Kivett

GOLF WORD SCRAMBLES   Chris McMullen and Carolyn Kivett

This Golf Word Scrambles book consists of 101 puzzles; each puzzle contains 10 golf-related words or phrases, like sand trap, nine iron, Tiger Woods, or St. Andrews. All 10 words from each puzzle are related – for example, they might all be common golf phrases, golf equipment, professional golfers, or famous golf courses. Knowing that the words in each puzzle are related may help you unscramble any words or phrases that you don't see right away. You can check all of your answers with the solutions in the back of the book. The puzzle pages are decorated with golf holes. This puzzle book is great for both golf lovers and word puzzle enthusiasts.

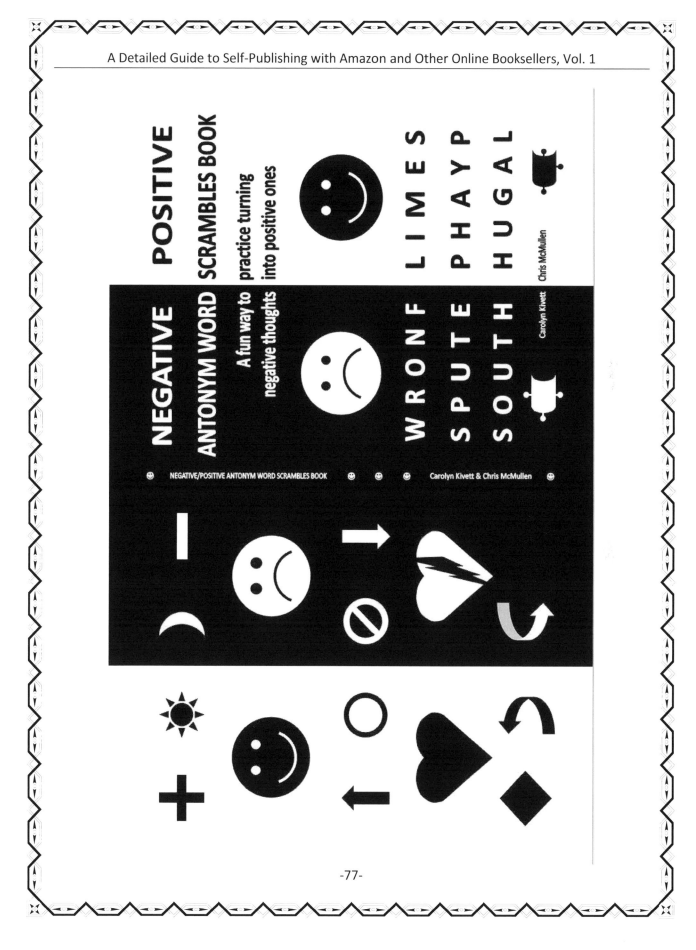

Watch a tesseract unfold. See how the 3D cross section of a hypercube changes as the hypercube rotates. Explore the world of 2D humanoids, and also take a tour through a 4D hyperuniverse. View 4D wheels with axles with a spherinder or cubinder structure. Imagine climbing a 4D staircase. Find 10 out of 120 dodecahedra of a hecatonicosachoron highlighted... all on this visual tour of the fourth dimension.

Anyone who is curious about the fourth and higher dimensions can enjoy the detailed concepts of this text. The book is much more visual and conceptual than algebraic, yet it is detailed and technical, with the intention of satisfying the needs of mathematically-minded readers familiar with the fundamentals of algebra, geometry, and graphing.

Chris McMullen earned his Ph.D. in particle physics with a thesis on the collider physics of extra dimensions. He has also published a half-dozen papers and taught winter courses on extra dimensions.

$15.99

Chris McMullen, Ph.D.

The Visual Guide to Extra Dimensions, Volume 1

The Visual Guide to

EXTRA DIMEN-SIONS

Volume 1

Visualizing the Fourth Dimension, Higher-Dimensional Polytopes, and Curved Hypersurfaces

Chris McMullen, Ph.D.

3.1.2 What Should You Include on Your Cover?

Your front cover must include the full title and the names of all of the authors. The full title on your front cover file, the title on the title page, the title on the copyright page, and the title that you enter when you go to publish your paperback book must all match exactly. However, you don't need to include the subtitle on your cover; this is optional. Spell the names of all of the authors exactly the same way on the cover, title page, copyright page, and as you enter them when you go to publish your book. You might have an illustrator or editor, for example, to acknowledge in addition to the authors.

All of the text of the title does not need to be the same size, does not need to lie on the same line, can have a symbol replace a letter (like a planet replacing an 'O'), and can even be separated or spread out considerably (as long as it is reasonably obvious how to correctly read the words of the title in order). You probably want a few key words to be larger and to stand out effectively. The key words should be easily visible in the thumbnail image.

Most front covers feature some art. However, many very appealing and effective covers don't have anything that you might normally regard as art – many just have simple patterns of solid colors, stripes, or simple shapes. You don't necessarily need good drawing or art skills in order to design a great cover. You probably observed some simple covers that were very nice when you were browsing through covers. When it comes to the thumbnail image – and this is where most Amazon buyers will first see your book – simple is often much more effective than complex. The main ingredients are key words that stand out and are easy to read combined with an appealing color scheme (note which combinations of colors seemed appealing to you when you were browsing covers – and if you're not confident with your own judgment or those of your friends, you can search for opinions about good color schemes on your favorite internet search engine).

If your book has 130 pages or more, include a label on the spine, too. In fact, it is worth having this many pages (in case you were planning to submit a slightly shorter book) so that you can add spine text to your cover. A book looks more professional when you see the title and a combination of the author, publisher, and a logo on the spine. Also, it makes the book much easier to find when it is sitting on a bookshelf: So if you have any aspirations of getting a local bookstore to buy and sell copies of your book, you really need to include spine text. If your book has over 100 pages, you can still include spine text, but due to printing tolerances, there is a chance of the edge of the spine text wrapping onto the front or back cover; also, the spine text is required to be quite small on a thinner book. A book of 100 pages or less can't have spine text on the cover. (We will describe how to add spine text in Sec. 3.1.7.)

Keep in mind that buyers will see the back cover of your book when they use the Search Inside feature on Amazon. The back cover can be decorative, or it can be functional, or both. One way to make the back cover functional is to include a description of your book. If your book has been professionally reviewed, you can include a quote from the review on your cover. The back cover can also include a brief biography of the author, or highlight the author's qualifications. The back cover provides an opportunity to help market and sell your book. You can even put a table or picture on the back cover that may be helpful to the reader – like a map, if you are writing a fantasy book, or a multiplication table, if you are writing a math workbook. I included pictures of a variety of my book covers on the back cover of this book because I thought that these color pictures of covers might be helpful to some of my fellow, soon-to-be self-published authors when they go to design their covers.

Your back cover will automatically include a bar code and ISBN number. You can predict precisely where this will be placed, as described in Sec. 3.1.5. (If you really would like it placed elsewhere, try contacting the company with whom you self-publish your paperback – such as CreateSpace. After logging into your account, click Contact Support on the left side of the screen.) Consider including the list price on the cover, too. Big chain bookstores, like Barnes & Noble, require the list price of the book (which is the list price that shows on Amazon's listing) to be on the cover in order to be eligible to have your book stocked in their stores. However, this does not affect eligibility for online sales, and it is not easy to get big chain bookstores to stock your book on their shelves (see Sec. 4.1.7 and Chapter 8).

3.1.3 Design With Both the Paperback and Thumbnail Image in Mind

It's very important for the front cover of your book to look nice as a thumbnail image because this is the first thing that prospective buyers will see on Amazon and any other websites where you paperback book is sold. The thumbnail image helps customers to visualize holding your paperback book in their hands. The actual cover of your paperback book – including the front cover, spine, and back cover, is also important because customers who buy your book will see it firsthand (their friends and family members will likely see it, too).

Many people are significantly influenced by the cover of a book. Do you know anybody who has a coffee table book decorating their living room, who mostly appreciates that the cover looks nice? You're not trying to sell a coffee table book, and you want people to read your book and value it for the content, but my example does show one common way that a cover is important to buyers. Similarly, some customers like holding a book that looks nice and sounds interesting when they read it in a bus or on a plane, for example. You may find that you have friends or family who have some books that they bought because they looked or sounded interesting, but never got around to reading. Again, you don't want your book to go unread, but you can see in this case that the appearance of the book may factor into the purchase decision.

The content is important, but many readers will not judge your book solely by the content. The thumbnail image helps to draw interest in the book, and the actual cover helps to continually recall interest in the book – and to interest other potential readers. If a customer buys your book online, it may be a week or more before the book arrives in the mail. When the customer opens the box, you want the cover to revive his or her interest in your book. When the customer sees your book lying around, you want the cover to remind the customer to read your book (of course, captivating content can achieve this, too – but the customer has to start reading your book before he or she can be captivated by the content; the cover can help to capture the reader's interest before the book is ever opened).

The cover should do more than just catch attention or create interest. It should look professional in appearance in order to make a good impression. The cover can also provide information about the book and/or the author, and can help to sell or market your book.

Several factors affect how professional your cover looks. Any misspellings or grammatical mistakes on the cover give a poor impression right off the bat, so it's definitely worth very carefully proofreading all of the text on your cover. Also, check the images over carefully when you review your proof to ensure that there aren't any formatting errors – such as intersecting lines that should meet at their edges, but are a little misaligned. The cover text should be easy to read in person, and the key words should be easy to read on the thumbnail image. The color combinations that you see on the cover should look appealing both on the screen and in print. (Even if you publish your book with a black-and-white interior, the cover will be color.) Overall, the cover should have a good aesthetic feel to it. Including spine text and centering it properly on the spine and including the list price on the cover can also help to create a professional look. A professional cover is also tasteful and inoffensive.

It doesn't take a Picasso for a cover to draw interest from readers. A simple cover is often more effective than a complex cover. You also don't want the cover to seem too busy.[19] Books with the best-looking covers don't always sell well. Although the appearance of the cover is important, it's not the only factor that affects sales – content, reviews, qualifications of the author, recognition of the publisher, and so on, are important, too.

Here is one way that a cover can be quite simple, yet still be effective. The cover could have a few large, key words that are easy to read on the thumbnail image, and the background could include a few large rectangles (one above the other) – all with an appealing color scheme. Without even a picture, such a cover can be effective. It is easy to vary this approach – change the large rectangles to some other pattern, or add an image. I'm not saying that you should avoid anything more complex: Rather, I'm saying that if your goal is to keep the cover design as simple as possible, your cover could still be effective. I have a few sample thumbnail images below that exemplify this simple scheme. These thumbnail images aren't for real books – I just made them up to illustrate a few ways that the design scheme of a cover can be simple.

---

[19] A couple of my own covers are a little too busy, such as the astronomy book shown on the front cover. For the most part, I have tried to keep my covers from looking too busy, and I recommend this as a general rule.

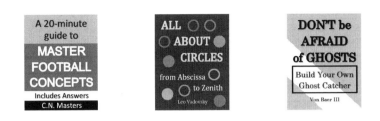

You don't make both a cover file and a thumbnail image for your paperback book. If you publish your book with CreateSpace, they will create the thumbnail image for your Amazon and other online bookstores' listings from your cover file. So you want to anticipate how the thumbnail page will look, based on your file for the entire cover that includes the front cover, back cover, and spine. After you make the cover for your book, you can preview how the cover will look as a thumbnail image as follows:

1. Add (so remember to remove them afterward) a few large rectangles (click Shapes in the Insert tab) that block out the back cover, spine, and any background that extends beyond the edges of the cover (you will be able to do this easily the same way that you draw the temporary edges of the cover, spine, and bar code in Sec. 3.1.5).
2. Change the zoom (the Zoom button is in the View tab) to a small number, like 10% to 20% (it depends on how large your monitor is, for one).
3. Open Amazon and adjust the zoom until your cover looks about the same size on the screen as the thumbnails that you see there.

This will give you an indication of what your book's cover will look like as a thumbnail image. You will also get to preview the thumbnail image of your book when you proceed to publish your book (as described in Sec. 4.1.9). If you're not satisfied with the preview, it's worth making some adjustments.

3.1.4 Color Shifts and Other Printing Issues

Beware that the colors that you see when you view your cover on the screen in Microsoft Word (or your PDF file) may not look exactly the same as when you receive a copy of your paperback book. This is not the publisher's fault; instead, it has to do with the difference between how colors are made on a computer monitor versus how they are printed on paper.

Here is the technical reason for the variation. Many computer monitors use a RGB (red, blue, green) color scheme. This is a color addition scheme where the combination of two or more colors can be used to make any other color. The monitor shines light from two or more colors at the same point on the screen to create the desired color there. Printers generally use a CMYK (cyan, magenta, yellow, black) color subtraction scheme. In this case, you view reflected light from the page. Here, the colors mix according to the rules for pigmentation, which is different than for mixing light.

The CMYK process used by printers is, from a conceptual standpoint, more limited than the RGB process. As a result, it is difficult to achieve the exact same color with a printer as that color appears on a screen. There may also be a difference in brightness, contrast, and other qualities between the image that you see on the screen and the actual cover.

The printing process used by CreateSpace is excellent, but – as with printing in general – does not perfectly reproduce the colors that you see on the screen. You may notice slight variations in color. For example, a blue may appear a little darker on the printed page and a little brighter and lighter on the screen. You can print your cover if you have a color printer (scaled down to a smaller size, unless your printer accepts large sheet sizes – like 11" x 17"): Although it won't be the same printer that is used by the publisher, it might be better than only looking at the screen.

On a related note, you can draw with hundreds of colors on your computer monitor, but the publisher's printer won't print in this many different hues and shades. So if your cover has three different shades of green, for example, you might only see two different shades of green on your actual cover. If you use a few different shades or hues of the same color, try to ensure that no two of the colors look too similar.

	Color	Red	Green	Blue
	Aqua	0	255	255
	Black	0	0	0
	Blue	0	0	255
	Fuchsia	255	0	255
	Gray	128	128	128
	Green	0	128	0
	Lime	0	255	0
	Maroon	128	0	0
	Navy	0	0	128
	Olive	128	128	0
	Purple	128	0	128
	Red	255	0	0
	Silver	192	192	192
	Teal	0	128	128
	White	255	255	255
	Yellow	255	255	0

There is one thing you can do if want to try to control the colors to some degree: When you choose a color, select More Colors, choose the Custom tab, and enter precise values for Red, Green, and Blue. The table on the previous page lists the RGB values for the 16 standard basic web colors. If you want to look up the RGB values for additional colors (such as orange or brown), try searching for "red green blue values colors," for example, with your favorite internet search engine. The previous table appears in color if you are reading the eBook version of this book with an eReader that supports color. Unfortunately, most of these 'standard' web colors are not the same color as Microsoft Word 2010's default colors. For example, when you select 'green' in the list of what they call Standard Colors, it turns out to be different than the 'green' that you get when you manually type in the standard RGB values for 'green' from the previous table.

Another issue that you might have with your images is termed 'flattening.' The publisher flattens images when they convert the PDF file that you submit to the final PDF file that will be used to print your book. Usually, if anything, the color may shift a little bit due to flattening. You can flatten the image yourself if you purchase Word-to-PDF conversion software that has an option to flatten the images. However, this is probably an unnecessary expense. Alternatively, you can convert the images to JPEG files following the instructions of Sec. 2.2.5 – although the quality of the image in the paperback book or its cover may be better by not converting the image to a JPEG file. At least, see if you are content with your images after first trying the free PDF conversion that is available with Microsoft Word 2010. If not, keep in mind that it might not be flattening that is the problem: As we just mentioned, color-shifting may also be attributed to inherent differences between printing and producing an image on a screen.

Not every effect that you can create on the screen will show up in your physical paperback book, and in some cases the effect may look somewhat different. This may be an issue if you use some of the fancier options – like setting transparency, or choosing a default texture or pattern. The pattern may be scaled differently in the printed image than it appears on the screen, for example. The printing process is excellent overall – I'm very pleased with the results, and continue to use CreateSpace for my self-publishing needs – but I have observed occasional discrepancies. If you are a perfectionist and notice subtle details, you must realize that the printing process is not a perfect reproduction of what you see on the screen.

There are also sometimes slight variations in positioning, alignment, and the cut of the book cover. You have to allow for slight printing tolerances. I've ordered hundreds of books, and very rarely had more than just a slight issue. I have had a couple of noticeable problems, which were promptly resolved, and these haven't occurred for a couple of years. If you see a significant printing problem – like something being off by ¼", you should contact CreateSpace to report it along with the number printed on the very last page of your book (which will help them track the problem to its source). After logging into your account, click Contact Support on the left side of the screen. Be courteous in your communication and keep an open mind – a mistake could turn out to be your own.

3.1.5 First Draw Temporary Edges of the Cover, Spine, and Bar Code

The first step in creating a cover is choosing a sufficient page size and then marking on the page where the boundaries of the cover, spine, and ISBN bar code will be. This is pretty straightforward to do as you will be able to follow step-by-step instructions.

When you open a new Word document to serve as your cover file, you will need to adjust the page size in order to accommodate the front cover, back cover, spine, and room for images to bleed at the edges. There is a simple formula that you can use to calculate precisely what the minimum page size will be. I will provide the formula with CreateSpace in mind; if you use a different publisher, the calculation may be a little different.

The first step is to compute how wide the spine will be. Since the thickness of your book depends upon how many pages there are in the book, you will need to know the page count for your book. When you open the file for your book's interior, Microsoft Word shows the page count in the bottom left corner. If the page count is an odd number, add 1 to the page count since you must have an even number of pages (this is because each piece of paper has 2 pages – one page on each side). As examples, if your book has 133 pages, count this as 134 pages instead; but if your book has 152 pages, just leave it as 152. (If you have an odd number of pages, you might consider adding 1 more page to it – otherwise, the last page will just be blank. Actually, there will be another two or four pages after that: The very last page will have a bar code and date of manufacture on it. However, any pages that CreateSpace adds at the back do not affect your royalty calculation.)

You also need to decide whether you will print your book on white or cream paper because the thickness is slightly different. (However, if your interior will be in color, then white paper is your only option.) In order to determine the spine width, multiply your page count by 0.002252" (0.002347" for color) for white paper and by 0.0025" for cream paper:

For white paper: spine width = number of pages x 0.002252 inches (0.002347" for color).
For cream paper: spine width = number of pages x 0.0025 inches.

For example, a 150-page black-and-white book on white paper has a spine width of 0.3378" (that's 150 x 0.002252), while a 150-page book on cream paper has a spine width of 0.375" (that's 150 x 0.0025).

Next, what is the trim size of your book? You had to select this before you set the page size for the interior of your book. Note that the trim size is not the same size as the page size if you allowed room for images to bleed. The actual dimensions of your book will match the trim size (within reasonable tolerance). You might want to recall the available trim sizes listed in Sec. 2.1.4.

The first dimension of the trim size is the book's width, while the second dimension is the book's height. For example, an 8" x 10" book has a width of 8 inches (across from left to right, when the book is closed) and a height of 10 inches (top to bottom).

Now we can calculate the trim size of your cover. The width of your cover will be two times the width of your book's trim size plus the spine width. The height of your cover will equal the height of your book's trim size.

Width of cover trim size = (width of trim size x 2) + spine width.
Height of cover trim size = height of trim size.

For example, suppose that we have an 8" x 10" book with a spine width of 0.42". The cover trim size will have a width of 16.42" (that's 8" x 2 + 0.42") and a cover height of 10".

If you want to have images (such as a color background) extend all of the way to the edge of the cover (as opposed to live elements – like text – which must be 0.125" from the cover edges), you must submit a cover file image that measures 0.25" wider and 0.25" taller than your cover trim size in order to allow for images near the edge of the cover to bleed. (The extra 0.25" allows for 0.125" bleed on each side – left and right or top and bottom.)

So if the cover trim size is 16.42" x 10" (as it was in the previous example), then the image in your cover file must be at least 16.67" x 10.25" (where 0.25" was added to both the width and height).

CreateSpace permits you to submit a larger cover image than needed, provided that you center everything on the page (there is a simple way to do this with Word, which we will learn shortly). However, I do not recommend this because it often results in unexpected changes to your cover file during file review. Change the page size by clicking the Size button on the Page Setup group of the Page Layout tab, then More Paper Sizes at the bottom of the list. Enter the values of the width and height, including bleed. In my previous example, the width would be 16.67" and the height would be 10.25". Be sure that everything is centered properly on the front cover, spine, and back cover of the PDF cover file that you submit. You're much less likely to have resizing or repositioning issues if you size the cover perfectly.

Let me describe conceptually what we are going to do, and then I will provide step-by-step instructions, followed by a couple of illustrations. We're going to set the page size and then add 5 rectangles. The 5 rectangles will serve as guides to show you the boundaries of the front cover, back cover, spine width, and ISBN bar code (yep, that's only 4 – the 5th will serve to help place the ISBN bar code rectangle correctly). When your cover is completely finished, you will delete these 5 rectangles. They are temporary, but very useful as they serve to help you place your cover text and pictures exactly where you want them.

Following are the instructions for adding the 5 guide rectangles:

1. First, set the page size to a size that is equal to your cover trim size plus bleed, or to a size that is larger than this. In my example with an 8" x 10" book with a spine width of 0.42", we determined that the cover trim size plus bleed was 16.67" x 10.25". In that example, the page size needs to be at least 16.67" x 10.25". I recommend 17" x 11", unless the cover trim size plus bleed turns out to be larger than this. Go through the calculation of the spine width and the cover trim size plus bleed for your book, following my examples.

2. Go to the Page Layout tab, click Size, choose More Page Sizes at the bottom of the list, and enter the width and height for your cover file.

3. Also in the Page Layout tab, click Margins and set all of the margins to 0". You will receive an error message in a popup window: Click Ignore.

4. In the View tab, click One Page so that you can see your entire cover on the screen.

5. Go to the Insert tab. Choose Shapes. Select the rectangle that has square corners (not the one with rounded corners). Since there are two rectangles that look similar, be sure to choose the right one.

6. Your cursor will now look like a plus (+) sign (like the crosshairs of a scope). Place the cursor somewhere on the page and press the left button on your mouse. A rectangle will appear on the screen.

7. With the rectangle selected (it was already selected unless you have since clicked somewhere else – if so, click on the rectangle to reselect it), go to the Format tab. (This Format tab only appears when a drawing object is selected.) Click on Shape Fill (but not the left part of the button). Choose No Fill (beneath the Standard Colors) so that you can see through the rectangle.

8. With the rectangle still selected, return to the Format tab. Click on Shape Outline (but not the left part of the button). First choose Black (near the top). Then go back into Shape Outline, click Weight, and choose 1 pt or less (in order to decrease the thickness of the outline).

9. With the rectangle still selected, again return to the Format tab, and on the far right change the width and height to match the trim size of your book. For example, for an 8" x 10" trim size, set Width to 8" and Height to 10".

10. With the rectangle still selected, click Copy in the Home tab (or hold down the Ctrl button while pressing C on your keyboard). Then click Paste (or Ctrl + V) twice. Now you will see 3 rectangles. One rectangle is for your front cover, one is for the back cover, and the third is for the spine width. Grab one rectangle (but the edge – you can't grab the middle when the color has been set to No Fill) and change its width to match the spine width of your book. Recall the results of your spine width calculation. This third rectangle should be very narrow (probably less than one inch unless you have a very long book).

11. Grab one of the large rectangles and move it to the far left of the screen. To do this, click the edge of the rectangle with the left button of your mouse and hold the left button down as you drag it across the screen. Release the button when you finish.

12. Grab the narrow spine width rectangle and place its left edge against the right edge of the far left large rectangle. After you get it close, with the spine rectangle selected click the left (←) or right (→) arrow keys to line the edges up as well as you can.

13. Now grab the second large rectangle and place its left edge against the right edge of the spine width rectangle. Line up the edges as well as you can.

14. Select all three rectangles. There are a couple of ways to do this. One way is to click on one rectangle, press the Ctrl button on your keyboard, and while you are holding down the Ctrl button, click the other two rectangles. This way is frustrating if you mis-click anything before you finish. The other way is to click one rectangle, go to the Format tab, and click Selection Pane. A selection pane will appear at the right of the screen. Click on the word Rectangle 1 (or any other number) in the selection pane, hold down the Ctrl button on your keyboard, and then click on the names of the other two rectangles.

15. With all 3 rectangles still selected, in the Format tab, click the Align button and choose Align Top (this will line all 3 rectangles by their tops).

16. With all 3 rectangles still selected, in the Format tab, click Group and then select Group from the list.

17. Click elsewhere on the screen to deselect the rectangles, then select the group of rectangles (be sure to click the group only once). Go to the Format tab, select Position, choose More Layout Options (at the bottom of the list), choose the Position tab in the window that pops up, and in both Horizontal and Vertical, click Alignment and choose Centered. This will center the group of 3 rectangles on the screen.

18. Insert a fourth rectangle following Steps 5-8 again. Set the size of the rectangle to 2" x 1.2" following the instructions in Step 9.

19. Insert a fifth rectangle (you can use copy/paste instead of making a new one – this way you don't have to set the fill and outline again) and change its size to 0.25" x 0.25".

20. Position the small square (0.25" x 0.25") in the bottom right corner of the large (like 8" x 10") rectangle on the left. Then position the ISBN bar code rectangle (2" x 1.2") so that its bottom right corner touches the upper left corner of the small square.

21. Group all 5 rectangles together like we did in Steps 14-16.

If you followed all of the steps correctly, your cover guide will look like the illustration on the next page. I suggest saving just the guide by itself (before completing your cover) in case you publish more books in the future. The second illustration that follows shows the cover spread for this book (shrunk down to fit on the page of this book) with the guide rectangles on it. This will help you see the purpose of the guide rectangles that you made.

Top left corner of page

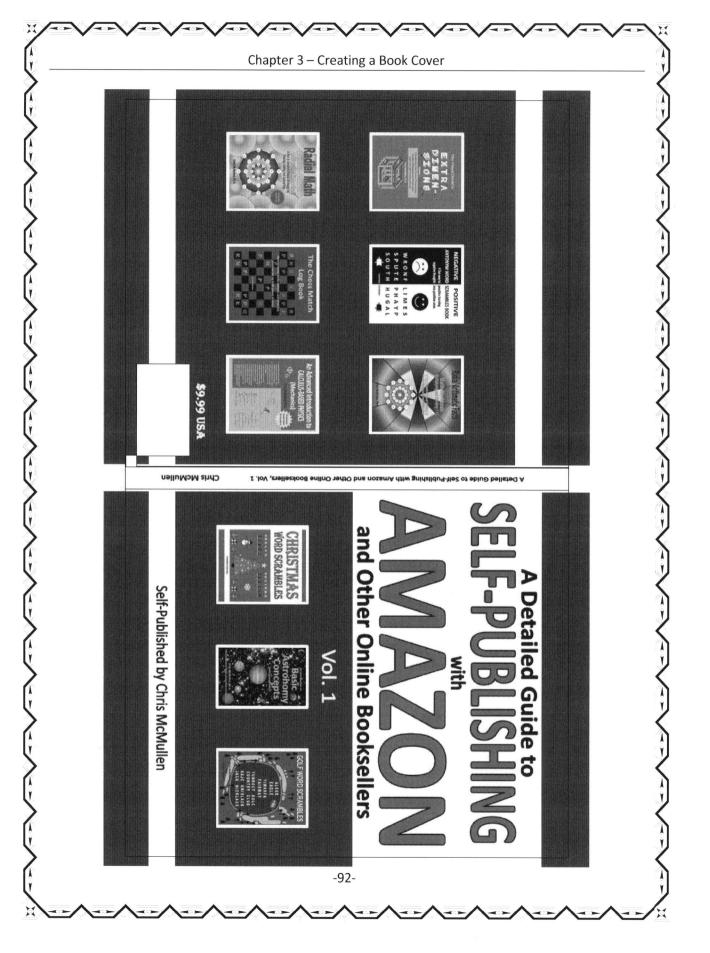

The gray border in the first illustration just serves to show where the page boundary is. View each of the previous two pages with the book turned sideways with the spine at the top – i.e. the 'bottom' of each page is at the outer page edge, while the 'top' of each page is at the spine. Doing so, you can see that the 'left' rectangle represents the back cover and the 'right' rectangle represents the front cover.

In Sec. 3.1.6, we will learn how draw and format textboxes and WordArt, and, then in Sec. 3.1.7, we will apply this to add text for the title, author, spine, description, price, etc. In Sec.'s 3.1.8 and onward, we will learn how to draw, format, and insert pictures. You will want to make one large picture for your background (which you will learn how to do in Sec. 3.1.10) – which could simply be a very large solid rectangle.

Remember to allow room for images to bleed 0.125" (or slightly more, but not less) beyond the cover guide that we made. For a simple background, add a rectangle the size of the page of your cover trim size + bleed (width = trim width x 2 + spine width + 0.25", height = trim height + 0.25"), center it on the page, change Wrap Text to Behind Text, and set Shape Fill to a color of your choice. Remember to keep all text within 0.25" of your cover guide boundaries. Don't put anything where the ISBN bar code will go (otherwise the bar code will cover it up). Any images that extend near the edge should either stop 0.25" before reaching the edge of the cover guide or should extend 0.125" beyond the edge to allow for bleed.

3.1.6 Formatting WordArt and Textboxes

WordArt and textboxes allow you to create text that can grouped together with images to form pictures, to create floating text that can be placed anywhere in the document, or to create text that can be rotated. The text in text boxes and WordArt can be formatted just like ordinary body text using the features in the Font group in the Home tab, and also fancier text effects that can be found in the Format tab. In older versions of Microsoft Word, there were significant differences between textboxes and WordArt,[20] but now you can achieve the same effects with either textboxes or WordArt. The main distinction now is that WordArt starts out looking a little fancier than a textbox when you first type your text. I prefer WordArt for short phrases or single words, and textboxes for sentences or paragraphs.

This is a textbox. You can remove the 'box' from the textbox if you want to. You can also format it to look like WordArt, if you want.

---

[20] There used to be fancier text effects for WordArt, but only more basic formatting options for textboxes. In Microsoft Word 2010, you can find the same features for textboxes and WordArt in the Format tab.

Is this a textbox or WordArt? Actually, it could be made either way.

To create WordArt, go to the Insert tab, click WordArt, and choose any of the 𝔸's as a starting point. A rectangle will appear on the screen with a message that says, "Your text here." Place your cursor in the message, delete the message, and type your text into the WordArt.

Grab the WordArt by placing the cursor over the dashed rectangle that surrounds the WordArt and clicking the left button of your mouse once; this causes the rectangle to become solid instead of dashed. Go to the Format tab (which only appears when the WordArt is selected) in order to change the style of the WordArt. Since the same formatting options are available for both WordArt and textboxes, let's discuss how to insert textboxes before we describe the various formatting options.

To insert a textbox, go to the Insert tab and click Text Box. I prefer to pick the basic textbox in the top left corner, and then format it to my liking. Set your cursor on the screen and click the left mouse button to insert the textbox. Place your cursor inside the textbox in order to type text into it. Grab the textbox the same way that you grab WordArt. However, unlike WordArt, the rectangle always looks solid.

A variety of things that you can do with a textbox or WordArt includes:

➤ Select the textbox or WordArt by clicking the edge of the rectangle.

➤ Edit the text by placing your cursor within the text.

➤ Note the distinction between selecting the box versus editing the text. Select the box by grabbing the edge of the rectangle, and edit the text by putting the cursor where the text is. In both cases, you click on the textbox or WordArt, but in different ways. WordArt will have a dashed rectangle when you are editing the text and solid rectangle when you select it, but a textbox will look solid either way. For either one, you will see 8 tiny white circles (at the corners and midpoints of the sides) when it selected, and your cursor will be flashing when you are editing text. Sometimes, when you try to select the box, the first time that you click the box it is ready to type instead; in that case, click the rectangle a second time to properly select it.

➤ Move a textbox or WordArt by selecting it and dragging the mouse (move the mouse while holding down the left button). Once it is very close to where you want to place it, use the arrow keys ($\rightarrow$, $\leftarrow$, $\uparrow$, and $\downarrow$) on the keyboard to move it a small distance in order to position it precisely where you want it.

➤ Resize the textbox or WordArt by first selecting it. When it is selected, you should see 8 tiny white circles – one at each corner and the midpoint of each side. When you place your cursor over one of these circles, you will notice (without clicking) that it turns into a double arrow (↔). Place your cursor over one of the circles and drag the mouse (hold down the left button while moving the cursor) to change the size of the box.

➢ You can rotate a textbox or WordArt. One way to rotate the entire box is to go to the Format tab and click Rotate. You can quickly rotate the box 90° clockwise (Rotate Right) or counterclockwise (Rotate Left). For other angles, click More Rotation Options and enter the angle directly into the Rotation field in the Size tab. If you Flip the entire box, the text will still read forward, not backward. Another way to rotate the entire box is to select the box and place your cursor over the green circle above it. Then drag the cursor to rotate the box (click the left button of your mouse and hold it down while moving the mouse).

➢ You can also rotate the text within the box as opposed to rotating the entire box. To do this, go to the Format tab and select Text Direction.

➢ Change the style and size of the font in the Home tab the same way that you format ordinary text. This, along with other standard text formatting options available in the Home tab, such as boldface and highlighting, were described in Sec. 2.1.11. You can also include standard paragraph formatting from the Home tab in textboxes and WordArt, such as bullets and linespacing (as described in Sec. 2.1.10). For the fancier formatting options available in the Format tab, see the remaining bullets on this list.

Some standard formatting options:
❖ Bullets.
❖ **Boldface**, *italics*, underline.
❖ Highlighting, ~~strikethrough~~.
❖ Superscript, subscript.

➢ Insert an equation into a textbox or WordArt by clicking Equation from the Insert tab (see Sec. 2.1.13).

$$y = \sum_{i=1}^{N} x_i^2$$

➢ Note that, in the Format tab, there are a Shape Fill and Shape Outline in addition to a Text Fill and Text Outline. This is because you can fill the box itself with color and also outline the box, and you can also fill and outline each letter of the text. Compare the WordArt examples below to see the distinction between filling and outlining the shape versus the text.

➢ Both Shape Fill and Text Fill allow for gradients and patterns in addition to solid colors. You can find more options within Gradients by selecting More Gradients, such as choosing a preset gradient pattern or changing the direction of the gradient.

GRADIENT

➤ Shape Outline and Text Outline each allow for a variety of solid and dashed outlines (choose Dashes) – including double or trip lines (choose More Lines and then select Compound Type) – as well as the option to vary thickness (select Weight).

➤ Change the shape of the box by clicking Edit Shape in the Format tab. Alternatively, you can insert a shape from the Insert tab, click to insert the shape, right-click the shape, and select Add Text. Note the Callouts available in the selection of shapes, which are designed to have text pointing to a picture (of a person, for example). When you select a callout (by clicking at its edge), look for the tiny yellow diamond (near the point), and drag it (by left-clicking it and moving the cursor while holding the button down) to move the pointer of the callout.

➤ You can find fancy text options in Text Effects in the Format tab, including Shadow, Reflection, Glow, Bevel, 3-D Rotation, and Transform. For example, in Transform you can make the text follow a path or you can warp the text. Find more options at the bottom of each list (such as 3-D Options or Shadow Options).

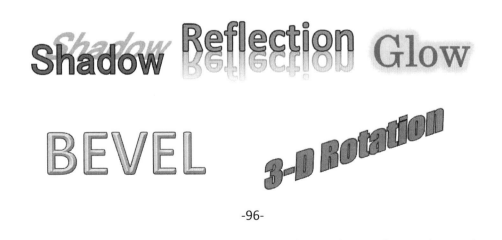

➤ You can also apply Shadow, Reflection, Glow, Soft Edges, Bevel, and 3-D Rotation to the shape of the box – as opposed to the text – by choosing Shape Effects in the Format tab. Note the distinction between Shape Effects and Text Effects.

➤ Note that there are several preset styles to choose from in the Shape Styles group of the Format tab.

➤ You can also change the way that a textbox is wrapped in your document by selecting Wrap Text in the Format tab. In your book cover, choose In Front of Text so that you can position the textbox wherever you want. In the interior file for your book, choose In Line With Text or Square instead of In Front of Text, as this reduces the complexity of your file. When you choose In Line With Text, you can also center it or align it with either margin using the icons in the Paragraph group of the Home tab. When adding a textbox to a drawing that you make in Word, select In Front of Text (for every item in the group – drawing or textbox), group the textbox(es) and other drawing elements together (choose Group in the Format tab), and then change Wrap Text to In Line With Text (you must select the entire group, without also selecting a specific item in the group, in order to do this). For a wrapped textbox or WordArt, modify the distance between the box and body text choosing Wrap Text in the Format tab, then More Layout Options, and finally the Text Wrapping tab.

➤ If you are using a textbox or WordArt as a label in a diagram, remove the outline of the textbox and the fill by selecting No Fill in Shape Fill and No Outline in Shape Outline.

➤ Change text alignment by selecting Align Text in the Format tab. Click the little arrow in the bottom right corner of the WordArt styles group in the Format tab and select TextBox in order to adjust the internal margins.

Once you have made one textbox or WordArt, if you wish to make another one similar to the first it may be more convenient to copy/paste the original (using Ctrl + C and then Ctrl + V) instead of making a new textbox. However, if you do this, be sure not to accidentally paste a textbox into a textbox (this happens if you have a textbox selected when you paste).

3.1.7 Title, Author, Spine Text, Cover Price, and Other Text

In this section, we will discuss how to use textboxes and WordArt to make all of the text for your book's cover. Then, in subsequent sections, we will describe how to draw images and how to add drawings, photos, clipart, and other images to your cover. I suggest not adding a background for your cover until later, as this will make it easier to select objects on your cover without accidentally grabbing the background. We will also discuss how to make a background in the following sections.

It will probably be useful to switch back and forth between zoom options as you make your cover. When you want to see the entire cover on your screen, select One Page in the View tab. When you prefer a close-up so that you can read small text easily and place images or text precisely, try Page Width, 100%, or click Zoom to choose another value, such as 200%, in the View tab.

You should presently have a file started with a large page size and 5 rectangles positioned to serve as the guides for the front cover, back cover, spine width, and ISBN bar code, as described in Sec. 3.1.5. It should presently look like the image below:

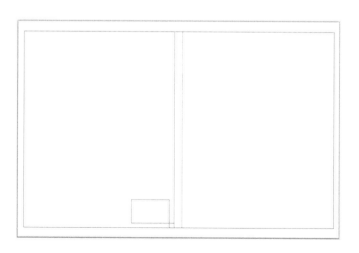

Start out by typing the full title of your book in one or more textboxes. Your front cover must contain the full title exactly as you enter it when you publish it if you choose to publish with CreateSpace (but the subtitle – if you have one – is not required to appear on your cover; that's optional). Your title can be split over multiple lines, and words on one line do not need to read perfectly straight across, so long as the order of the words is clear and each word can be clearly made out. If you want any words to appear larger or in a different font, for example, create different textboxes or WordArt for them. You can even use a picture for a letter, such as a basketball for an 'O' in the title of a sports book. You can even make the individual letters of a word separately – for example, you can make every letter of a word outlined with a circle and then stagger the letters (the sample below was made by grouping each letter together with a circle and then using the Bring Forward option in the Format tab; use Wrap Text to position the WordArt in front of the shape). There is ample opportunity to be creative, should you wish to exercise it, in the design of your cover. You may wish to read Sec. 4.1.3 before finalizing your title.

If your title extends onto two or more lines, consider entering each line in a different textbox or WordArt instead of using the Enter key to go onto the next line. This will allow you to place the text closer together, vertically, for example. If you do use two or more textboxes or WordArt for your title and you want the font to be the same throughout, double-check that the font has the same size in each box (it's also a good idea to visually check that the letters of each textbox or WordArt appear exactly the same if you're trying to match them – in addition to checking the font size number).

If you would like a textbox or WordArt to be centered on the front or back cover, one way to do it is to make the textbox or WordArt the same width as the front cover and center the text within it. Be sure to check that the text does not extend all of the way to the edge of the cover, though: The text must be at least 0.25" from the cover edge. Remember, the cover guide that you made includes a rectangle to show you the front and back cover edges. Copy and paste the 0.25" x 0.25" square, then move this square (drag it with the cursor) to any cover edge if you want to check that there is at least 0.25" between the text and cover edge. Alternatively, you can make a narrower textbox or WordArt, center the text within it, and align the box with the cover rectangle – by selecting both the textbox/WordArt and the front or back cover rectangle (it must be ungrouped from your cover guide before doing this – click

Ungroup in Group in the Format tab), clicking Align in the Format tab, and then Align Center. (Select multiple objects by clicking one, holding Ctrl, then clicking the second – or select one on the Selection Pane available from the Format tab, hold Ctrl, then click the second.)

You may want a few words of your title to be readily visible in your thumbnail image. If so, you need a very large font size for these words. If you would like the font to be larger than 72 pt – the maximum default font size that you get when you click the arrow next to the font size in the Font group of the Home tab – click on the font number (which will highlight the number in blue) and type the number that you would like to try (such as 96 or 144). You may wish to refer to the end of Sec. 3.1.3, where we discussed how to preview what the thumbnail image will look like as you design your cover in Microsoft Word.

Remember that you want your cover to look good both as a thumbnail image and as a softcover book. While a large font size helps to make text more readable on the thumbnail image, it might not look as good to have a very large font when holding the book itself. With this in mind, you might just want a few key words to be very large, and many of the words to be much smaller. Consider both how the actual cover and thumbnail image will look as you design your cover.

We discussed a variety of text effects in Sec. 3.1.6, which you can apply to your textboxes and WordArt. Bear in mind that you want the text – especially, key words – to be easily read. Some font styles and text options are easier to read than others. You also want to apply an appealing color scheme. See what the text looks like with and without **boldface** – some fonts look better on the cover one way or the other. Similarly, explore the difference between having a Text Outline color as well as setting the Outline color to No Color; also, try making the Text Outline the same color as Text Fill, compared to making the two colors contrast. Trying out various options is the best way to help you make decisions.

You must also include the full name(s) of all of the authors on the front cover, and spell each name the same way that you enter it when you publish your book. Other names of contributors, like an illustrator or editor, may not need to be on your cover, but should be mentioned somewhere – like the title page and copyright page. See Sec. 4.1.9 regarding contributors that you might acknowledge, and also about author names and pen names.

You may wish to use a smaller font for the author's name than for the title, unless you have name recognition – as is the case with celebrities and already popular authors, but is also the case for authors who write a nonfiction book in a field of their recognized expertise, for example. On the other hand, if you're really proud to have your name on the book and want it to stand out, go ahead and make it large – remember that it is your book, so you should be happy with the design of your cover. If an author has special qualifications that relate to a nonfiction book – such as professional experience or a relevant degree – you may want to include this information with the author's name.

If you want to center the author's name on the cover page, or align it with other text, for example, select the items (click on one, hold Ctrl, and click the others – you can also select the items in the Selection Pane from the Format tab), go to the Format tab, and choose the Align button.

You can include the subtitle of your book on the front cover, if you have one, but you may also choose not to do so. A subtitle may provide additional information that may be useful to a potential buyer who is looking at your book in person. This may not be important unless you have plans where many potential customers will be checking your books out in person compared to the number of sales that may come from browsing for your book online. You may find it difficult to fit a subtitle on the cover in addition to the title, author(s), and whatever artwork or pictures you may have in mind, yet still have the cover look nice as a thumbnail. If so, it may be best to leave the subtitle out.

Think about the positioning of any images that you plan to use when you place your title and author text on the front cover. You could have the title at the top, name at the bottom, and a large image in between, for example – but if you view dozens of book covers, you will see that there are many other ways that you can choose to place the title, author(s), and images. If your cover will feature one main image, you probably want to design the title and author text around it. If you plan to use multiple images of about the same size, think about how you want to place them – e.g. you might scatter the images around, or you could group them together or place them symmetrically. In these cases, you should also plan the position of the images first, then place the title and author text around them. If, on the other hand, your cover design will feature a pattern that is uniform throughout, your cover text will not be dictated by the position of your images.

You might want to highlight a brief, important note on your front cover in a way that stands out. For example, if you write a workbook, you might want to emphasize that it includes the answers; or if you are writing a book in a mystery series, you might want to highlight the series name. One way to do this is with a starburst or a callout. In order to do this, follow these instructions:

1. Go to the Insert tab and select a shape of your liking, such as one of the stars.
2. Click on the arrow in the bottom right corner of the Size group on the far right of the Format tab and check Lock Aspect Ratio in the Size tab.
3. Adjust the size of the shape by selecting it, placing your cursor over one of the small white circles at the corner (but not a side) of the rectangle, and dragging your cursor.
4. Select a Shape Fill, Shape Outline, and other formatting of your liking.
5. Insert a textbox or WordArt and add text. Adjust the font style, size, and formatting.
6. Select the shape and the textbox (or WordArt) by clicking on one, holding down Ctrl, and clicking on the other.
7. Choose Align in the Format tab, then Align Center and Align Middle. If you're not happy with the centering, you can always use the arrow keys on the keyboard to adjust it.

8. While the shape and textbox (or WordArt) are both selected, group the objects together (available in the Format tab).
9. Position the combined shape where you would like it by selecting the shape and dragging your mouse.

It is also possible to add text directly to a shape (by selecting the shape, right-clicking it, and choosing Add Text), instead of making them separately and grouping them together. However, by making them individually, it is generally easier to center the text precisely and you can also position text with much narrower margins between the text and the shape.

Does your book have enough pages to include spine text? A book of 100 pages or less is not thick enough to include spine text (if you include it with a cover file that you submit to CreateSpace, they will remove the spine text if your book doesn't have more than 100 pages). If your book has fewer than 130 pages, the spine text will have to be very narrow in order to allow for printing tolerances so that the spine text does not wrap around to the front or back cover. Thus, it may be better to omit spine text if your book is under 130 pages. If your book has 130 pages or more, you should take full advantage of the opportunity to add spine text to your cover. In fact, if your book is presently a little short of 130 pages, this is a good incentive to add a few more pages.

In order to add spine text to your book, first insert a textbox. Type the text for your title and author(s) into this textbox on a single line. Actually, it would be better to copy and paste (using Ctrl + C and Ctrl + V) the text for your title and author from the copyright page of your interior file into the textbox for the spine text in your cover file (since it's easier to check for spelling mistakes and other typos on the copyright page than it is in the spine text). You can enter the text in separate textboxes, but you know that they will be perfectly aligned if they are in the same textbox. Add several spaces between the title and author(s) to create some separation between them.

Select the textbox, go to the Format tab, choose Rotate, and click Rotate Right 90°. Be sure to choose right, not left, in order to achieve the proper orientation: This is an industry standard so that all books have their writing in the same direction on the spine. Your library would look funny if a few books had the spine text rotated the other way. Find some of your own books and study the orientation of the spine text and check that yours is rotated correctly. When you receive a proof of your book, remember to compare the orientation of your spine text to that of traditionally published books.

Be sure to center the spine text within the textbox. After you choose a font style and other formatting of your liking, adjust the font size and the number of spaces between the title and author(s) until your spine text has suitable length, thickness, and positioning. You can place the spine text exactly on the center of your cover file by clicking Position in the Format tab, going to More Layout Options, and changing Alignment to Centered in both Horizontal and Vertical. If you happen to change the height of thickness of your spine text (which could simply result from changing the font style, for example), you will want to re-center the spine textbox on the page.

Ensure that you leave at least 0.0625" on either side of your spine text between the two cover folds. If your book is short (around 130 pages), this may require using a smaller font size than you would prefer. If you submit your cover file to CreateSpace, they will let you know if you did not leave enough room on either side of your spine text, and will shrink the spine text down, if necessary, in order to allow for reasonable printing tolerances. (You will also have the opportunity to view a proof of your book, and revise the cover if you aren't satisfied with the adjustment.)

Remember to account for the ISBN bar code placement when designing your back cover. You don't want an important image or text to get covered up by it. Recall that the cover guide that you made in Sec. 3.1.5 accounts for the precise placement of the ISBN bar code.

Most books have some text on the back cover, although occasionally a book will only have a picture and the ISBN bar code. A back cover description can provide a sample of your writing, and also provides the opportunity to do one or more of the following:

☺ Describe your book and draw interest in your work.
☺ Explain how your book is distinguished from similar titles.
☺ Include a biography of the author(s).
☺ Highlight your experience and qualifications.
☺ Help to market your book. For example, if any magazines have reviewed your book, you can include quotes from them.

If you write a book with a black-and-white interior, the cover is the only place that you can include color pictures. If you are writing a chemistry book, you can include a periodic table on the back cover, and if you are writing a fantasy book, you can include a map on the back cover. Should you have valuable content that you would like to appear in color, but you have a black-and-white interior, consider adding it to your back cover. The back cover of this book (if you are reading the paperback edition) includes both descriptive text and thumbnails of some of my book covers. I included these color pictures of front covers as a sample of book covers to supplement the large black-and-white covers from Sec. 3.1.5.

Your book will look more professional if you add a cover price. There is no standard location for the cover price. However, you should find some position where it looks natural, and there shouldn't be any alignment concerns that may stand out in the reader's mind (like feeling that it isn't quite centered within its area). If you will be making your book available on Amazon UK and Amazon Europe (meaning continental Europe) through CreateSpace (this option is free, so why not take advantage of it – unless you happen to have content that isn't supposed to be sold in one or more of those countries), your book might look a little more impressive if you state your price in USA dollars, UK pounds, and EUR euro. For example, your cover price might be $8.99 USA, £5.59 UK, €6.98 EUR. To add these symbols, go to the Insert tab, click Symbol, choose More symbols, go to the Symbols tab, change From to ASCII (decimal), and enter the character code. The character code is 0163 for the pound symbol (£) and 0128 for the euro symbol (€).[21] In Sec.'s 4.1.4-5, you will learn how to set your price in pounds and euro in addition to dollars.[22]

The picture below shows an example of what your cover might look like when your text is complete, prior to adding any images and before removing the guides. The layout of your cover may be somewhat different, but you should presently have a title, author(s), spine text (if your book has at least 100 pages), a cover price, and other text (such as a description). The main point is to see how your text appears before adding other images.

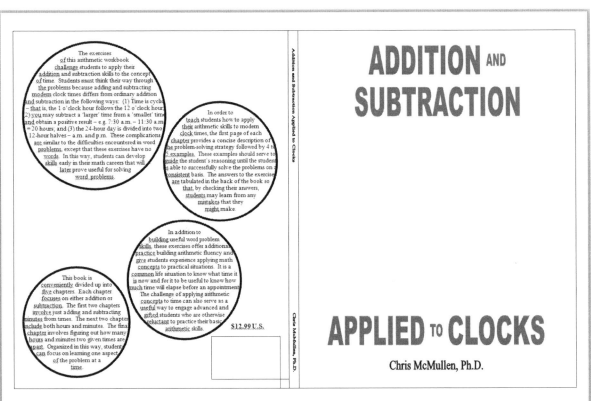

Be sure to remove the guides when your cover is in its final form. However, it would be wise to save a version of your cover (with a different file name, of course) that includes the guides, just in case you need to modify your cover later (e.g. if your page count increases with revisions).

---

[21] If you're having trouble finding a specific symbol that you're looking for, try typing "shortcut key for ___" in your favorite internet search engine. You can very often discover the character code this way.

[22] Did you know that euro should not be capitalized and that the plural does not have an 's'?

3.1.8 How to Make Illustrations Using Microsoft Word's Drawing Tools

If you wish to make your own pictures, I highly recommend using Microsoft Word. It is very easy to use – especially, if you read this section and try making each image as you read the instructions. You can make very professional images simply by drawing in Microsoft Word.

I do <u>not</u> recommend using Paint. I have had many students express a preference for Paint when I teach them how to use Word, but the only reason for their preference was that they were already used to Paint. Many pictures that I have seen drawn in Paint look very unprofessional. For example, diagonal lines often look noticeably jagged in Paint, but straight in Word. There are many more features in Word to help you align images and enter values for width and height, for example, which help you draw with precision. Use Word instead of Paint, and make your book look much more professional. (Better yet would be Adobe PhotoShop.) It is easy, and you <u>can</u> do it. If you really want to learn how to draw pictures in Microsoft Word, sit down at your computer as you read this section, open Microsoft Word, and try to make each image yourself. Again, I'm preparing instructions with Microsoft Word 2010 in mind; Microsoft Word 2007 is similar.

Before we get started, let me remind you of the color issues that we discussed in Sec. 3.1.4. Strangely, the preset colors in Microsoft Word 2010 do not include many of the 16 standard web colors, and a few colors that seem like standard colors are not quite the same as the 16 standard web colors. Even what Microsoft Word calls 'Standard Colors' when you click on Shape Fill or Shape Outline are not all the same as the standard web colors. As a result, if you go with the defaults instead of entering RGB values, you might find (as we discussed in Sec. 3.1.4) that the colors that you see on the cover are slightly different from what you see on the screen. I recommend using the RGB values in the table in Sec. 3.1.4 for the 16 standard web colors. You will also want to look up the RGB values of other useful colors which are not in the table – like orange and brown. You can easily find a more comprehensive table by searching for "RGB values" with your favorite internet search engine.

Here is how to enter the RGB values for a color: When you are choosing Shape Color or Outline Color, go into More Shape Colors or More Outline Colors and enter the RGB values in the Custom tab. Once you have used a color once, you will be able to quickly find it in Recent Colors the next time that you click on Shape Fill or Shape Color (until you close Microsoft Word – then the next time you open the program, you need to do it again).

Avoid drawing a picture from scratch inside your book interior file. Instead, first draw the picture in a new blank document (with your book file closed – and any other programs that take a significant chunk of your computer's memory closed). Save your picture file (so you have a backup copy, just in case). Group the images of your picture together and, for an interior image, also change Text Wrap to In Line With Text. Then you can open your book interior file or cover file, and copy and paste the completed picture.

This will minimize the risk of running into memory problems – like having to restart your computer or having a file become corrupt. Drawing the image in your book file sometimes causes problems, but pasting the completed picture already grouped together and in line with text usually doesn't cause a problem. We will learn how to group objects together and change the text wrap later in this section.

So let's get started. Go to the Insert tab and click on Shapes. This is the place to start anytime you want to draw a picture. Note the New Drawing Canvas at the bottom of the list that appears when you click on Shapes. You don't have to use a drawing canvas, but you might find it convenient to draw your picture on a canvas. You can try drawing the pictures with and without a canvas, and see which you prefer.

Select a shape and adjust its formatting as follows. It would be good practice to see if you can make each of these images.

1. Go to the Insert tab, click Shapes, and choose one of the shapes.
2. When you select one of the shapes, your cursor will change into a plus (+) sign. Place your cursor on the screen and click the left button of your mouse to insert the shape.
3. Select the shape with your mouse. When a shape is selected, a Format tab will appear at the top of the screen. Go into the Format tab.
4. Set the Shape Fill and Shape Outline. Choose More Shape Colors or More Outline Colors to set the RGB values (see Sec. 3.1.4). Note the distinction between White and No Fill: If you place one shape over another, No Fill will let you see through it. If you use No Fill, you will have to grab the edge of the shape in order to select it. Similarly, remove the outline from a shape by choosing No Outline.
5. If you want to blend multiple colors together in the fill, select Gradient (in Shape Fill), then More Gradients, and then Gradient Fill. Note the preset color schemes available for gradients.

6. In Shape Outline, you can change the thickness of the line in Weight and the pattern in Dashes. At the bottom of each list, More Lines offers more options, like a double line.
7. If you change your mind about which shape you want, you don't actually need to delete it and start over. Instead, you can simply select Edit Shape in the Format tab, and then choose a new one.
8. Explore the variety of Shape Styles available in the Format tab. You can certainly create many more effects than just what you see in Shape Styles, but it's nice to be familiar with preset styles, since they are easy to make.

9. When you click on a shape, you will see 8 little white circles – one at each corner and the midpoint of each side. For many shapes, if you look closely you may also find one or two little yellow diamonds. If you grab and drag (hold the left button of your mouse while moving the cursor) the little yellow diamond, it will adjust the shape's shape. For example, the four different pictures below were all made from the 5-point star shape – the only difference is that the little yellow diamond was used to adjust the shape.

10. Resize a shape as follows. Select the shape. Place your cursor over one of the 8 little white circles and your cursor will transform into a double arrow (↔). Drag the cursor to resize the shape. The corners allows you to change the width and height together, while the sides allow you to change just the height or just the width. Another way to resize the shape is to click on the shape, go to the Format tab, and enter the Width and Height directly. This is especially useful if you want to create different types of shapes and make them all the same height or width.

11. Sometimes you want to lock the aspect ratio so that the shape looks the same when you resize it. To do this, select the shape, go to the Format tab, click on the little arrow in the bottom right corner of the Size group (on the far right), choose the Size tab in the popup window, and check the box to Lock Aspect Ratio. For example, if you want to make a circle and change its size without having it turn into an ellipse, you must lock the aspect ratio before you resize it.

12. There are two different ways to rotate a shape. One way is to select the shape, place your cursor over the green circle, and drag the mouse. Alternatively, you can set the rotation angle precisely by going to the Format tab, selecting the little arrow in the bottom right corner of the Size group, choosing the Size tab, and typing an angle in the Rotation field. If you click Rotate in the Format tab, you can quickly rotate the shape 90° or flip the object horizontally or vertically.

13. In the Format tab, if you click Shape Effects, you can choose from Shadow, Reflection, Glow, Soft Edges, Bevel, and 3-D Rotation. You can find Options at the bottom of each list. For example, in 3-D Rotation Options, click 3-D Format in the popup window and enter a value in order to increase the Depth (otherwise, the shape won't look 3-D). Note that 3-D Rotation Options allows you to rotate a shape in ways that aren't possible with the other two methods of rotating a shape (described in Bullet 12). All six images below are the same basic plain rectangle with different Shape Effects.

14. You can really alter a shape by clicking Edit Shape and then Edit Points from the Format tab. For example, insert a circle and choose Edit Points. You will see 4 small black rectangles appear; these are the 'points' that define the shape. Place your cursor over one of these small black rectangles and drag your cursor. The shape won't look much like a circle when you do this. As you drag your cursor, note the blue line that appears. Try rotating this blue line to learn how it affects the shape. Also, try stretching the blue line. Next, right-click a point and choose Delete Point. Now right-click somewhere on the boundary of the shape and select Add Point. Right-click a point and switch from Smooth, Straight, and Corner. As you can see, you can make all sorts of custom shapes using the Edit Points feature. Each image below was made simply by editing the points of a basic circle.

15. If you want to move a shape, just grab it and drag your mouse – unless you want to move it just a little bit, then use the arrow keys (↑, ↓, ←, and →) on your keyboard to place it at a precise position on the screen.

16. Don't forget the value of the undo and redo buttons at the top of the screen (or use Ctrl + Z and Ctrl + Y).

Next, explore the assortment of lines, arrows, and curves that you can make:

1. In the Insert tab, click Shapes, and first select the basic Line tool. Position your cursor somewhere on the screen and click the left mouse button to insert a line.

2. When you select the line, you will see a tiny white circle at each end. Place the cursor over one of these little white circles and drag it to reposition one end of the line.

3. Grab and drag the little white circle at one end of the line to change the length of the line and its orientation. See if you can make a horizontal line and a vertical line by doing this. If you look closely, you can see a subtle difference between a line that is perfectly horizontal and one that is close but not quite – the one that is not quite horizontal will appear just slightly jagged. When making horizontal and vertical lines, be sure to get the orientation just right.

4. If the line is horizontal or vertical and you want to resize it, just type the new Width or Height at the right of the Format tab. If the line is tilted and you want to resize it without changing the tilt, first lock the aspect ratio (see Bullet 11 in the previous list) and then enter a new Width or Height.

5. Format the line by clicking Shape Outline in the Format tab. Here, you can change the color, width, and pattern. Explore the options in Width and Dash in Shape Outline, and look for More Lines while you are there to find more effects.

6. You can also insert a single (→) or double (↔) arrow by clicking Shapes. The formatting options for arrows are just like lines, except that you can also change the style and size of the arrowhead. In the Format tab, choose Shape Outline, click Arrows, select More Arrows, then pick Line Style in the popup window in order to change the size and style of the arrowhead. You can turn a line into an arrow following these same steps.

7. The Arc tool in Shapes in the Insert tab allows you to draw a circular arc. You can format it just like lines; you can even add an arrowhead to it. If you add a Fill Color to the arc, it will look like a pie slice. If you want to draw one-half of a circle, one way to do it is to use the arc tool, draw a semicircle, and add a Fill Color. Lock the aspect ratio of the arc before you resize it (see Bullet 11 of the previous list) – otherwise, it will stretch into an ellipse, instead of being circular.

8. There is another tool that allows you to draw a curve that doesn't look circular. Find the shape called Curve and select it. (When you click Shapes in the Insert tab, just place the cursor over a shape without clicking and wait a minute – the name of the shape will pop up in a moment.) As usual, the cursor will turn into a plus sign (+) when the Curve tool is selected. What's different is how you insert the curve: Place the cursor somewhere on the screen and click the left mouse button once to begin using the Curve tool, then move the cursor to another point and click again, move the cursor to a third point and click again, and continue doing this until your curve is complete – and then press the Enter key on the keyboard. You can format a curve the same way that you can format a line, and in addition you can Edit Points on a curve (as described in Bullet 14 in the previous list).

9. If your third (or more) click when using the Curve tool is on the initial point, a closed curve will result. Note that all of the shape formatting options apply to a curve (whether it is open or closed), including Shape Fill and Shape Effects.

10. The Freeform tool (also in Shapes in the Format tab) works the same way as the Curve tool, except that it connects straight line segments together instead of fitting a curve through the points. The Freeform tool is useful for drawing irregular polygons, for example. If you are trying to draw something rectangular using the Freeform tool, try turning on the Gridlines (see Bullet 4 of the next list).

11. The Scribble tool allows you to "draw" by holding down the left button of your mouse and dragging it, but you might find it challenging to draw smoothly with this tool. If you happen to have a touchscreen monitor, you can probably draw freehand much better with that than you can with the Scribble tool. If you do have a touchscreen monitor, there will be a special tab for the touchscreen drawing tools.

12. If you just want to draw a tiny point, there are a couple of ways that you could do it. One way is to insert a circle from Shapes (in Insert), lock the aspect ratio (see Bullet 11 in the previous list), and make the circle much smaller (see Bullet 10 in the previous list to recall how to resize a shape). You can also reduce the circle's size by setting Shape Outline to No Color – or making it the same color as the background and increasing the Width of the outline. Another way to draw a tiny point is to type a period (.) into a textbox or WordArt – or enter a dot from the symbols menu (click Symbols from the Insert tab) if a period is too small.

● ● ·

Shapes, lines, arrows, arcs and other curves, and textboxes and WordArt form the building blocks with which you can draw just about anything on Microsoft Word that you could create on paper by hand. Following are some tools that are useful for combining shapes together to form composite images:

1. Select multiple objects by first clicking on one, and then holding down the Ctrl button on the keyboard while selecting the others. If you open the Selection Pane in the Format tab, it will help you select objects that are not easy to grab.

2. Use the Align button in the Format tab to align two or more objects – after selecting them – according to Left, Right, Center, Top, Bottom, or Middle. Note that Center means horizontally, while Middle means vertically. There are also new buttons in Microsoft Word 2010 to align a picture to a page or a margin.

3. Another new feature in Microsoft Word 2010 is the Distribute option available when you click Align in the Format tab. Create even spacing between multiple objects by using Distribute Horizontally or Distribute Vertically.

4. You can place objects at precise points on the screen and draw right angles with the Freeform tool (described in Bullet 10 of the previous list), for example, with the aid of the gridlines. In Microsoft Word 2007, you could simply turn the Gridlines on or off in the View tab. In Microsoft Word 2010, they have revived some of the Microsoft Word 2003 flexibility of gridlines and placed these features with the Align button in the Format tab. When you click Align, you can toggle between viewing and not viewing gridlines, and you can also adjust the Grid Settings. Turn the gridlines on when you want place objects on the grid and check the box to Snap Objects To Other Objects when you want objects to meet together – but remove these options when you want the freedom to place an object anywhere. You can also change the grid size.

5. The Bring Forward and Bring Backward buttons in the Format tab help to layer objects – i.e. to control which object is placed before another. If you click the bottom part of these buttons, you find more options – like bringing an object all of the way to the front or back.

6. Use copy/paste (Ctrl + C and Ctrl + V) to make quick reproductions of any image. For example, the circular object that appears to the right was made by inserting a circle, changing the color, removing the outline, locking the aspect ratio, copying the circle, pasting 4 copies, setting the sizes from 0.2" to 1", changing two of the colors, aligning the centers, and then aligning the bottoms.

7. When multiple objects are selected, you can group them together using the Group button in the Format tab. You can also Ungroup them the same way.

8. If you select multiple objects and rotate (see Bullet 12 in the first list of this section) them, they will rotate individually unless you first group them together – in that case, the group will instead rotate as a whole.

9. A group of images may not look as nice if it is resized. Even if you lock the aspect ratio, there may be some noticeable and undesirable changes. One problem is that the thicknesses of the lines do not change automatically if you resize an image. Similarly, text does not change size when you resize a group. Alignment imperfections can also be magnified when a group is enlarged. There is a definite advantage to drawing the picture the right size the first time.

10. Drawing elements have a default Text Wrap that is In Front of Text. When your image is finished, if you insert it into your interior book file, you can change the Text Wrap to In Line With Text or Square in the Format tab. Grouping multiple objects together and wrapping them In Line With Text will help to minimize the risk of complex file issues; keep the number of free-floating (In Front Of Text) pictures to a minimum (only do that when there is no other way to position the picture exactly where you want it). In your cover file, on the other hand, you should use In Front Of text: This file just has one page, and you need the flexibility of placing images anywhere on the screen. If you change Text Wrap to In Line With Text or Square, for example, you won't be able to use some drawing features unless you change it back to In Front Of Text. So if you need to revise a text-wrapped figure, first change Text Wrap to In Front Of Text temporarily.

If you have figures and/or tables that you will be describing in the body of your text, your book will look more professional if you include numbered captions below each figure. For example, many books have a numbered caption of the form, "Fig. 3. The total United States budget is plotted over the course of 100 years." This helps readers quickly find the figure that you are referring to, and the description below the figure helps readers understand what the figure represents. I didn't include figure captions with this book, however, since most of the figures are simple shapes and it didn't seem necessary to include a sentence between the pictures of the book covers to tell you that they are book covers. Well, I did include one caption in the figure below so that you could see an example of a caption.

Add textboxes and WordArt to label your figures. If you do, change both the Shape Outline and Shape Fill to No Color and No Fill, respectively – it doesn't look nice when all of the text labels are surrounded by black rectangles, for example.

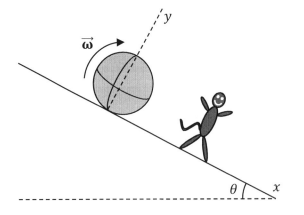

Fig. 1. A ball rolls without slipping down an incline, chasing a frightened monkey.

3.1.9 Sample Drawings and How to Make Them

Here is a brief sample of the variety of pictures that you can draw with Microsoft Word 2010 by applying what you learned in Sec. 3.1.8. It would be good practice to see if you can reproduce some of these pictures.

Let's begin with a few basic three-dimensional geometric objects. There are few different ways that you can draw a cube. The simplest way to make a cube comes with the least flexibility in customizing it: Go to Insert, select Shapes, and choose Cube (by clicking on its picture). If you look closely, you'll notice that the sides are shaded differently. One option that you do have with this preset cube can be found by clicking the tiny yellow diamond (◊) near its top left corner (visible only after you select the cube). If you click the tiny yellow diamond and drag it, it will reshape the cube.

If you want more flexibility with your cube, there are two other ways that you can draw it. One way is to insert a square and two parallelograms from Shapes, and join them together to form a cube. One parallelogram will need to be rotated. You will also have to drag the little yellow diamond to change the shape of each parallelogram, and also adjust the height and width of each. It will take some trial and error to make the three pieces fit together precisely in the shape of a cube.

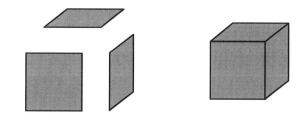

A third way to draw a cube is to first make a hexagon and then add three edges to it. Turn on the Gridlines and use the Freeform tool to make a hexagon (or insert a hexagon and select Edit Points to reshape it). You can draw dotted edges to show the hidden back side of the cube by copying and pasting the solid front edges.

Yet another option is to draw a rectangle and add thickness to it in the 3-D Rotation Options (you must switch to 3-D Format in the popup window). If there is a specific way you want the object to look, you might find it challenging to make a cube this way.

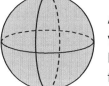

A sphere can be drawn by first inserting a circle and then using the Arc tool (in Shapes) to help illustrate the three-dimensional roundness. Once you make one arc, you can copy and paste it to quickly make the others. Including both solid and dashed arcs can help to distinguish between the front of the sphere and its back.

If you are clever with gradients and shadows, you can also use these tools to draw a sphere. In the sphere at the right, the Gradient is a preset color choice (Fire) with Radial Type and the rightmost Direction selected. The Rotation Angle was set to 330° to make the gradient's direction match that of the shadow. Play with the Shadow Options to try to get the shadow to match the sense of light created by the gradient's effect.

You can find a basic cylinder in Shapes (called Can), where the end will be lighter than the body. A cylinder can also be made by increasing the Depth (you can also change the Depth Color) in 3-D Format within the 3-D Rotation Options. However, you gain the most flexibility in creating a cylinder from two Ovals with Shape Outline, one Rectangle with Shape Outline set to No Color, and two straight lines, as illustrated below. The rolling hollow cylinder illustrated below was drawn from three Circles, one Rectangle, some Lines, an Arc with an Arrow end, a Brace, and some equations that were inserted into textboxes.

Most objects can be drawn by putting common geometric shapes together, as we will see in the following examples. For example, a flower can be drawn by using Circles for petals, a Curve for the stem, and combining Arcs together to form leaves. Similarly, a football can be drawn using arcs and lines. The bunch of grapes illustrated below was made by stacking numerous copies (use Ctrl + C and Ctrl + V) of an Oval atop one another.

You can draw a present by adding some ribbon and a bow to a cube. In the present that follows, two rectangles were used for the ribbon, while the bow was made out of a Circle and six Ovals. Rectangles can also be used to make a piano or organ keyboard.

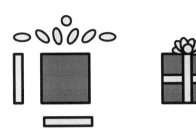

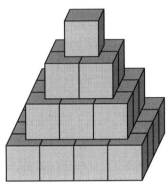

A cube can be copied and pasted several times, and these cubes can be stacked together to form a pyramid. To make the pyramid shown to the right, first make one cube. Then copy the cube and paste two copies of it. Place the two copies side by side and Align them by their bottoms. Group the two side-by-side cubes together, then copy and paste the group. Place one group in front of the other. Next, make three cubes in a row, then make two copies of that row. Make the bottom layer the same way. Finally, group each layer together, and then stack the layers.

The concave lens in the ray diagram below was actually made from two Moon shapes and two Triangles. Another way to make it would be two add two arcs with white Shape Fill in front of a Rectangle.

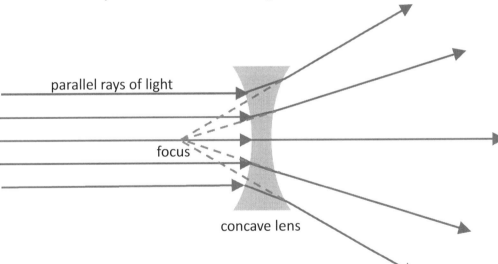

The easiest way to construct a complex image is to break it down into a combination of simpler shapes. For example, if you want to draw a person, the simplest way to do it is to make a stick figure. The following illustration shows how a snowman was created from Circles, Lines, Rectangles, Arcs, and Ovals. If you want to draw a monkey, for example, you could make a stick figure person and add a tale; an improvement upon this would be to use ovals and circles instead of lines.

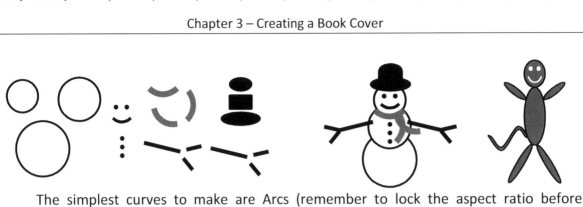

The simplest curves to make are Arcs (remember to lock the aspect ratio before resizing an Arc if you want it to remain circular instead of becoming elliptical). Other curves can also be made quite nicely using the Curve tool, but you have to practice with this tool and exercise some patience to perfect your curves. Now would be a good time to review how to use the Curve tool (see Bullets 8-9 in the second list of Sec. 3.1.8) and how to Edit Points (see Bullet 14 in the first list of Sec. 3.1.8).

The green and fairway of the following golf hole were drawn using the Curve tool. When you first attempt the Curve, just try to get something close – you aren't going to make the perfect curve on your first try. <u>Don't</u> delete the curve and start over until you get it right; instead, once you get one in the ballpark, use the Edit Points feature. The fairway below has 11 points – see if you can find the 11 'corners.' (The fairway's 11 points are fairly easy to find, whereas some of the green's 7 points are more subtle). You can reproduce the fairway by making a closed Curve with 11 points that are in roughly the same positions as the 'corners' of this fairway. Remember that you can right-click a point and adjust the blue line to reshape the curve at that point. As I said, it takes some practice and patience to perfect use of the Curve tool, but you can create more complex images if you master this tool. The bunkers are Ovals and the trees were made from Circles. The tee boxes are Rounded Rectangles.

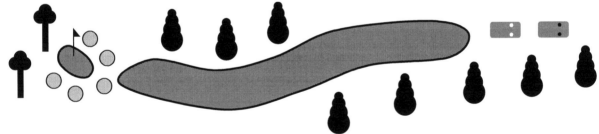

The right-handed coordinate system below was drawn with Curves, Arcs, Lines, and Arrows.

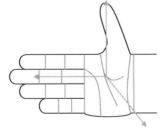

3.1.10 Making a Background for Your Cover

One way to make a background image for your book cover is to simply add a large rectangle. The rectangle could have a single color, or it could be a gradient or a pattern, for example. See the first list of bullets in Sec. 3.1.8 regarding how to insert a shape, change its color, and add a gradient or pattern to a shape. If you would prefer to use an imported picture as your background, see Sec. 3.1.12 regarding how to insert and format a picture.

After you insert a background rectangle, select the background rectangle and change Wrap Text (in the Format tab) to Behind Text. Now you will see all of the text and pictures of your cover in front of the background rectangle.

Change the size of the background rectangle to match the cover trim size + bleed (width = trim width x 2 + spine width + 0.25", height = trim height + 0.25"). For example, for an 8" x 10" book with a spine width of 0.42", the cover trim size plus bleed is 16.67" x 10.25". Type the dimensions directly at the far right of the Format tab. After centering the background rectangle (see the next paragraph), be sure that your background rectangle extends at least 0.125" beyond the cover edges marked by your guide (so that the colors will 'bleed' all of the way to the edges); it's okay if the rectangle extends more than this amount.

Now center your background rectangle: Click Position in the Format tab, go to More Layout Options, choose the Position tab, and change both Horizontal and Vertical to Center.

You can make more than one background rectangle. For example, you may want to have a different background for the front cover, spine width, and back cover. You can even add a border to your front and back covers. The cover guide that we made in Sec. 3.1.5 will help you piece your background together. Make rectangles for the front cover, spine width, back cover, and border, then position these rectangles where you would like them, and group them together. They should line up precisely where they meet and fill the entire page. Change the position of the background rectangle group to Behind Text.

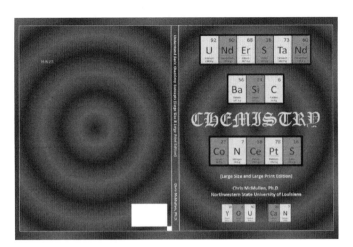

Consider saving your background rectangle for last – otherwise, when you select text and images on your cover, you might find that you accidentally grab the background instead.

3.1.11 Copyright Restrictions on Photos, Clipart, and Other Images

If you will be publishing a book that will be available for sale, you need to be aware that most clipart and photos have a copyright restriction that does not allow them to be used for commercial use. Including a picture in a book or on its cover is considered to be commercial use if the book will be available for sale. If you violate the copyright policy of the copyright holder, you put yourself in a situation where you may be sued by the copyright holder.

Unfortunately, if you click on Clip Art in the Insert tab, the clipart available from Microsoft Office's website is <u>not</u> available for commercial use (which you will see if you read the fine print, which is not always easy to find). Much of the clipart and the vast majority of photos that you may find on the web are also <u>not</u> available for commercial use. Even if you purchase a cd with thousands of photos or clipart images, these are <u>not</u> available for commercial use unless you find a statement on the box that clearly states that you may use it for commercial use.

Some clipart collections do allow commercial use of the clipart and photos, but many do not. Those that do write this statement clearly on the box – they want you to notice this statement on the box, as it may increase your chances of buying their product. Those that do not allow commercial use sometimes do not mention this anywhere on the box – you have to hunt through all the legal fine print later to discover that you can't use the images for commercial use. Sometimes you have to buy a more expensive edition to get the license for commercial use, but beware that some products still are <u>not</u> available for commercial use even if you buy the most expensive version. Make sure that you find the statement in writing before purchasing a collection.

A few companies may allow you to purchase a commercial use license if you write to them. They may ask you for specific details in writing – like how you intend to use the image and how many books you expect to sell. They might also ask you to include a specific statement in the book, declaring the origin of the image. It is also common that they won't allow you to use the image as it is, but will request that you either use it as part of an image or make some change to the image – this way, everyone that uses the image will have a different variation of it. (However, it's <u>not</u> acceptable to make a variation of an image or use an image as part of another picture when commercial use is not permitted.)

There are even special fonts that do not permit commercial use. Microsoft Office itself even comes in student, personal, and professional editions (and even that license doesn't extend to everything, like clipart).

On the other hand, you can sometimes find clipart, photo collections, and fonts that are available for free and allow commercial use, so it pays to do some research. Many of the photos available from NASA (www.nasa.gov) are available for free download and do allow for commercial use, provided that you make it clear that NASA did not participate in the writing or publication of your book.[23] Even then, you must be careful, because some of their photos do have copyrights held by individuals (you have to read the photo credits of each photo to find out).

If there is a specific photo that you want to use, try contacting the copyright owner. You may use the image for commercial use if you obtain written permission. Make sure that you obtain permission in writing – and check with an attorney to make sure that the writing is satisfactory – from the copyright owner (check on this, too) and that the writing clearly allows commercial use of the specified image. If you have written permission to use an image, acknowledge the copyright holder in the caption below your figure.

Similarly, when you are browsing covers to get ideas for your cover, don't copy covers that you see. Focus on understanding your design options – like how to layout the cover, which color schemes work well, and what features you could include (like starbursts or book reviews from magazines) – but don't copy specifics (like sentences from the cover or diagrams that you've seen). Copying or paraphrasing text is also a copyright violation called plagiarism. You're also not allowed to reproduce a picture (unless you've been granted commercial use). Note that drawing from scratch a copy of a picture that you've seen is a copyright violation, too. There are even some places or images that you aren't allowed to photograph – such as taking a photo of the Eiffel Tower at night – and use commercially.

---

[23] If you want to use these images, first read their "Image Use Guidelines."

3.1.12 Inserting and Formatting Pictures and Clipart

As mentioned Sec. 3.1.11, don't use the Clip Art button in the Insert tab to find clipart and other images because you're not permitted to use any pictures that have a copyright restriction against commercial use.

Instead, you will need to either draw your own figures, take your own photos, or find a library of clipart and pictures which clearly states that commercial use is allowed.

First, turn off picture compression. Go to the File tab, look for Options, which is hiding below Help and Save & Send. Click Options, pick Advanced, scroll down to Image Size and Quality, and check the box for Do Not Compress Images in File. Choose the maximum PPI.

To insert a photo, clipart, or any other picture that you don't draw in Word, go to the Insert tab, click Picture, browse for your picture, click on the picture's filename, and click the Insert button on the popup window. If you select the picture (by clicking on it), a Format tab will appear at the top of the screen (only when the picture is selected). In the Format tab, there are several tools that you can use to format the picture in Microsoft Word.[24]

1. You can remove a background by clicking Remove Background. When you select this, a square will appear in the picture, which you can resize (by placing your cursor over one of the little circles or squares that appear at the corners and midpoints of the sides, and holding down the left button while moving the mouse to drag the cursor). When you finish resizing the square, click anywhere else on the screen outside of the picture. The black space in the background of Venus[25] was removed from the photo below following this procedure.

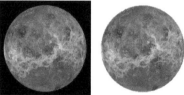

2. If you want to remove a color from the picture and Remove Background doesn't do the job, you can make one color in your picture transparent. To do this, click Color, choose Transparent Color, and click somewhere on the picture that has the color that you want to make transparent. Beware, though, if you make red transparent – for example – it will make every red in the picture transparent. Also, you will be able to see anything that may be behind the transparent color (such as the background).

---

[24] If you have some fancy photo-editing software, you may find a greater variety of options by editing your pictures in that program instead of Word. Also, when you publish an eBook, adjustments that you make in Word may not show up (i.e. you might see the original image instead) unless you copy and paste the modified image into Paint (see Sec. 2.2.5) and save it as a new image.

[25] This photo is from NASA's image gallery (www.nasa.gov). NASA did not participate in the writing or publication of this book.

3. It is often useful to crop a photo – i.e. to remove part of the background or to select just a particular image from a picture. Click on the bottom half of the Crop button (on the right side of the Format tab) to find the cropping options, which include Crop To Shape, Aspect Ratio, Fill, and Fit.

4. Crop To Shape can serve a similar purpose compared to removing a background, but it can also be used in other ways. If you want to take a close-up, or frame a picture with a different shape, for example, Crop To Shape will be useful. In the photo below, Uranus' moon Titania[25] was cropped to the shape of a circle. Note that removing the background or setting black to transparent would also have removed the dark surface of the moon in addition to the black space. The Apollo 17 photo[25] below was cropped to the shape of a trapezoid. When cropping to a shape, after you select the shape, deselect the object (by clicking elsewhere on the screen), reselect the object, and then click the top half of the crop button to adjust the boundary of the shape. (If instead you try adjusting the boundary without first deselecting the object, the aspect ratio of the object will change as you adjust it.)

  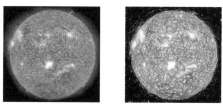

5. If you make a mistake or change your mind after formatting a picture, click Reset Picture to revert back to the original. This button (on the left of the Format tab) can be very handy (so can the Undo and Redo buttons at the top of the screen – or use Ctrl + Z and Ctrl + Y).

6. You can adjust the color and tone of your picture by clicking Color (at the left of the Format tab). Also, explore the variety of Artistic Effects (this button is next to the Color button). The photo of the sun[25] below was recolored in Pencil Grayscale.

7. You can add an outline to a picture by choosing Picture Border. In addition to choosing a color for your border, you can adjust the Width and select from a variety of solid and dashed outlines in Dash (which includes double lines – choose More Lines at the bottom to adjust settings like Compound Type and Dash Type). The 1969 moon landing photo[25] featuring Buzz Aldrin (taken by Neil Armstrong) below has a gray picture border.

8. Compare the two photos of earth[25] below. If you click Remove Background or set a Transparent Color and then add a Picture Border, the border will have a rectangular outline, as in the photo on the left. If instead you Crop to Shape and add a Picture Border, the border will have the outline of the cropped shape, as in the right photo.

9. There is a good selection of preset Picture Styles available in the center of the Format tab. You can customize your own style by clicking Picture Effects, which has the following options: Shadow, Reflection, Glow, Soft Edges, Bevel, and 3-D Rotation. You can find more options at the bottom of each list – when you click 3-D Rotation Options, for example, in the popup window you can also explore 3-D Format options. The Sombrero galaxy[25] below is shown in a few different styles.

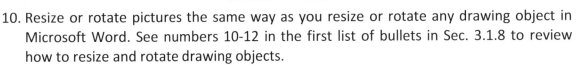

10. Resize or rotate pictures the same way as you resize or rotate any drawing object in Microsoft Word. See numbers 10-12 in the first list of bullets in Sec. 3.1.8 to review how to resize and rotate drawing objects.

11. There are also several standard formatting features that are often useful. In Wrap Text, choose In Front of Text when you want to make a composite picture from multiple pictures. Use Group to group them together when the picture is complete, and change Wrap Text to In Line With Text when inserting a picture into your book's interior. Set Wrap Text to In Front of Text when adding a picture to your cover so that you can place it anywhere on the screen. The Align button is helpful for aligning two or more pictures by their tops, left sides, or centers, for example.

12. You can also edit a picture by using Microsoft Word's drawing tools (described in Sec. 3.1.8), and you can insert a textbox or WordArt (see Sec. 3.1.6) to add labels.

If you edit a picture in Microsoft Word, note that the picture will generally revert back to its original form in an eBook. Word does not change the file for your picture – it just displays the edited picture when you open Word. However, when you submit your Word document for your eBook, the original picture is loaded when the file is converted into your eBook. Fortunately, there are ways around this. For example, if you crop a photo in Word, you can delete the cropped portions of the photo by clicking on the Compress Pictures button in the Format tab and checking the corresponding box. To save other changes, you can copy and paste the edited photo into Paint (see Sec. 2.2.5), save the new photo as a JPEG file, and insert this modified photo back into Word. Don't do this with the paperback version of your book – just the eBook version.

If you crop and otherwise edit pictures in their native program (such as photo-editing software), you may find more editing options than Word has. Also, make sure that any changes to the pictures are permanently saved before inserting them into the Word file for your eBook.

A tool that can be particularly handy is a Snipping Tool. Many new computer models have a Snipping Tool on the Start Menu. If not, you may be able to find this tool online. When you open the Snipping Tool, it allows you to make a rectangle, capture an image on the screen, and save it as a JPEG file. (Again, you must be careful that anything you copy is not protected by copyright, trademark, or commercial use restrictions.) For example, suppose that you want to enlarge an image from your paperback book for use in an eBook: You could zoom in on the image in Word, use the Snipping Tool to capture the enlarged image, and save it as a JPEG file for your eBook. Also, note that the latest version of Microsoft Word has a Screenshot tool. To use it, first open the image in a separate window (it can't be in the same file that you are using), and adjust the window exactly as you want the Screenshot to appear. Click the top half of the Screenshot button (in the Insert tab) to select an available Screenshot.

Another way to make a picture is to scan it. If you draw a colorful children's book, for example, you can scan the images with a scanner (or even photograph them), save them as JPEG files, and insert them into your Word document. Test this out before scanning on a large scale to check the resolution of your scans. Insert a sample scan into a Word document, click Save As and choose PDF, then print out the page from your PDF file. It may not be the same quality as your final book, but it will help to give you some indication of how the PDF file's resolution compares to what you see on the original paper.

It's important to have high-quality images, both in print and in eBook format – especially, if you have several pictures in your book. It is not uncommon when publishing an eBook for the author to begin with high-quality images, but discover that the pictures aren't nearly as good when reading the eBook on one or more devices. It would be wise to make a file with a few representative pictures, go to Amazon's Kindle and begin the publishing process (don't fill out everything – just the bare minimum for it to let you upload the file), upload the file that just has the few sample pictures, and view converted eBook file on the

Kindle previewer to see what the pictures will look like (view them both in the black-and-white version and in the Kindle Fire version). If you're not happy with them, strive to find ways to improve them (you can find suggestions in Sec. 4.2). Also, look at the file size, calculate the number of pictures that you plan to make, and estimate the total file size. We will discuss how to publish an eBook on Kindle (and other platforms), along with the issue of file size, in Sec.'s 4.2.2, 4.2.4, and 4.2.8-11.

Some documents do <u>not</u> scan well. For example, if you have a pile of lecture notes and just want to scan them in, you might find that the resulting book does not have sufficient quality – especially for an eBook, if the images are highly detailed. However, some images <u>do</u> scan well with a high-resolution scanner or camera. You may be able to make the background pictures for a full-color picture book this way – but if the pictures include writing, that may be too detailed (instead, add the writing with textboxes after inserting the pictures into Word). If you will be making an eBook version of your manuscript, it is smart to preview how the images will look before you begin converting your book into an eBook.

Finally, let's briefly discuss two other types of pictures that you may wish to make: graphs and flowcharts. You can find all of the ingredients for making these by clicking Chart (for graphs) or SmartArt (for flowcharts) in the Insert tab. If you have two columns of data and want to make a graph, you probably want to make an X Y (Scatter) plot instead of a Line (even if the data set is linear, you probably don't want what Word calls a Line graph). There are also a variety of Bar and Pie charts to choose from. In SmartArt, there are several different types of flowcharts that you can make; once you choose a basic design, you can modify it to suit your needs.

When inserting a figure into the interior file for your book, consider adding a caption to describe the figure (as described in Sec. 2.1.14). This is common in traditionally published books, and will help your book appear professionally edited.

3.1.13 Adding Photos, Clipart, and Other Images to Your Cover

Most of the images that you include on your cover should in some way relate to your book. For example, if you publish a puzzle book, you could include a close-up of the puzzle on the front cover, or if you publish a fiction book that features hockey players, you could include a photo that relates to hockey. Pictures on your front cover can help show customers what your book is about.

Insert pictures, clipart, and other images into your cover – and format them – as described in Sec. 3.1.12. In your cover file, change Wrap Text (in the Format tab) to In Front of Text for all of your images except for the background (which should be Behind Text). If you want to draw your own figures, see Sec.'s 3.1.8-9. Select multiple objects and use the Align button in the Format tab to center or otherwise align images (e.g. you might want to center an image with the front cover rectangle of your cover guide by selecting both and aligning them – but be sure to ungroup your front cover rectangle first).

Group multiple images together (by selecting them – hold down Ctrl while selecting the images, or use the Selection Pane in the Format tab to select them while holding down Ctrl – and clicking on Group in the Format tab) to help minimize the risk for PDF conversion issues, objects wandering around as you move other objects, and to help reduce problems that may arise from the file becoming highly complex. In Word 2007, for example, it wasn't uncommon for the cover file to look quite different in the PDF than it did in Word unless you grouped multiple images together.

Some authors include a picture of themselves either on the cover (the back cover is probably more common) or on an author page near the end of the book. Many readers are curious about the person behind the words. If you are not too shy, consider doing this. If you are attractive and photogenic, maybe it is even worth including on the front cover. But remember, customers are buying your book, not your photo. Also, consider whether you have a face that suits the type of book that you are writing – survey some people (not just close friends and family, who may offer a biased opinion) to see what they think.

If you draw an image in Microsoft Word and need to resize it, group all parts of the images together, lock the aspect ratio (click on the little arrow at the bottom right corner of the Size group in the Format tab), and then resize the picture (either by dragging a corner or by manually entering the width or height on the Format tab – sometimes, you have to open the Size popup window to make this work). Unfortunately, an enlarged or reduced image doesn't always look the same, so sometimes you have to ungroup the parts of the picture, resize text, adjust thicknesses, and improve alignment by moving objects around.

If you would like to use a photo as a background, see Sec. 3.1.12 regarding how to insert, resize, and format the photo. Also, recall that we discussed how to insert a background, in general, in Sec. 3.1.10. Change the Text Wrap of the background to Behind Text. I suggest saving the background for last – otherwise, you may find yourself accidentally grabbing the background when you are trying to select and edit other objects.

When your cover is complete, place a sheet of paper over the back cover to study how the front cover looks (and similarly analyze the back cover and spine). Then zoom out considerably (look in the View tab), place a sheet of paper over the back cover, and study how the thumbnail image looks. Solicit opinions from friends, family, and acquaintances.

Remember to remove the cover guides that we drew in Sec. 3.1.5 when your cover is finalized. However, you should save a next-to-final version of your cover file (with a different file name, of course) with the guides included, just in case you need to revise your cover.

3.1.14 Cover Help, Including Free and Paid Cover and Illustration Services

In case you may be interested in receiving help – free or paid – creating artwork or designing your cover, we will discuss some alternatives to doing it all by yourself in this section.

First, CreateSpace has a free Cover Creator. (KDP now has this, too, for eBooks.) This program is easy to use – it launches directly from the page where you publish your book. It includes free artwork and fonts to choose from, and makes the cover design simple. Designing your own cover following the instructions in this chapter provides the most flexibility – and is also pretty straightforward to do – but if you want some free artwork to choose from and a way to make design even simpler, you should check out Cover Creator. Since Cover Creator is free, you should at least give it a try before investing in any paid services. We will describe how to launch Cover Creator in Sec. 4.1.9.

CreateSpace also offers another free service that can help you with your cover design: CreateSpace can build you a cover template in a PNG or PDF format. (If you want a template in Word, I recommend following the step-by-step instructions in Sec. 3.1.5.) You can get a PNG or PDF template for your cover by following these steps:

1. Visit CreateSpace's website: www.createspace.com.
2. Click the Books tab near the top left.
3. Choose Publish a Trade Paperback.
4. Select the Cover tab.
5. Click on the Submission Requirements link (under the heading, "Want to build your own book cover from scratch?").
6. Scroll down to the heading, "Get a headstart with one of our cover templates," and click Download Cover Templates.
7. Select the interior type and the trim size of your book, enter the page number, and choose the paper color. Then press the Build Template button.
8. Now you can download a PNG or PDF template of your book cover.

Before we discuss paid services, let's talk about one more thing that you can get for free: help and advice. If you have questions about the publishing process, you can contact CreateSpace by clicking the Contact Support button after you login to your CreateSpace account. You can also get help from fellow authors by asking questions in a community forum – for CreateSpace, Kindle, etc. The link to the community forum for CreateSpace is
https://www.createspace.com/en/community/index.jspa
Whether you have a specific question or even a general topic in mind, if you type your issue into the search field of your favorite internet search engine, there is a good chance that you will find the answer there, too.

CreateSpace and other companies do offer professional (paid) services to help you with your cover design. This includes purchasing artwork, hiring an illustrator, or even paying to have the entire cover designed for you. Awesome artwork could make your book very eye-catching and help you fall in love with your own book, but it's probably the content that should be more meaningful than your cover. Like any investment, paying for artwork is a risk. Think about how many books you will have to sell just to break even if you invest money in the production and publication of your book. If instead you publish your book for free, you won't be starting out in the hole. For this reason, I recommend doing it yourself – or at least give it a shot and see how it turns out. Back to the comment I made about loving your cover – when you put your own creativity, time, and effort into the book cover project, that can also help you enjoy your own book cover.

If you want to explore CreateSpace's paid services, go to their website and click Design under Comprehensive Book Services. If you would like professional artwork for your interior and/or cover, click on Custom Illustrations. Browse the sample artwork there. You can request a specific artist: If you find a sample that you like, you can request to have the same artist make your illustrations. In addition to Custom Illustrations, there are a handful of links for various Cover Options. If you want to explore paid services from other companies and individuals, try searching for them with an internet search engine, asking questions in community help forums for authors, talking to other authors that you know, and looking for friends or family members who have artistic talents. Do some research and be wary of paying for services from entities or people that you don't know: It would be wise to find a sample of the service first and also find fellow authors who can vouch for the service.

3.2 Converting Your Cover into an eBook Thumbnail Image

3.2.1 Why You Need a Different Thumbnail Image for Your eBook

Paperback books and eBooks have different types of covers. There are obvious structural differences: The cover file for your paperback book includes a front cover, spine, back cover, and extra room around the edges for colors to bleed, whereas your eBook cover just needs a front side. Also, the front cover of your paperback must be designed to match the trim size of your book, which probably won't be the ideal aspect ratio for the cover of your eBook. Furthermore, when you submit your paperback book cover, it will be in the form of a PDF file. When you submit your eBook cover, it will be in the form of a JPEG file.

Another difference is that your paperback book cover needs to look good both as a thumbnail image and in person, but your eBook's cover will primarily be viewed as a thumbnail image. Sometimes, it is wise to refrain from making the font too extremely large for a paperback cover, thinking of how it will look in person; instead, easy-to-read is very important for the eBook cover. In this case, you might make some of your text larger. Since your eBook cover will primarily function as a thumbnail image, it's not necessary to include finer details that will be difficult to make out in the thumbnail.

Even the rules for making the paperback and eBook covers differ: The front cover of your paperback must contain every word of your book's title in order, but this is not required for eBook covers with some eReader companies. If you do include every word of your title on the cover and try to make every word easy-to-read on the thumbnail image, if you have a lengthy title there will scarcely be room for images. Consider highlighting key words and increasing their font size, while still leaving ample room for images on your eBook cover.

You also have the opportunity to make a higher-resolution image for your eBook cover. I recommend making the highest-resolution image that will be accepted. We will return to this point – including how to do it – in the next section; for now, it is one more reason to design a new cover for your eBook.

For these reasons, I recommend modifying your paperback cover file to create your eBook cover file (instead of copying the thumbnail image from CreateSpace, for example). It's easy to do, as explained in Sec. 3.2.2: You already have the ingredients for your cover, we're just going to modify them – so it will be much easier than starting from scratch.

If you do modify your paperback book's cover, which I'm suggesting is worthwhile, to make your eBook cover, also consider having the two covers look similar, though not exactly the same. If the covers look considerably different, readers may be confused into thinking that they are really two different books instead of two editions of the same book. A reader who unknowingly buys the same book twice may not be too happy about it. (You also have the opportunity to make this clear in your book's description.) If the books look similar, but a little different, that will be consistent with having two different editions – one paperback, one eBook – of the same book.

Let's discuss how you can use the exact same image for your eBook cover and paperback book front cover. Although I don't recommend this, I will still tell you how to do it. First, if you publish your paperback book with CreateSpace, there are two ways that you can get a copy of the front cover of your book. You could open your book's detail page, right-click on the front cover image, select Save As, and save the file to your computer (in a PNG or BMP format). However, you will still need to convert your file to a JPEG or TIFF file format, and you will probably want to increase the resolution. You can get a better image by clicking the Publish Your Book on Kindle link from your book's detail page. This image will be a JPEG file.

If you have a Snipping Tool on your computer, Microsoft Word 2010, or any other program that offers a Screenshot, you can take a Screenshot of your cover. Adjust the View until you can see (at least) the whole front cover. With a Snipping Tool, make a rectangle that just outlines the front cover and capture this image. With Microsoft Word 2010, open a new document (leaving the front cover open), go to the Insert tab in the new document, click the top half of the Screenshot button, and select an available Screenshot. Copy and paste the

Screenshot into Paint (see Sec. 2.2.5), crop the image as desired, resize the image (see Sec. 4.2.2), and save your eBook cover as a JPEG file.

3.2.2 Designing Your eBook Cover

Before you design your eBook cover, browse a variety of eBook thumbnail images. For some of the books, compare the eBook thumbnail image to the paperback or hardcover thumbnail image – this will help you gauge how similar or dissimilar a typical eBook cover looks compared to its paperback or hardcover counterpart. Following are a couple of sample thumbnail images for some of my own eBook covers for which there is a corresponding paperback cover. The eBook thumbnail appears at the left side of each pair, while the paperback thumbnail appears at the right side of each pair. In each case, observe that the paperback cover is more detailed, the text in the eBook thumbnail is easier to read, and the eBook thumbnail is wider. (Yes, I broke my own rule by not making them very similar...)

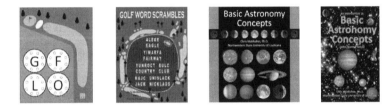

Following are a few of my eBook covers for which I don't have a corresponding paperback book.[26]

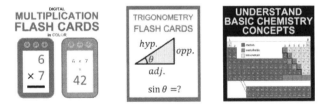

You will need to submit a cover file as a JPEG file. (Amazon's Kindle also accepts TIFF images, and other eReader requirements will differ. We will discuss eBook publishing requirements for a variety of companies in Sec.'s 4.2.1, 4.2.4, and 4.2.8-11.) I suggest making your eBook cover in Word, using many of the same elements from your paperback cover – but perhaps modifying their sizes.

---

[26] Actually, I do have a paperback book with a title that begins, "Understand Basic Chemistry Concepts," but it doesn't match the eBook cover depicted here. I have two different chemistry books that both begin with these four words.

You can easily make a JPEG file from an eBook cover that you create in Word. When your eBook cover is ready, select the entire image (change View to One Page and click in the gray area to the left of the page to do this quickly) and follow the instructions in Sec. 2.2.5 to convert your cover into a JPEG file.

Set the page size in Word using the Page Layout tab. You can make either dimension – height or width – as large as 20". I recommend making the height 20" in order to maximize the resolution of the cover that you make in Word. You can have a square cover, which would then be 20" x 20"; this will give you a square thumbnail image. When a website – such as Amazon – displays their eBooks side-by-side with equal cover heights, some books appear wider than others because they don't all have the same aspect ratio. A square book with maximum resolution will appear widest. It may not be the case that wider is better. However, if you want wider, go with 20" x 20".

When you decide on your aspect ratio, keep in mind that your cover JPEG file may be added to the beginning of the eBook (in addition to your title page) – depending on the eReader company. In this case, you may want the aspect ratio of your cover to match the aspect ratio of the eReader. For example, if you want to match the Kindle Fire and Nook Color aspect ratios, choose 11.7" x 20"; for the Kindle eInk 6" and black-and-white Nook, choose 15" x 20"; and for the Kindle Fire HD 7", choose 12.5" x 20". Another consideration is that your thumbnail may look more uniform if it matches the aspect ratio of most of the other eBooks of its genre.

To make your eBook cover, you can simply copy (Ctrl + C) and paste (Ctrl + V) textboxes, WordArt, drawings, photos, and other pictures from your paperback book cover into your eBook cover. You will probably need to resize most, if not all, of the textboxes and images. Remember that if you click on the little arrow in the bottom right corner of the Size group at the far right of the Format tab, you can choose to lock the Aspect Ratio before resizing. Also, a group of images may not look as nice when it is first resized – you may need to change the font size, line thicknesses, and adjust alignment to recreate the quality of the original image. You can Zoom out in the View tab to preview what the eBook will look like as a thumbnail image, and you will also get a preview of the thumbnail when begin the publishing process (although the actual thumbnail usually looks sharper than the preview).

Amazon recommends an eBook cover with an aspect ratio of 5:8 and a longest dimension with 2500 pixels. The width will then be approximately 1563 pixels. A page size of 12.5" by 20" creates this aspect ratio. While 5:8 matches Kindle Fire devices, it's more important how the thumbnail looks before buying the book. With that in mind, 5:8 may be too narrow; many designers prefer 6:9. **Note that KDP now has a Cover Creator.**

If you do this, you will need a different cover for a Nook eBook since a Nook cover can't have more than 2000 pixels on the longest side. You can simply open your JPEG file in Paint and resize the longest dimension to 2000 pixels. If you use the 5:8 aspect ratio, your width will have about 1250 pixels.

Chapter 4

Self-Publishing Your Book

Chapter Overview

4.1 Publishing Your Paperback Book with CreateSpace
4.2 Publishing Your eBook Online

This chapter answers questions about the following topics, and more:

- ☑ Detailed instructions for how to publish a paperback book with CreateSpace.
- ☑ Pricing your book, selecting categories, adding a second Browse category at Amazon, choosing keywords, adding a subtitle, and a discussion of CreateSpace services.
- ☑ Making your paperback book available in bookstores and libraries.
- ☑ Detailed instructions for how to publish – with information about pricing – an eBook on Amazon's Kindle, Barnes & Noble's Nook, the Sony Reader, and more.[27]
- ☑ The problem of using the brand of the eReader in the description of your eBook, why it's not really a problem, and what to do instead.
- ☑ Important differences between the paperback and eBook versions of your book's description, keywords, and categories.
- ☑ Your paperback Amazon listing and Kindle Amazon listing will be linked together, such that either page shows both versions of your book.
- ☑ An introduction to Smashwords[27] – a free publishing service that makes your eBook available on a variety of eReaders.

---

[27] Kindle and Amazon are trademarks of Amazon.com, Inc. Nook and Barnes & Noble are trademarks of Barnes & Noble, Inc. Sony is a registered trademark of Sony Corporation. Smashwords is a registered trademark of Smashwords. These trademarks and brands are the property of their respective owners.

4.1 Publishing Your Paperback Book with CreateSpace

4.1.1 About CreateSpace and Amazon[28]

I recommend publishing the paperback edition of your book with CreateSpace, for reasons that I described in Chapter 1. CreateSpace is an Amazon company. I love and trust Amazon as both a consumer and as an author. I gave CreateSpace a shot because of Amazon's reputation, and have come to love and trust CreateSpace, too. These bookselling and publishing giants have created many opportunities for small business owners and self-published authors. Amazon frequently features success stories of small, family-owned businesses that sell their products on Amazon as well as success stories of self-published authors. I'm happy to support a huge business that gives the small guy a fighting chance.[29]

We all know that Amazon is an online bookstore giant (which also sells many other products besides books). As a potential self-published author and Amazon customer, you may want to take a moment and consider how Amazon's history impacts you. When Amazon emerged as a giant online bookseller, they made a very bold move: They allowed customers to resell their used books (regardless of where they were purchased), and listed the used book sales on the same detail page for the new books. Traditional publishers and bestselling authors were not happy about this, as they did not (and still don't) draw royalties[30] on the resold copies: Customers who visited Amazon online to order a bestselling book could choose – as an alternative to paying the cover price for a new book – to purchase a used book for as little as one penny (and bestselling mass market paperbacks often were selling for just one penny). Traditional publishers were a major supplier to Amazon, yet Amazon went against their wishes, benefiting the small guy – consumers could buy books for less, consumers could resell their books (many used books sold very quickly and brought a much better price than a yard sale ever would), and many small businesses found a great avenue for selling new and used books.

Amazon's next major moves, which significantly impacted the publishing industry, were to introduce the Kindle and to advertise CreateSpace. Both Kindle and CreateSpace

---

[28] CreateSpace and Amazon are trademarks of Amazon.com, Inc. These trademarks and brands are the property of their respective owners.

[29] I was not endorsed to write this book by Amazon or CreateSpace. I was not paid nor encouraged in any way to show my support of these companies in my book. Neither company was aware that I was writing or self-publishing this book until the work had already been completed (and these companies are probably too huge to ever take notice of this book, let alone read it and see that I have recommended them). These are my honest opinions; you are encouraged to do some research and form your own opinions.

[30] Don't freak out about this. In Sec. 4.1.7, I will explain how the sale of third-party used and new books probably helps the self-publisher much more than it hurts.

provided (and continue to provide) incredible self-publishing opportunities for authors. I first learned about CreateSpace when I was shopping at Amazon. I found the link at the bottom of their webpage that says, "Independently Publish with Us." This link briefly describes Kindle and CreateSpace, and invites you to visit their websites. There are now millions of paperback books and eBooks being published this way. The editors of big publishing houses have long decided what books we should be able to read (and write), but now Amazon (and other companies, like Barnes & Noble and Sony, with their eReaders) are providing millions of new books to choose from. I recognize and appreciate what Amazon has done for both self-published authors and consumers, and so I continue to support Amazon both ways.

CreateSpace is an Amazon company that has been helping authors, musicians, and filmmakers make their work available through Amazon and other distribution options (such as other booksellers and libraries). CreateSpace is a print-on-demand service, meaning that they print and bind your book when it sells. This way, there is no inventory to manage, and your book is always in stock and never goes out of print (unless, for some reason, you decide to discontinue production of your book). Your book will show as 'in stock' on Amazon's website, and is ready to ship if a customer purchases it. The print-on-demand technology is what makes self-publishing possible – you can self-publish for free (there are no setup fees). You don't have to purchase any of your own books (unlike old-fashioned self-publishing, where you would buy hundreds or thousands of copies up front and try to sell them directly to bookstores). Since CreateSpace is an Amazon company, your self-published book will be listed with Amazon,[31] available for purchase by millions of potential customers around the globe. You can even make your book available for sale in Europe (if so, they will print your book on demand in Europe and ship it from Europe to save shipping costs). There is also an Expanded Distribution option, which allows other booksellers and libraries to buy copies of your book and sell them. Your book will also have an eStore on CreateSpace, where customers can purchase your book directly (this is useful if you have your own webpage – you can add a link from your website straight to your eStore). CreateSpace also provides tools, resources, customer service, and a community forum, all of which provide help for you to self-publish your work. The royalties are excellent, too (see Sec.'s 4.1.4-5). I don't imagine that you will find another self-publishing service that makes your book more visible, offers better royalties, and also comes for FREE. It's an amazing combination!

Most of the material from Sec.'s 4.1.2-8 – such as preparing your book description and choosing key words – will apply regardless of where you publish your paperback book, even though I will generally speak with CreateSpace in mind. In Sec. 4.1.9, I will specifically outline how to publish your paperback book using your CreateSpace account.

If you would like more information about CreateSpace, you can visit their website directly (www.createspace.com); or you can visit Amazon's website (www.amazon.com),

---

[31] This is provided that your book doesn't have unacceptable content, such as pornography, offensive material, and public domain content.

scroll down to the bottom of the page, and click Independently Publish With Us. You can sign up for an account for free. Then, when you login, it is very easy to contact them if you have any questions that you would like to ask. In your Member Dashboard (this shows up automatically when you login), click the Contact Support bar on the left side. You can send an email, or you can click Call Me to speak with someone over the phone. The phone will probably ring almost immediately. I've used this option myself a few times, and always found a courteous, knowledgeable support specialist on the other end of the line. Other ways to get questions answered include the Frequently Asked Questions at the bottom of the Contact Support page and the Community Help forum (click Community on the left side of the screen from your Member Dashboard), where you can speak with other self-published authors.

4.1.2 Preparing a Description and Biography

You will need to prepare a description of your book for online booksellers. Amazon will use your description on your book's detail page, and it will also appear in your CreateSpace eStore. Most other online booksellers, like Barnes & Noble, which are available through the Expanded Distribution, are not presently using this description – it's up to them. Therefore, you should focus on your Amazon audience when you prepare your description, and then revise your description if you also publish an eBook version of your book.

Customers browsing through Amazon who come across your book will be able to read your book's description. Therefore, the purpose of your description is to inform potential readers what your book is about in order to help them make their purchase decision. Your main goal is to provide a clear indication of what the customer is buying. If your customer expects your book to be one thing, but it turns out to be something else, the result could be a negative review. Thus, you don't want to 'oversell' or 'under-describe' your book: If your book sounds like the best thing since sliced bread, but doesn't live up to the description, or if there isn't enough information for the customer to understand exactly what he/she is getting, the customer may leave a negative review – which will affect potential sales in the future.

Your book will have a Search Inside feature on Amazon (though it may take a few weeks before this feature is added to your book), which allows the customer to preview the contents, introduction, other front and back matter, the back cover, and sample pages. Because of this, some authors make the mistake of not describing the book well, thinking that the customer will be able to sample the book firsthand. The problem with this is that many customers purchase books without using the Search Inside feature. You just have to accept this fact and make your description clear. The consequence for an unclear description could be a negative review; it doesn't help to be able to say, "You could have looked inside!"

In addition to providing a clear picture of what your book is about, your description provides a writing sample. Customers won't assume that the author of the book also wrote the book's description (unless you want to advertise this point in the description – it might be more professional to write in the third person, as if someone else is describing your book), unless perhaps the customer is another self-published author (which is not at all unlikely, as many self-published authors like to support the self-publishing concept). Rather, the description is the first form of writing that the customer associates with your book: If there are obvious spelling or grammatical mistakes in the one-paragraph description, in the customer's mind, that won't bode well for the quality of the book itself.

There is a limit to how long your description can be: When you self-publish with CreateSpace, your description must be 4,000 characters or less (estimated at about 760 words). The character limit is the same for Kindle, but some eReaders may have a different restriction on the character limit.

I recommend typing your book's description in Microsoft Word. There are a few advantages of doing this and later using copy/paste to transfer your description to the publisher:

- You can easily check the character count. Click the word count in the bottom left corner of the screen, and a window will pop up to show you the character count. You want "Characters (with spaces)."
- Use Word's spelling and grammar checker to help reduce the chance for such mistakes. These checkers are not foolproof, though, so you still need to read the description carefully (and have friends/family check it, too). These checkers will help to catch a few obvious mistakes, though.
- It will be easy to find your description if you need to modify it for your eBook.

The nature of your description depends on what type of book you are publishing. For fiction, you want to inspire interest in your story without giving away the plot (definitely, don't spoil the ending). Since characters can attract interest in a book, describe key characters involved in the story. The setting of the story may also draw interest: A reader might want to enjoy the feeling of living someplace exotic, or might appreciate being able to relate to a story from their home city, for example.

In nonfiction, you want to make the range and depth of the content very clear. While you should mostly describe your book, you want to show how it is distinguished from similar titles (not by mentioning other books directly or putting other authors down, but by describing what is unique about your book). Describe any special features that your book includes, such as an answer key, a glossary, or over a hundred figures. Readers will want to know such things as whether your book is comprehensive or focused on a narrow topic, whether it is an introduction for beginners or presented at a high level for experts, and whether it is written with clear language that anyone can understand or written at a technical level. You want to make the contents clear (since not everyone will Search Inside to see the table of contents). If the author has any special qualifications that relate to the book (such as a degree in the subject area, or several years of experience in the field), highlight this.

I suggest reading descriptions of other books for inspiration (but don't plagiarize the content). Browse descriptions on Amazon and also read back covers and dust jackets of books that you have (or visit a library or bookstore).

You are not permitted to include contact information in your description, such as an email address or even a website URL. Also, you may not include any reviews, quotes, or testimonials in your description. If you have a professional Editorial Review, Amazon will post that review separate from your description. You can't use your description to ask customers to review your work. You're not allowed to advertise or promote in your description. Also, you can't use DHTML, Java Scripts, or any executables in your description.[32]

While you want to provide sufficient detail so that the potential reader has a clear description of what your book is about, having a description that is too lengthy might also deter some readers. A concise description is often effective, provided that it doesn't omit important details. A shorter description may be better for fiction; leaving an air of mystery might even stir a little interest. On the other hand, I've come across many short descriptions that didn't tell me what I really wanted to know: If you take a chance on such a book, you're not going to be happy if it doesn't turn out to be what you were looking for. There is a balance somewhere in between, where you provide all of the pertinent information in a concise description. I suggest erring on the side of too much, rather than too little, information in the case of a nonfiction book.

If you have a long description, you may want to find a way to organize it into parts to help readers find what they are looking for. Unfortunately, if you use the tab key to make indentations, the paragraph breaks will not show up in the description for your book on Amazon (although they will show up for a Kindle book). There are some alternatives. You could use one-word section headings in CAPS (but don't use CAPS extensively – it's unacceptable), as illustrated in the following sample description. You can also number the sections of your description – like (1), (2), etc. – or use symbols – like the asterisk (*), but many nonstandard symbols won't show up – in order to help show the divisions. **Once published, you can format your description better at Author Central (see Sec. 6.1.4).**

Following, I have a couple of my sample descriptions to help get you started. These descriptions are for nonfiction books. The first description is fairly long, and features occasional use of the CAPS key to create divisional breaks. The second description is fairly concise. Again, I selected my own descriptions because it was easy to get permission to use them, not because I thought you'd be interested in a book about chemistry or the fourth dimension. I recommend that you check out a variety of other book descriptions.

---

[32] This covers most of what you need to avoid including in your description for Amazon. Visit Amazon and other booksellers' websites to learn all of the exclusions that apply.

Understand Basic Chemistry Concepts

OVERVIEW: This book focuses on fundamental chemistry concepts, such as understanding the periodic table of the elements and how chemical bonds are formed. No prior knowledge of chemistry is assumed. The mathematical component involves only basic arithmetic. The content is much more conceptual than mathematical. AUDIENCE: It is geared toward helping anyone – student or not – to understand the main ideas of chemistry. Both students and non-students may find it helpful to be able to focus on understanding the main concepts without the constant emphasis on computations that is generally found in chemistry lectures and textbooks. CONTENTS: (1) Understanding the organization of the periodic table, including trends and patterns. (2) Understanding ionic and covalent bonds and how they are formed, including the structure of valence electrons. (3) A set of rules to follow to speak the language of chemistry fluently: How to name compounds when different types of compounds follow different naming schemes. (4) Understanding chemical reactions, including how to balance them and a survey of important reactions. (5) Understanding the three phases of matter: properties of matter, amorphous and crystalline solids, ideal gases, liquids, solutions, and acids/bases. (6) Understanding atomic and nuclear structure and how it relates to chemistry. (7) VErBAl ReAcTiONS: A brief fun diversion from science for the verbal side of the brain, using symbols from chemistry's periodic table to make word puzzles. ANSWERS: Every chapter includes self-check exercises to offer practice and help the reader check his or her understanding. 100% of the exercises have answers at the back of the book. COPYRIGHT: Teachers who purchase one copy of this book or borrow one copy of this book from a library may reproduce selected pages for the purpose of teaching chemistry concepts to their own students.

The Visual Guide to Extra Dimensions, Volume 1

Watch a tesseract unfold. See how the 3D cross section of a hypercube changes as the hypercube rotates. View 4D wheels with axles with a spherinder or cubinder structure. Imagine climbing a 4D staircase. Find 10 out of 120 dodecahedra of a hecatonicosachoron highlighted... all on this visual tour of the fourth dimension. The book is much more visual and conceptual than algebraic, yet it is detailed and technical, with the intention of satisfying the needs of mathematically-minded readers familiar with the fundamentals of algebra, geometry, and graphing.

You can also add an author biography to your book's Amazon detail page. (This is separate from a biography that you can add to an Amazon Author Page, if you choose to create one. Author pages will be described in Chapter 6.) Since many books do not include an author biography below the description, including one can add a professional appearance to your book's Amazon page. Of course, a biography will also help readers learn more about the author behind the book, and any relevant experience and qualifications.

When you publish a book with CreateSpace, you can include a biography with your submission, which will automatically appear (within a few days, usually) on your book's Amazon detail page. It will also appear – along with your description – in your CreateSpace eStore. As with your description, I recommend first typing your biography in Word to check for spelling and grammar mistakes, and to check the character count. Save your biography – since you will need one for your Author Page, too (the Author Page biography should probably be longer, the detail page biography a shorter version – the former will be described in Chapter 6). Your biography must be written in 2500 characters (including spaces) or less, which is estimated to be about 475 words. Of course, the same provisions outlining what you can or can't include with your description also apply to your biography.

What do you want your readers to know about you? They might be curious about your background, relevant qualifications, or previous publications. Some will wonder what your hobbies and interests are. Readers will probably appreciate being able to see some of your personality as they read your biography. As it is another writing sample (though again, it will seem more professional if it is written in the third person so that it appears that another person wrote about you – rather than speaking in the first person as if you wrote it yourself, even if that was the case), it's very important to make a good impression by avoiding spelling or grammatical mistakes. If you struggle with spelling and grammar, it will be worthwhile to receive proofreading assistance with your description and biography.

If you publish multiple books, you can include a different biography with each book. However, the biography that you post on your Amazon Author Page (see Chapter 6) will be the same for all of your books.

Following is a sample biography that I included with my books on the fourth dimension. It is a bit long because I felt the need to establish my qualifications in this field. In general, I would suggest a shorter biography on your book's detail page, but include a longer biography on your Author Page.

Chris McMullen is a physics instructor at Northwestern State University of Louisiana. He earned his Ph.D. in phenomenological high-energy physics (particle physics) from Oklahoma State University in 2002. Originally from California, he earned his Master's degree from California State University, Northridge, where his thesis was in the field of electron spin resonance. He has published several papers on the prospects for discovering large superstring-inspired extra dimensions at the Large Hadron Collider, which is his area of specialization. Dr. McMullen published The Visual Guide to Extra Dimensions, Volumes 1 and 2, to share his passion for the geometry and physics of the fourth dimension. He also wrote these books, Full-Color Illustrations of the Fourth Dimension, Volumes 1 and 2, to help illustrate the geometry of a fourth dimension of space. Dr. McMullen was fascinated with a fourth dimension of space when he first read Rudy Rucker's introduction to the subject during high school. He happened to be working on his Ph.D. in particle physics when Arkani-Hamed, Dimopoulos, and Dvali wrote a famous technical paper motivating large superstring-inspired extra dimensions, which transformed the subject of the fourth dimension from philosophy to a plausibly experimental science. Dr. McMullen has published these general-audience books on the fourth dimension to share his passion for the math and physics of extra dimensions. One of his favorite sayings is: May your contemplation of a fourth dimension of space enhance the dimensionality of your thoughts.

The following sample biography is for a Christmas word scrambles book that I coauthored. It is somewhat more concise than the previous biography, and also illustrates how you can divide the biographies of two coauthors in a single biography field.

Chris McMullen and Carolyn Kivett are a son-and-mother combination who teamed up to write a variety of word puzzle books and, recently, some children's books, such as math flash cards for the Kindle. CHRIS MCMULLEN holds a Ph.D. in theoretical high-energy physics (aka particle physics) from Oklahoma State University. He teaches physics at Northwestern State University of Louisiana. In addition to solving verbal and math puzzles, he enjoys playing chess and golf and writing books in his spare time. His mother, CAROLYN KIVETT, loves solving verbal puzzles, such as anagrams and crossword puzzles. She runs a small business in southern California where she manufactures covers for outdoor entertainment centers and golf cart enclosures from scratch. She enjoys the challenge of sewing materials into new geometric shapes, which is a three-dimensional visual puzzle. She loves to collect teddy bears and sunflowers, and also enjoys playing golf.

4.1.3 Selecting a Browse Category, Keywords, and Title/Subtitle

You will need to select a browse category for your book's detail page on Amazon. If you also publish an eBook, you will need to select two browse categories.

Visit Amazon's website and browse through the books. Click Books on the left of their home page, then choose Books from the list. On the left-hand side, you will find a list called "Books Categories." Explore these categories and their subcategories to discover what options are available.

Next, type in key words that relate to your title in the Search field at the top of the screen. Make sure that 'Books' is selected (as opposed to 'All' or a specific category) because you want books from various book categories to show up in your search. Find books that are similar to your book, open their detail pages, and see what browse categories they are listed in. This will help you decide which categories are a best fit for your book.

When you publish your book with CreateSpace, you only get to select one browse category. However, if you feel strongly that a second browse category is relevant for your book, you can politely ask them to consider having a second browse category added to your book at Amazon by clicking Contact Support from your Member Dashboard. You will also be able to select two browse categories when you publish an eBook.

In addition to selecting a category, you will need to add keywords to associate with your book. Keywords help potential buyers find your book when they use the search field at Amazon.[33] Your book will already be searchable at Amazon using any combination of words from your title and subtitle. In addition, your book will be searchable using up to 5 keywords that you enter when you publish your book. Each keyword may actually be a combination of words. Unfortunately, CreateSpace won't allow you to enter a keyword that exceeds 25 characters (including spaces) – which is a shame because sometimes there are highly relevant, very popular keywords that exceed 25 characters.

You want to find the best 5 keywords that relate to your book. If you will be publishing an eBook with Kindle, they will let you use 7 keywords, so you may as well find 7 now (and Kindle doesn't impose the 25 character restriction). For most books, it's easy to find dozens of relevant keywords. Unfortunately, you can only choose 5. So you need to try to determine which 5 are the best to use. (You can also change them later if you think of something better or if you want to see whether changing the keywords might affect your sales.)

I recommend typing possible keywords into the search field at Amazon to test out the popularity of the keyword. Plus, as you do this, you may discover keywords that you hadn't thought of. After you type a few letters, you will see a list of popular searches come up. Keep in mind that a keyword is not necessarily a single word, but may be a group of words or a phrase. Make a list of all of the relevant keywords, and make notes about which ones seem more popular. This list will help you choose the 5 best keywords.

---

[33] Other online booksellers, like Barnes & Noble, which may sell your book through the Expanded Distribution channel, will probably not use these keywords. If not, you can always consider contacting them and inquiring about the prospects of having relevant keywords added to your book. First, give them plenty of time (a month or more) to get your book properly listed, then see if your book comes up in the keyword search at their website (I mean to check if it comes up at all – it probably won't be on the first page if it comes up).

The most important factor in choosing your keywords is that they be very relevant to your book. It's not just popularity that you're looking for. It doesn't do you any good to use a very popular keyword that doesn't relate to your book, like using Tiger Woods as a keyword for a book that doesn't even mention Tiger Woods (that will just upset customers). Ensure that the keywords closely relate to your book's content. The keyword could relate to your content (like "medical thriller"), the setting (like "San Diego"), or the type of book (like "workbook"), for example. The keyword may even be another term for a word used in your title. For example, a book that is entitled, *Scary Word Search Puzzles*, should have "word find" as one of the keywords because some people will be typing "word find" instead of "word search," and the book should show up either way.

Another factor is the popularity of the keyword. If you want your book to be discovered in searches at Amazon, you want to use a keyword which potential buyers will be searching for frequently. If your keywords are only searched for once every few months, almost nobody will discover your book through your keywords. When you start typing a keyword in a search at Amazon, if the keyword does not show up at all, you know that it will be a very rare search. You definitely want to use keywords that have been typed frequently enough to show up on the list of keywords. Very popular keywords will show up after just typing a couple of letters, less popular keywords require typing more letters.

However, using the most popular keywords might not be the best idea (as long as the keywords that you do use are searched for with a reasonable frequency). Here's why: If the keyword is exceedingly popular, the keyword search will pull up thousands of matches, and your book may be way down at the end of the search (where it is unlikely to be found). If instead your keyword is moderately popular and pulls up, say, 50 matches, there is a much better chance of your book being visible in the search results. (Even if your book is way down at the end of the search results, it may still be discovered – as explained in Chapter 7.)

The points below relate to keywords. **Learn how to get into special categories at** https://kdp.amazon.com/self-publishing/help?topicId=A200PDGPEIQX41.

- Popularity changes with time. If you check the popularity of keywords today, you might find that the order of their popularity is different next month. A keyword that you choose today could even become obsolete in the future. The current popularity is based on the frequency with which that keyword has been used recently.
- Plurals may make a difference. For example, if you search for "fraction book," the order of the search results changes if instead you search for "fractions book." However, you probably don't need to make separate keywords for both singular and plural – as long as you have one, your book will probably show up the other way, too. For example, if you use "fraction book" for one keyword, you probably don't need to waste a second keyword for "fractions book." You can always test this out after your book is published (and waiting a reasonable time period for all of the keywords to be added to your book's Amazon detail page).

- The word "book" may be implied. For example, if you have the word "pirates" in your title, your book will probably show up in a search for "pirates book" without having to waste one of your keywords to make "pirates book." You can always test this out after your book is published (and keep in mind that your book could be way down at the end of the search results).
- The order of your keywords may make a difference. For example, "writing practice" is different from "practice writing." If the keyword is popular both ways (i.e. compared to reversing the word order), you could choose one of the keywords and see if your book is searchable both ways. If not, and you want it to be, you will have to change one of your other keywords to accommodate this (since you can only have 5).
- The popularity of the keywords (and the order of the search results) changes when you search in 'All' compared to searching in 'Books' or even searching in a specific category (and it's also different when searching for your eBook in Kindle). Explore all of these options when choosing your keywords.

Keywords help to make your book searchable, but not necessarily visible: Your book might not be in the first several pages (though it could be on the first page – you won't know until you try it out), and it could be down at the end of the pack (if so, that could change in time). In Chapter 7, we will discuss how customers will be able to find your book if it is way down at the end of the pack, and how your book might become more visible as time passes.

One way to decide which 5 keywords to use is to conduct a survey among family, friends, and acquaintances. Ask them what they would type into a search if looking for a book like yours and see what the common responses are.

You should have keywords in mind when you develop the title and subtitle for your book, since your book will also be searchable through combinations of words in your title and subtitle. Note that words in your title are more important than words in your subtitle because your book may not be searchable by words in your subtitle in Amazon's European (and other) websites or with other online booksellers (if you use these distribution channels).

A title or subtitle that simply consists of keywords probably won't be the best title. A catchy or interesting title can be very effective, and often such titles only include a few keywords, if any. Most fiction titles are catchy, but have no keywords of their own. Nonfiction titles tend to include a few keywords that help to indicate what the book is about.

A subtitle is optional. When your book shows up in search results at Amazon, the subtitle will appear after the title, separated by a colon. So if you have a long title and subtitle, the overall title will look very long. Sometimes, concise can be more effective. If you don't have any keywords in your title, you may want to include a subtitle in order to add a couple of keywords which briefly help readers to see what your book is about.

It's very important to spell the title and subtitle correctly: Since this is the first thing that a potential buyer will read, you don't want these to make a poor impression. The title and subtitle also need to sound good – which may be more important than keywords.

If you are publishing a series of books with volume numbers, you may want to consider adding the volume number to the title or subtitle. There is also a separate place to enter the volume number when you publish your book.

4.1.4 Calculating the Cost of Your Book and Your Royalty

In this section, I'll show you how to calculate your royalty for books published with CreateSpace. In Sec. 4.2.5, we'll discuss eBook royalty calculations. In order to calculate your royalty, first you need to figure out the author's cost of the book. The author's cost is how much it costs the author to buy the book directly from the publisher. Unless you have a lengthy book and choose a color interior, the author's cost is actually quite affordable:

- $ A black-and-white book costs $2.15 plus 1.2 cents per page over 108 pages.
- $ A color book costs $3.65 plus 7 cents per page over 40 pages.

Note that if you have an odd number of pages, you have to add 1 page to your page count (since there are two sides to every sheet of paper).

Here is an example: Suppose that you have a 200-page black-and-white book. The author's cost is $3.25. The breakdown is as follows. Subtract 108 from 200 to find that it is 92 pages over. Multiply 92 by $0.012 (that's 1.2 cents expressed in terms of dollars) to get $1.10. Add this to $2.15 to get the author's cost of $3.25.

If you want to skip the math, don't worry – you can. CreateSpace has a calculator on their website that will figure the author's cost for you. From their homepage, click Books, then Publish a Trade Paperback, and click the Buying Copies tab. Scroll down, enter the information, and press the calculate button. The 'per book' cost is the author's cost.[34]

Let us first discuss the royalty calculation for books sold directly by Amazon.[35] When a customer buys your book directly from Amazon, CreateSpace pays you 60% of the list price minus the author's cost of your book. For example, if the author's cost of the book is $3.25

---

[34] You don't get a discount by buying in bulk. Rather, since the cost is quite cheap, they don't charge us more when we buy a small quantity. However, you do save on shipping if you purchase multiple books.

[35] If a used or new book sells from a third-party seller at Amazon, you earn no royalty. However, if you use the Expanded Distribution, there will be some sellers offering copies of your book (usually new, but sometimes they call it used) who purchase their wholesale copies from CreateSpace. If this happens, you will earn royalties from the Expanded Distribution channel when they purchase your book wholesale. For reasons that I will explain in Sec. 4.1.7, there are some incentives for customers to buy your book directly from Amazon – instead of buying new or used copies (whether they are from customers reselling theirs or Expanded Distribution sellers).

and the list price is $9.99, the royalty will be $2.74 per book. To figure this out, multiply the list price by 60% as follows: $9.99 x 60% = $5.99. Then subtract the author's cost: $5.99 – $3.25 = $2.74.

CreateSpace also has a royalty calculator on their website. From their homepage, click Books, then Publish a Trade Paperback, and click the Distribution and Royalties tab. Scroll down, enter the information, and press the calculate button. You will also be able to play with the list price and royalty calculation when you enter the list price for your book during the publishing process (see Sec. 4.1.9).

You make a different royalty if you sell books through distribution channels other than Amazon. In addition to selling books on Amazon, you can sell books directly from an eStore on CreateSpace, through Amazon Europe, and through the Expanded Distribution channel. You can use CreateSpace's royalty calculator to see what royalty you will draw in each of these distribution channels; you will also have the opportunity to play with the numbers (i.e. type in different list prices and see what the royalties will be) when you go through the process of publishing your book.

The royalty rates for Amazon sales, your CreateSpace eStore sales, and Expanded Distribution sales are summarized in the table below.

Distribution Channel	Royalty
CreateSpace eStore	80% minus author cost
Amazon's Website	60% minus author cost
Expanded Distribution	40% minus author cost

For example, if you set your list price at $7.99 and the author's cost of your book is $2.51, your royalty would be $3.88 for sales in your CreateSpace eStore ($7.99 x 0.8 – $2.51), $2.28 for sales at Amazon ($7.99 x 0.6 – $2.51), and 69 cents for Expanded Distribution sales ($7.99 x 0.4 – $2.51). Each sales channel is optional: You get to choose which sales channels you would like to offer. All of the sales channels are free, including the Expanded Distribution channel (see Sec. 4.1.7). (Expanded Distribution used to cost $25, but now it's free.)

The royalty is also 60% minus the author cost for sales through Amazon UK and Amazon Europe. The difference is that sales through Amazon's UK and other European websites (including France, Germany, Spain, and Italy) have a different author cost and may also have a different list price.

When you select distribution options for Amazon UK and continental Europe, books purchased through Amazon UK and Amazon's other European website are manufactured in Great Britain or continental Europe. This way, European customers can purchase your book without having to pay an outrageous shipping charge to send the book from the US to Europe.

The list price for books sold through Amazon UK is set in pounds (£); this is called Great Britain pricing (GBP). The author's cost and royalty are also figured in pounds. The author's cost for GBP is £0.70 plus £0.01 per page for black-and-white books and £0.70 plus £0.045 per page for color. (Unlike Amazon US sales, these per page charges apply to every page in the book – not just the number of pages over 108 or 40.) For example, a black-and-white book with 150 pages has an author's cost of £2.20 in GBP (£0.70 + £0.01 x 150).

The list price for books sold through Amazon's continental Europe (EUR) websites is set in euro (€). The author's cost and royalty are also figured in euro. The author's cost for EUR pricing is €0.60 plus €0.012 per page for black-and-white books and €0.60 plus €0.06 per page for color. For example, a black-and-white book with 150 pages has an author's cost of €2.40 in EUR pricing (€0.60 + €0.012 x 150).

To figure your royalty for GBP and EUR sales, multiply your list price by 60% and subtract the author's cost of your book. For example, if your book has list prices of £5.50 and €6.82 and author's costs of £2.20 and €2.40, respectively, your GBP and EUR royalties will be £1.10 (0.6 x £5.50 – £2.20) and €1.69 (0.6 x €6.82 – €2.40). Of course, you may choose to have these royalties deposited into a US bank account in US dollars (but if you prefer to be paid in pounds or euro and have it deposited in Europe, that's possible, too).

4.1.5 Setting the List Price and Royalty for Your Book

When you self-publish a book, you control the list price. Since your royalty depends on the list price, you control how much royalty you make for each book that you sell. It's not the royalty that you make per book that matters, though: If you're trying to maximize your income, it's how much royalty you draw overall that counts. For example, if you could sell many more books by dropping your price a little, you might make more royalty overall. However, book sales do not always increase when the price is dropped. You want to choose a lower list price if it means more royalty overall, but you don't want to lower your price when it won't improve sales enough to increase your overall revenues. It's a challenge to set the perfect price. In this section, we will describe a few different methods for setting the list price of your paperback book, and explore a variety of factors that you may want to consider when you set the list price for your book.

The standard royalty for a traditionally published book is 15%. For comparison, you should see what list price would give you the standard 15%. I'm not saying that you should use 15% to determine your royalty. Rather, a self-published book should probably draw a greater royalty than 15%. For one, there is no guarantee that you will sell a large number of copies, so you want to ensure a fair royalty on those that you do sell. A second reason is that you're doing your own editing and publishing services: You're not just being paid as the author, but as the editor and publisher, too. Hence, you should make more than just the author's standard share. Nonetheless, it's a useful starting point to see what list price would give you a 15% royalty, and then you can go from there.

The formula for making your CreateSpace royalty for Amazon sales equal to 15% is:

$$\text{list price} = \text{author's cost} \times 20 \div 9$$

For example, if the author's cost of your book is $2.38, a list price of $5.29 would give you a 15% royalty for sales at Amazon (since $2.38 x 20 ÷ 9 = $5.29). Your royalty would be 79 cents per book – that's 15% (since $5.29 x 0.15 = $0.79). You should calculate what the 15% royalty list price is for your book, just for your reference. (First, you will need to calculate the author's cost of your book, as described in Sec. 4.1.4. Remember, you may use CreateSpace's book cost calculator to figure this out; then use CreateSpace's royalty calculator to check that the royalty is indeed 15% – multiply the list price times 0.15 to check.)

One problem with a royalty of 15% through Amazon sales is that you probably won't make any royalty (or significant royalty) through Expanded Distribution sales (this sales channel is now free). While the royalty for Amazon sales is 60% of the list price minus the author's cost, the Expanded Distribution royalty is 40% of the list price minus the author's cost. In the previous example, with a list price of $5.29, if you calculate 40% of the list price, you get $2.11 (that's 0.40 x $5.29) – there's nothing left when you subtract the author's cost of $2.38. Therefore, the list price would need to be higher in order to offer books through the Expanded Distribution channel.

As I already mentioned, it is reasonable to draw a royalty of greater than 15% for a self-published book, since you're doing more than just writing the book – you're editing it, formatting it, publishing it, designing your own cover, etc.[36] Therefore, it may be more reasonable to make your Expanded Distribution royalty (instead of your Amazon royalty) equal to 15% of your list price. Let's see what this comes out to. The formula for setting the list price so that the Expanded Distribution royalty will be 15% is:

$$\text{list price} = \text{author's cost} \times 4$$

For example, if the author's cost of your book is $2.38, a list price of $9.52 would give you a 15% royalty for Expanded Distribution sales (since $2.38 x 4 = $9.52). Your royalty would be $1.43 cents per book sold through the Expanded Distribution channel – that's 15% (since $9.52 x 0.15 = $1.43). In this case, your Amazon royalty would be $3.33 (that's $9.52 x 0.6 – $2.38), which is 35% for Amazon sales. You should apply the above formula to your book for your reference, and also figure out what the royalty would be for both Amazon sales and Expanded Distribution sales.

Setting your royalty to make 15% on Expanded Distribution sales is not necessarily the best list price for your book. We will now consider a variety of factors that may influence what list price you set:

---

[36] If you invest money in any of these services, you also want to recoup some of your start-up funds.

$ Check out the competition. Search for other books that are similar to yours to see what the going rate is. Potential buyers will be comparing book prices when they shop. If your book is way overpriced, they may prefer a more economically priced title. On the other hand, if your book significantly cheaper, they might assume (perhaps incorrectly) that your book is shorter, less detailed, or lesser quality – i.e. they might believe that "you get what you pay for." If you just blindly price your book for a 15% or 35% royalty, for example, you may lose sales if it turns out that your book is not competitively priced.

$ Pay attention to details when you price the competition. For example, paperback books generally cost less than hardcover books. Your book will be softcover[37] if you publish with CreateSpace, so you should base your price on paperback editions. Look at how much material you get for your money: A book might be cheap if it has little content, and it might be more expensive if it is very long. Other details that you should consider include whether the book is in color or black-and-white, whether it has several quality illustrations, and special qualifications of the author. A book with unique features might earn a higher price. Is there anything special about your book that would drive buyers to spend a little more?

$ Keep in mind that your book is self-published. If buyers will be comparing your title to traditionally published books – especially, if the other titles include bestselling authors or major publishing houses – consider how the price of your title might influence a potential customer's purchasing decision when your book appears alongside these other titles in their Amazon search results. You can take this two ways, though, so it's not entirely clear cut: You might think that your list price should be a little less to entice readers your way, or you might think that you need to draw a higher royalty if your expectation is that you're not going to sell as many books.

$ Who is your primary audience? If you're hoping for most of your business to come from new customers who happen to find your book in Amazon search results, you may want your book to sell for a little less than traditionally published titles that are similar to yours. However, if you're planning to drive many of your sales through marketing (or sell books in person, after a seminar, or from your own website, for example), then your price can be somewhat higher (and help you recover any marketing expenses, too).

$ There are occasionally special offers. For example, until recently, books priced $9.99 or less were eligible for Amazon's 4-for-3 program (where customers could by 4 books for the price of 3). The 4-for-3 program was apparently discontinued in February of 2013. Browse books to see if there may be any special offers going on at Amazon.[38]

---

[37] If you're interested in a hardcover option, see Sec. 4.1.9.
[38] It's possible that the 4-for-3 program will return someday. It wouldn't hurt to check.

$ Another very important number to have in mind is $35. When a purchase (of eligible items) totals $35 or more, Amazon buyers can choose free shipping (called FREE Super Saver Shipping). If you were planning to set a list price in the mid-twenties, you may want to set the list price high enough for Amazon customers to receive free shipping.[39] Similarly, if you are planning to have a two-volume set, if the list price of each volume is high enough for the pair to total $35 or more, customers will be able to purchase the pair with free shipping.[40] If there are any Special Offers available, customers can take advantage of those and also receive free shipping if the total comes to at least $35.[41] If you have a series of books that you were planning to price at $5.99 each, if instead you price them at $6.25 each customers will be able to buy 4 and qualify for free shipping (without having to hunt for a cheap fifth book).

$ You should consider FREE Super Save Shipping even if you only plan to publish a single book and your price will be well below the $35 threshold: Explore which books customers are likely to buy in addition to yours. You want typical combinations to come out just over $35 rather than just under $35. Books do tend to sell in combinations at Amazon: After a few customers buy the same combination of books, when a future customer buys one book, Amazon has many marketing tools that help to promote the sale of other books in the combination (such as notes that other customers who bought this book also bought these other books).

$ The list price is not the same as the selling price. Amazon (and other booksellers, if you opt for Expanded Distribution) may choose to sell your book at a discount from the list price. If so, you still receive royalties based on the list price, not the actual selling price. A book with a higher list price is more likely to be on sale compared to the list price than a book with a lower list price. If you were thinking of selling your book for $15 to $18, for example, it's possible that if you go with $18, it will wind up being on sale. There is no guarantee that a book of any list price will be discounted, and is totally at the discretion of Amazon (or other bookseller); you have no say in this.

$ Contrary to common economic intuition, a lower list price does not always produce more sales. Why not? Some customers believe "you get what you pay for." Some have bought cheap books and found them to be shorter than they were expecting, lesser quality than they were hoping, or were otherwise dissatisfied. There may also be a critical price where the book is already such a good value that dropping the price won't make any difference. Thus, a lower price won't guarantee improved sales.

---

[39] However, you must also consider the possibility that Amazon may offer customers a discount, placing your book on sale for a price less than your list price.
[40] Again, if you price each volume at $12.50 and Amazon places either volume on sale, the customers won't qualify for free shipping – so you might allow a little room for a possible discount.
[41] When the 4-for-3 program was available, customers could qualify for free shipping if all four books added up to $25 (this is now $35), even if the total was less than $25 after removing the cost of the free book.

$ On the other hand, sometimes a lower price will drive many more sales. This is especially true when many customers perceive a book to be noticeably overpriced. If a book is significantly more expensive than similar titles, a few customers may buy it with the "you get what you pay for" mentality, but many customers may also feel more comfortable going with the lesser risk of the average price range. If a lower price affects FREE Super Saver Shipping, that may also play a significant role in how frequently the book sells.

$ Who is your audience? If many of the potential customers looking for books similar to yours tend to like good deals, then a lower price is more likely to drive more sales. If you're writing a nonfiction book about saving money or finding great bargains, for example, then your book *should* be economically priced. At the other extreme, customers tend to spend more money on technical textbooks and luxury books.

$ The effect of price is not easy to predict. A lower price provides a better deal. In some cases, the deal attracts more customers and pays off; in other cases, the lower price may actually hurt sales. A higher price sometimes suggests that a book is more serious, more detailed, or otherwise better; other times, a higher price deters sales.

$ You do have the option of changing your price if you want to experiment and see how price impacts sales. If you do this, it may be better to err on the high side to begin with and try lowering your price; if instead you raise your price, it may deter any customers who have observed the price hike.

$ Don't focus solely on how price will affect whether a potential customer will purchase your book: You must also consider how the customer will feel about the book's value after buying and reading your book. If a customer purchases your book, but later feels that it wasn't a good value, this increases your chance of receiving a negative review. When a customer opts for a more expensive book – thinking that "you get what you pay for" – the customer also has increased expectations. If you do price your book higher, you definitely want your readers to be satisfied with the value of their purchase.

$ Maybe royalty isn't your main concern. If you're more interested in selling as many books as possible (even if it means drawing less royalty income overall), or if a very affordable price is more important to you than your book revenues, then you might set your list price somewhat differently than an author who is mainly trying to maximize his or her overall royalties. This might be the case, for example, if you have written a book that attempts to spread awareness of a disease and how to prevent it.

$ You can't offer a list price that would make your royalty negative, so the absolute minimum list price is the list price for which your royalty would be zero. If you want to offer books for sale through the Expanded Distribution channel, your list price must also be high enough that the Expanded Distribution royalty is above zero. (You will be able to check these royalties when you go through the actual publishing process.)

$ You will probably have third-party sellers offering new and/or used copies of your book for sale at Amazon and other online booksellers. Some of these will be sellers who purchase your books through the Expanded Distribution channel, if you select it. Others will be customers who are reselling their used copies. If you choose a high list price (say, $15 or more), it's more likely for new or used books to sell for a healthy discount compared to Amazon's selling price, which will increase the temptation for potential customers to buy from a third-party. If you choose a low list price (say, under $10), third-party books will probably not seem as tempting – especially, if customers may buy enough books to qualify for FREE Super Saver Shipping.

$ Most list prices end with .99 or .95. Retailers have been doing this for ages: When buyers see a price of $7.99, they sometimes focus on the 7 – not seeing it as $8. For example, if you were planning to sell your book for $13, consider selling it for $12.99 instead. The reason is not to 'trick' your readers. Rather, the .99 and .95 ending is so common that your book might seem more professionally-priced if you have the common ending. If you strongly dislike this common pricing scheme, though, feel free to make a statement and end your list price with .50, for example. In rare circumstances, you might even be able to make the price relate to the theme of your book: For example, if you're writing a scary book, maybe the list price should end with .13 (as in $13.13); if your book relates to Las Vegas, how does a lucky $7.77 sound?

$ Basic economics[42] tells you that – assuming your main goal is to maximize your royalty income – the best price is a compromise between supply and demand. Basic economics also assumes that more people would buy your book at a lower price and fewer people would buy your book at a higher price – i.e. that the price will affect the demand. The latter is certainly true if you overprice your book: Try setting your list price at $500 and see how many copies you sell! There is also a psychological element involved: If the price is too cheap and customers don't recognize the value that they are getting (they recognize the great price, but wonder if it's because the product is cheap, too), they might choose to go with the middle price range instead. Since your book will be published on demand, you have virtually an infinite supply of books. So if you want to approach this from the perspective of economics, what you're really trying to gauge is the demand (and how it will be split between your book and similar titles). If you can create a higher demand through marketing, you can price your book higher; if there is little demand, it may take a lower price to attract customers.

---

[42] The entire subject of economics is based on maximizing your profits. Are people are more important than profits? Perhaps we should reinvent the subject of economics to maximize other things, like making the world (not just one individual's world) a better place. Just because you might make more money by charging a higher price doesn't mean that you *should* charge a higher price. However, I'm not trying to persuade you to make less royalty income than you can. I'm just trying to present a variety of perspectives to help you make an informed decision. The other side of this argument is that your hard work *deserves* every penny that you can earn.

$ Retailers often start out high and work their way down. There may be a high demand when a product is released to the market. Customers willing to spend more money buy products in this stage. As the price is gradually lowered, it becomes affordable to more customers. This strategy removes some of the guesswork from pricing the product. However, it can also create disgruntled customers (who might leave a negative review for a book) when they see it sell for less than they paid for it.

How did I set the price for this book? First, I searched for "self-publishing" and similar keywords on Amazon in Books. I ignored the eBooks when pricing the paperback. The first page of search results had paperback list prices ranging from $14.95 to $24.99. All of these list prices were discounted except for the $14.95 book. As I continued further into the search results, the first few cheaper self-publishing books that I came across (under $10) appeared to be shorter, less detailed works (or were much more focused – like how to publish an article rather than a book).

I observed that a list price between $15.99 and $19.99 would be competitive. Potential buyers might not take my book seriously if I made my list price well below $15.99, and I would probably lose many sales with a price of $20 or more. Also, a list price in the $15.99 to $19.99 range would increase the chances of having my book placed on sale at a discount. I feel that this book is highly detailed and quite comprehensive, focused on the information that many self-published authors would be looking for, and full of helpful ideas (these were my goals – you may judge the final product for yourself) – i.e. I didn't see a reason to set the list price below $15.99 based on content. Thus, I believed that this book would be a good value within the $15.99 to $19.99 price range.

Also, I felt that my book had a significant advantage over some of the competition. This book was clearly self-published (Amazon lists the publisher as CreateSpace Independent Publishing Platform) following its own instructions. What I was really amazed to see in my search results for self-published books was how many books about self-publishing were actually published by traditional publishers! If they know so much about self-publishing, why didn't they self-publish their own books about how to self-publish?[43] It seems reasonable to me that if you want to buy a book that will teach you how to self-publish, you ought to buy one from a self-published author who is successful enough at it to self-publish his/her own book. I knew that any potential buyer who checked out my book and clicked on my author profile would see that I have actually self-published dozens of books. I felt that this qualification – which helps set my book apart – could either merit a higher list price, or could make a list price of $15.99 or so seem like a better value.

---

[43] Mine is not the only self-published book about self-publishing that you can find in paperback. My point is that too many of the books on the subject of how to self-publish – and especially the top search results at the time – were not actually themselves self-published.

Secondly, my book on self-publishing describes both paperback publishing and eBook publishing, whereas most self-publishing books either do one of two things: (1) Focus on just one publishing platform, like CreateSpace or Kindle (but not both in detail); or (2) describe self-publishing in general terms (but not go into great detail for many of them). I want you to have an excellent paperback book and a well-formatted eBook, too, and so I have attempted to provide in-depth coverage for both formats. While I do mostly have CreateSpace and Kindle in mind, much of the content is also relevant for Nook, the Sony Reader, and other publishers; and later in this chapter I will lay down the details of how to self-publish an eBook with a variety of eReaders. This also helps my book on self-publishing stand out.

I therefore had a couple of compelling (or so I believed) reasons to put my list price at the higher end of the $15.99 to $19.99 bracket. I was planning to sell the paperback edition of this self-publishing book with a list price of $15.99, but as you can plainly see, I instead chose to set the list price of this paperback book at $9.99. I hope you appreciate the savings. ☺

Why did I set the list price at $9.99 instead of $15.99? Here are the reasons for my decision:

$ When I first published this book, Amazon's 4-for-3 program was still in effect. When the program was available, it was a great incentive for authors and publishers to price their books $9.99 or less. Although the 4-for-3 program was apparently discontinued in February of 2013, I opted to keep the original price. Personally, I'm very reluctant to raise prices (I'm sure you don't mind that I didn't). ☺

$ My audience mainly consists of aspiring self-published authors. Throughout this book, I've been advising you to keep your publishing investment to a minimum: Setting the list price at $9.99 instead of $15.99 helps you do this. $9.99 is my rock-bottom price – I only make about 50 cents when it sells through the Expanded Distribution, since this book has over 200 pages.

$ Almost all of my books are priced between $6.99 and $9.99. This price range has worked well for many of my other books. Once you find something that seems to work for you, it's hard to make yourself try something different. The only books that I have with a list price over $9.99 are technical physics books that have so many pages (like 500 pages) that I couldn't set the list price under $10 and still be eligible for the Expanded Distribution. If this book had another dozen pages or so, I wouldn't have been able to set the list price at $9.99.

I took a risk pricing this book at $9.99. Customers who see that my book is $5 below the typical price range of similar books might not see this as great savings – unfortunately, they might wonder what this book is lacking. I hope that you find that it's not lacking content or quality compared to similar titles – and even if the quality isn't lacking, potential customers won't know this (unless I'm so lucky to be blessed with reviews that say so).

I highly recommend that you conduct a survey among family members, friends, and acquaintances. They will help to give you some idea of what the book is worth. Your closest friends and family members may overprice your book: Your book and effort is likely to be worth much more to them than to a complete stranger. After they price your book, if you wind up selling it for less than they suggest, be sure to hit them up for a purchase: Tell them, "Look, I priced it less than you thought it was worth – so you have to buy one now." ☺ Be sure to say it with a smile!

Thinking about lowering your price? Consider this: For every $1.00 that you lower your price, you lose 60 cents from your royalty. In order for the price drop to increase your overall royalty income, you must not only sell more books, but the additional sales must be enough to compensate for the 60 cents per book that you are losing from your royalty.

Here is an example: Suppose that your book is priced at $9.99, your royalty is $3.00, and you presently sell an average of 30 copies per month. You're making an average of $90 per month presently. If you reduce your list price to $8.99, your new royalty will be $2.40. In order to still make $90 per month now, you must sell at least 38 books per month. In this example, you would have to sell at least 8 more books every month just to show a slight improvement in your monthly royalty income. The question that you have to ask yourself is this: Do you have reason to believe that 38 people were on the verge of buying your book last month, but 8 of them decided not to buy it because the price was $9.99 instead of $8.99? This is probably unlikely, in this example, unless there is a compelling reason – such as similar titles selling for $9.50, so now your book is 50 cents less instead of 50 cents more.

What if you dropped the price down to $7.99? Now your royalty would be $1.80 and you would need to sell 50 books per month just to make the same royalty – that's an extra 20 books per month. If you drop the price down to $6.99, your royalty would be $1.20 and you would need to sell 75 books per month. How about $5.99 – that's a bargain compared to $9.99, right? Well, you would make 60 cents per book, so you would have to sell 150 books at $5.99 just to make the same monthly royalty as you would with a $9.99 list price.

The point of my example is this: If sales aren't what you expect, dropping the price is not necessarily the answer. For one, you might not even increase your sales with a lower price (it happens). Even if you do sell more books by dropping your price, you have to sell many more books for the lower price to improve your monthly royalties.

However, lowering the price is sometimes the answer. It's important to price-match similar titles. If customers can find a book equivalent to yours for a lower price, then price may be more of a factor. However, if you are regularly selling copies every month, then price is probably not deterring customers from buying your book. On the other hand, if your sales are really slow and there are other equally visible similar titles selling for less, which also have frequent sales (as judged by watching the sales rank) – it could be that price is the hurdle (but there are other factors, too, including reviews, quality of the writing, quantity of content, publishing brand, appeal of the cover and description, better marketing strategy, etc.).

If price makes a significant difference for any Special Offers or eligibility for FREE Super Saver Shipping, then price may be more important. For example, when the 4-for-3 program was available, if your book was priced at $10.99, reducing the price to $9.99 *could* (but there are never any guarantees with sales) have made a significant difference. If there are currently any Special Offers like the 4-for-3 program, consider whether or not a small price change might significantly impact sales.

In general, unless the list price is quite low or quite high compared to the typical price range of similar titles – and unless the list price is on the verge of affecting eligibility for Special Offers – if you're not satisfied with your sales, it's probably not because of your book's list price. The best thing that you can do to impact sales is not changing the price, but developing effective marketing strategies and actively marketing your book (see Chapter 8).

I'm not trying to advise against giving customers a low price. I'm in favor good deals and savings, and most of my titles reflect this in the price. Rather, I'm trying to make two main points about low prices: (1) A lower price might not bring in more royalties, and (2) if you're not happy with your sales, lowering the price might not solve your problem. A lower price has its own advantages, even in the case where a lower price doesn't bring in as much monthly royalty. For one, the reader who purchases your book and recognizes that it's a great value will be happy to have found a good bargain. If it gets advertised that your book is a great value (that's a big 'if' – just because you feel that the list price is low doesn't mean that most customers will feel that your book is a good value) – as advertised by word-of-mouth or book reviews – this could have a significant impact on sales.

If you elect to sell your book at Amazon's European websites, you will also need to establish a good list price for your book in pounds (£) and euro (€). The same principles apply, but there are a few notable differences. For one, your author's cost in pounds and euro might be different from your author's cost in US dollars after conversions. You can calculate the cost of your book in each currency as described in Sec. 4.1.4, then look online for currency conversions to see if your book effectively costs you more or less in Great Britain and continental Europe. If so, you may want to take this into account when you set your list price. Another difference is that you may have a much greater demand in the US than you will have in Europe. This also may affect your choice of list price.

It would be wise to explore the list prices of similar titles in the UK. To do this, go to Amazon's homepage, scroll down to the bottom, and click on United Kingdom under the Amazon logo. Search Amazon's UK website the same way that you would search their US website – just type your keywords into the search field. You can similarly visit Amazon's websites in France, Spain, Italy, and German, but you'll encounter a significant difference: These websites are not in English. If you speak French, Spanish, Italian, or German, then it will be easier for you explore similar titles on one or more of those websites. If not, maybe you have a friend who speaks one of those languages. You can even find translation services on the web (including some that are free) to help you do searches on the European websites.

There is also a very easy way to set the list price for your book in GBP and EUR pricing: When you publish your book with CreateSpace, simply check the boxes that say to suggest a GBP or EUR price based on the US price. This suggested price is based on the average exchange rates over the past week. Although the exchange rate will fluctuate over the course of time, your list price will not change unless you manually go into your account and update the list price. Also, the suggested list price does not give you the equivalent US royalty.

4.1.6 Deciding on Your ISBN Option

If you self-publish with CreateSpace, you have four different ISBN options. Even if you publish your book elsewhere, you can still choose the fourth option, which we will discuss last.

The first option is free: You can choose to have an ISBN assigned by CreateSpace. If you choose this option, your imprint will be CreateSpace Independent Publishing Platform. On your book's detail page, the imprint will appear where it lists the publisher of your book. Other online booksellers – like Barnes & Noble – may shorten this to CreateSpace, but Amazon presently[44] lists CreateSpace Independent Publishing Platform as the publisher when you choose the free ISBN option with CreateSpace.

There are advantages and disadvantages of the free ISBN option. Obviously, you save money because it's free. A second advantage is that your book will also be eligible to be distributed to libraries and academic institutions if you select the Expanded Distribution option.[45] This is only an advantage if you choose the Expanded Distribution channel and if you expect to sell a significant number of books to libraries and schools through this channel. If you choose a different ISBN option, you may still be able to distribute your book to libraries – just not through the Expanded Distribution channel. See Sec. 4.1.7 regarding this possibility.

One disadvantage is that the free ISBN assigned by CreateSpace can only be used with CreateSpace. If, after self-publishing your book, you decide to republish your book with another publisher, you won't be able to use the same ISBN if you go with the free option.

The main advantage of spending money on the ISBN option is that you can choose your own imprint. This way, an imprint of your own choosing will show up for the publisher's name instead of CreateSpace Independent Publishing Platform. If you don't want it to be obvious that your book was self-published, for example, you could invest a little money (with any of the other three ISBN options) and choose your own imprint. If you plan to publish a series of books, it may have a more professional appearance if you add your own imprint (and design your own logo for your book cover and copyright page). Do some research before choosing an imprint name to be sure that you're not copying an imprint name that might be

---

[44] They used to list the publisher as CreateSpace instead of CreateSpace Independent Publishing Platform.
[45] As we will see in Sec. 4.1.7, the Expanded Distribution option is now free (it used to cost $25).

already used or even trademarked: If your imprint is similar to an imprint already used by a major publishing house, for example, you could get sued over it.

Personally, I'm proud to be a self-published author. I'm grateful for the self-publishing opportunities that Amazon has provided, and I'm pleased with my experience with CreateSpace. I choose the free ISBN option for all of my books. I happily wear the badge that identifies my book as having been self-published through CreateSpace. The more quality books that are easily identified as self-published books, the better will be the image of the self-published author, which will help to promote sales of self-published books. Also, there are hundreds of thousands of self-published authors, and many self-published authors support other self-published authors when they make their purchases. The self-published tag can work both ways: While it may deter some readers, it might attract others who support the concept. The genre of your work and the audience for your book may be significant factors, too, since self-publishing is viewed in a different light by different people. You have to decide for yourself which is better for your book. Choose carefully: Once you select your ISBN option, you're stuck with it for that title.

A second ISBN option is to invest $10 for a custom ISBN. The $10 ISBN option allows you to choose your own imprint. You won't be eligible for the libraries and academic institutions outlet through the Expanded Distribution channel. Like the free ISBN option, the $10 custom ISBN option can only be used with CreateSpace.

A third ISBN option is to invest $99 for a custom universal ISBN. The only difference between the $10 custom ISBN option and the $99 custom universal ISBN option is that the universal ISBN can be used with any publisher, not just CreateSpace. This option allows you to change your mind and publish the same title with the same ISBN with another publisher.

The fourth option is available no matter how you publish your book: You can purchase your own ISBN directly from Bowker at www.myidentifiers.com. It costs $125 (presently) to purchase an ISBN for a single book, and they entice you into buying ISBN's in bulk by offering multi-ISBN discounts. For example, you could spend $250 for 10 ISBN's instead of $125 for one. If you would like to use an ISBN for the eBook version of your book (optional), you will need a different ISBN for the eBook edition. Similarly, if you revise your book to make a second edition, offer a hardbound edition, or make a large print or any other edition of the same book, you will also need a new ISBN for each edition. If you decide to buy your ISBN's directly from Bowker, you should purchase at least 10 ISBN's unless you're 100% positive that you will only have one edition of your book (not even both paperback and eBook).

If you plan to publish several titles of your own, or if you plan to start your own publishing company, purchasing ISBN's directly from Bowker may be the way to go. Note that if you have a previously published book and now want to republish it and you have the necessary rights to do this and use your old ISBN, then your title, author, and binding type (paperback) must match exactly this information as it is already listed with Bokwer.

Regardless of whether you choose one of CreateSpace's three ISBN options or you buy your ISBN's directly through Bowker, your title will be registered with the Books in Print database, which lists the title and author information for all books that have ISBN's.

If you purchase an ISBN from Bowker, note that you do <u>not</u> need to purchase a barcode if you are publishing with CreateSpace: CreateSpace will automatically place an ISBN bar code on your back cover (as described in Sec. 3.1.5). Also note that you can't change the title, author name, or type of binding after you purchase your ISBN from Bowker and list this information with them.

4.1.7 Online Booksellers, Libraries, European Sales, and Expanded Distribution Options

In this section, we will first discuss how your book can potentially be distributed to online booksellers, libraries, schools, and even physical bookstores with CreateSpace's Expanded Distribution option. We will then describe Great Britain and continental Europe distribution channels through CreateSpace. The remainder of this section applies even if you don't choose to publish with CreateSpace: We will explore possible direct distribution of your books to libraries and physical bookstores – this second time, we will discuss how you might accomplish this without using the Expanded Distribution option.

If you decide to select the Expanded Distribution channel for a book that you publish with CreateSpace, you may do so for free (it used to cost $25). The Expanded Distribution opens up several avenues for selling your book other than direct sales at Amazon, including many other booksellers, libraries, and schools. However, you draw a greater royalty from Amazon sales and a lesser royalty from Expanded Distribution sales:

$$\text{Expanded Distribution royalty} = \text{Amazon royalty} - 20\% \text{ of your list price}$$

For example, if your list price is $8.99 and your Amazon royalty is $3.03, your Expanded Distribution royalty will be $1.23 (that's $3.03 – 0.2 x $8.99). See Sec.'s 4.1.4-5 for more details about the royalty calculation.

Note that there are some eligibility requirements for the expanded distribution:
- ✓ Your book will <u>only</u> be eligible for distribution to libraries and academic institutions through the Expanded Distribution if you use a free ISBN assigned by CreateSpace (see Sec. 4.1.6). If you purchase your own ISBN through Bowker, for example, you <u>won't</u> be able to select this Expanded Distribution channel.
- ✓ Your book will <u>only</u> be eligible for distribution to bookstores and online retailers if you use an industry-standard trim size (see Sec. 2.1.4). If you use a custom trim size, you <u>won't</u> be able to select this Expanded Distribution channel.

Since you make a greater royalty from Amazon sales than from Expanded Distribution sales, you may be wondering if it is actually worth the opportunity to make less royalty through other channels. If your book is only available for sale directly through Amazon, for example, then customers won't be able to buy your book through some channel that pays you less money. However, the Expanded Distribution does have some benefits that may make the investment worthwhile:

➢ Your book will be included in major catalogs – including Ingram and NACSCORP – available to bookstores and online retailers. Most bookstores and online booksellers – including Barnes & Noble – purchase their books from the catalogs of these major distributors. If a potential buyer who has heard of your book walks into Barnes & Noble, for example, he/she won't be able to order your book from them unless they find it in such a catalog listing.

➢ A variety of online booksellers – such as Barnes & Noble – will probably (there is no guarantee) create a listing for your book on their website. If you search for my name at Barnes & Noble's and Books-A-Million's websites, for example, you will find my books there – available directly from these booksellers, and listed as 'in stock.' I know that some of my books sell this way because many of my books have a sales rank at Barnes & Noble's website.

➢ Third-party sellers will probably list new and/or 'like new' copies of your book for sale at Amazon (in addition to any customers who may choose to resell or trade-in their used copies). They 'purchase' their books wholesale through the Expanded Distribution channel, and offer them for sale on Amazon. Actually, they probably will not buy your book in advance: Since your book is a print-on-demand title, they may only purchase your title if it sells – at which point it will be printed (not necessarily at CreateSpace – it could be a third-party printing service) and shipped. These third-party sellers lend credibility to your book: It looks like a popular, professional book when there are several retailers offering it for sale at Amazon. These third-party sellers probably help sales overall rather than cut into your royalties, as we will discuss soon.

➢ The more ways that your book is available for sale, the greater the chances of customers discovering your book. Greater visibility helps sales across all channels. Every customer who buys and reads your book has the potential to share your book with family and friends – or even post a note about your book on FaceBook or Twitter.

➢ Certified wholesalers can purchase your book directly from CreateSpace's wholesale website, called CreateSpace Direct: They can sign up to view their catalog at https://www.createspace.com/pub/l/createspacedirect.do?rewrite=true (or visit CreateSpace's home page, click Contact Us at the bottom of the page, and click CreateSpace Direct under Are You a Reseller?). If you choose the Expanded Distribution, you should visit local bookstores (and other retailers who sell books) and let them know that your book can be purchased wholesale through this link.

> ➤ If your book has a CreateSpace-assigned ISBN (see Sec. 4.1.6), your book will be listed with Baker & Taylor. In this way, your book will be available to libraries and academic institutions.

There is supposed to be a $25 book update fee with the Expanded Distribution channel, although this has never been charged. If you need to revise the files for your book interior or cover after your book is published, this is free for distribution on Amazon US, Amazon Europe, and your CreateSpace eStore, but is supposed to cost $25 if you have opted for the Expanded Distribution. It may also take 6 weeks for your changes to reach all of the Expanded Distribution outlets. If you feel that you may want to make revisions to your files after you publish your book, you should keep this in mind when you decide whether or not to select the Expanded Distribution outlet. Of course, if you proof your book carefully and don't have content that is likely to need updating, then you may not need to revise your book at all.

Let's return to a comment that I made about third-party sellers offering your book for sale on Amazon. First, Amazon is probably not the only place where third-party sellers may offer your book for sale – they may sell it from their own website, many other online booksellers (like Barnes & Noble or AbeBooks), European and other websites, or even their own physical bookstore (or other store that also sells books). If they purchase your book through the Expanded Distribution, you will earn royalties regardless of where or how they sell your book. So while you might draw less royalty when an Amazon customer buys your book from a third-party seller on Amazon than if the customer bought your book directly from Amazon, that same third-party seller (and several other booksellers that don't list titles on Amazon) may sell copies of your book a variety of other ways, too. Even if you don't select the Expanded Distribution option, there may still be third-party sellers offering your book for sale on Amazon – once a customer has finished reading your book, it may very well get resold on Amazon (by the customer, or buy a bookseller that received your customer's book by purchasing it a discount or through trade-in); in this case, you don't earn any royalty for the third-party sale. So no matter what, your book will probably be available for sale by other sellers.

Nevertheless, many customers will prefer to buy your book directly from Amazon instead of from third-party sellers. There are many incentives for customers to buy your book directly from Amazon, even if third-party sellers are selling new or like new copies of your book at a discounted price:

☺ Most customers trust Amazon more than the third-party sellers. Amazon does offer an A-to-Z guarantee, and allows sellers to choose Fulfillment by Amazon – both of which make buying used and new books from third-party sellers seem safer. Even so, most customers still prefer to buy their books directly from Amazon unless the savings is significant.

☺ Customers only earn FREE Super Save Shipping when they purchase new books or books where the seller chooses Fulfillment by Amazon. Many customers spend $35 or more when they purchase books (or have Amazon Prime membership) in order to qualify for free shipping. If a customer buys a third-party book that is not fulfilled by Amazon, the shipping charge is $3.99. A cheaper third-party book doesn't look as attractive when you add a $3.99 shipping charge to the total.

☺ Third-party books often do not qualify for Special Offers. If there are any Special Offers available (such as credits for MP3 downloads or the 4-for-3 program), this may be a great incentive to buy directly from Amazon.

I have added Expanded Distribution to virtually all of my books, and in every case I am quite pleased with my decision. This maximizes the visibility of my books, and even makes my Amazon listings appear more serious through the presence of the third-party sellers. Expanded Distribution is the reason that my books are available on Barnes & Noble's website, and some of my books are purchased there – you can tell from the sales rank.

The direct effect of the Expanded Distribution may not be as much as you might hope. For example, for my top two selling titles in 2012, Expanded Distribution accounts for about 5-10% of the quantity of books sold and about 2-5% of the royalties. For one of my top five selling titles, Expanded Distribution accounts for 25% of the number of books sold and 12% of the royalties. Every title is different. I have some titles that rarely sell through the Expanded Distribution, and I also have one title where 35% of the number and 20% of the royalty comes through the Expanded Distribution. Titles that sell regularly on Amazon (i.e. at least once every few days) also tend to sell occasionally (though not as frequently) through the Expanded Distribution channel. If your book sells at least once every few days (hopefully better) on Amazon, it would probably draw some sales through the Expanded Distribution, too. Since Expanded Distribution is relatively new, it is still growing and will likely improve.

As authors, we give up a substantial royalty (see Sec. 4.1.4) in order to sell our books through the Expanded Distribution channel (if we select this option) compared to direct sales on Amazon. We do this for the opportunity to sell some of our books through bookstores, libraries, schools, etc. We could sell a large number of books this way – hundreds, or even thousands – or we could sell 5% to 10% of our books this way. Like any investment, the best we can do is make an informed decision, but the outcome is not guaranteed. If you want bookstores and libraries to purchase your title – through the Expanded Distribution or via a more direct approach – you can improve the chances for this by targeting them in your marketing campaign. We will discuss how you might approach libraries and bookstores later in this section (while marketing strategies are described in Chapter 8).

Like CreateSpace, Kindle, Nook, and the notion of print-on-demand publishing, the Expanded Distribution channel is still growing. There are more self-published authors every day, there are more eBooks available on Kindle, Nook, and other eReaders every day, the way that booksellers and libraries purchase their books is still evolving, there are more small publishers each year, and even traditional publishers are adapting to modern technology. So keep in mind that sales through the Expanded Distribution may improve.

Let me make one more point about the Expanded Distribution channel: Whereas Amazon royalties are reported when CreateSpace manufactures your book, it may take a couple of months for a book sold through the Expanded Distribution to be included on your royalty report. So if you add the Expanded Distribution to your title, don't expect to see sales through this channel for a few months. Even then, the sales you are seeing through this channel have a lag of one to two months. If a bookseller does purchase several of your books, you may not even learn about it for a month or two. Thus, if you select the Expanded Distribution channel, you should prepare yourself to be patient as you monitor the progress of your Expanded Distribution sales.

Another way to improve the visibility of your book is to sell your book in Europe. You can do this by choosing the Amazon UK and Europe distribution channels. I highly recommend it, since this channel is <u>free</u>. When you select Amazon UK and Europe, your book will become available on Amazon's websites for the United Kingdom (amazon.uk), Spain (amazon.es), France (amazon.fr), Germany (amazon.de), and Italy (amazon.it). Not only that, but when your book is sold through these European websites, CreateSpace will print your book in the UK or continental Europe. This allows European customers to purchase your book with free or discounted shipping, for example. This gives you an advantage over any books that are not in stock in Europe – customers won't have to pay international shipping and handling charges in order to purchase your book.[46]

There are very good prospects for selling your book in the United Kingdom (at amazon.uk), as English is the national language in England, Ireland, and Scotland – and since there are many common interests among the United States and the United Kingdom. For example, in the first few months since the Amazon Europe channel has been launched through CreateSpace, Amazon UK accounts for 5% to 10% of my paperback sales for my top selling titles. I have a couple of titles where 20% of the sales come from Amazon UK, but also titles that sell much more rarely in the UK than in the US. The main factor is how relevant your book is in Europe. Also, if you can find ways to market your book to a European audience, that will help boost sales through Amazon Europe (Chapter 8 discusses marketing).

Another consideration is language. British English is similar to American English, but there is a different vocabulary and the grammar is not quite the same. For example, whereas we refer to the 'trunk' of a car, this is called a 'boot' in the UK. Spelling is a little different, too: For example, many words that end in -or in American English instead end in -our in British English, as in 'colour.'

---

[46] European customers will pay a value added tax (VAT), which varies from country to country. The VAT is 0% for books purchased in Great Britain, for example, and 7% in France and Germany. The VAT for Denmark is 25%. You can find a VAT chart at http://www.amazon.co.uk/gp/help/customer/display.html?nodeId=502578.

English is not the national language in continental Europe, which will make it tougher to sell books in Spain, France, Germany, and Italy. However, there is an audience for English books in continental Europe. For one, there are many Americans living in or visiting continental Europe. For another, many Europeans learn English as a foreign language (just as Spanish and French are foreign languages taught in the US). All of my books are written in English, but I do sell a few books to customers in continental Europe.

Amazon also has websites in Canada (amazon.ca), China (amazon.cn), and Japan (amazon.co.jp). However, unlike Amazon Europe, there isn't (yet) a CreateSpace distribution option for Canada, China, or Japan. If your book is available on Amazon US, it may also be available on Amazon Canada, China, and Japan. However, customers will have to pay for international shipping, which can be quite expensive. CreateSpace does not yet have a print-on-demand service for manufacturing books in these countries in order to offer local shipping to these customers. Maybe CreateSpace will launch an Amazon Canada option someday – it seems likely that we would have a significant audience for United States books in Canada.

Amazon Europe was launched only a few months prior to the publication of this book. It is still growing, and has much potential for significant sales – especially, in the United Kingdom. It also takes time for your book to develop associations with other titles in the UK.

You can also make your book available at your own CreateSpace eStore. There is <u>no cost</u> to select this option. Books sold through your CreateSpace eStore pay a higher royalty than books sold directly through Amazon.[47] However, nobody will ever discover[48] your CreateSpace eStore unless you provide the web address through marketing. You can even create discount codes for customers to use at your CreateSpace eStore. We will discuss the CreateSpace eStore in much more detail in Chapter 6.

We will now return our attention to libraries and bookstores – in particular, what more you can do besides simply purchase the Expanded Distribution option in CreateSpace and hope for libraries and bookstores to find your title in a very extensive catalog.

Libraries search for books through the Library of Congress Database. The Library of Congress homepage can be found at http://www.loc.gov/index.html. All books listed in the Library of Congress database have a Library of Congress Control Number (LCCN). Thus, you must have an LCCN if you want your book to be included in this database. If you publish with CreateSpace, they can apply for an LCCN on your behalf for $49. The application fee does <u>not</u> guarantee that your book will be included in the database. Also, the Library of Congress doesn't send out notices of rejection or acceptance. After applying for an LCCN, if you want to see if your book has been added to the database, you need to check the catalog

---

[47] However, there are advantages to having customers purchase your book directly through Amazon instead of your CreateSpace eStore, as we will see in Chapter 6.

[48] That is, you won't be able to find it by visiting CreateSpace's homepage and browsing for it. A link to the webpage is provided to the author. Customers will only find this page if the author provides this link through marketing (see Chapter 8). (You could use the search field at CreateSpace, changing Site to Store; not obvious.)

(http://catalog.loc.gov/). Not all books may be eligible: For one, think about whether your title would be a good fit for a library (a workbook or puzzle book where the reader would ideally write in the book is not good for a library, for example). Remember, you can contact CreateSpace by email or by phone (by clicking Contact Support from your Member Dashboard) if you have questions that you would like to ask a CreateSpace representative – such as inquiring for more details about the LCCN Assignment.

It's important to note that you can't add an LCCN after a book has been published. After you click Approve Proof, your book is published and it's too late to add an LCCN. If you're republishing material that was previously published, it's also too late to add an LCCN.

Traditionally published books that have an LCCN list this number along with the bibliographic information on the copyright page (in addition to the title, author, publisher, copyright notice, publication date, ISBN,[49] etc.). If you obtain an LCCN, your book will probably look more professional if you also do this; you can find a variety of traditionally published books to help you get ideas for how to add this to your copyright page.

The LCCN comes in two different forms – Cataloging in Publication (CIP) and Preassigned Control Number (PCN). Basically, all print-on-demand (POD) books – that includes any book published with CreateSpace – that are made available for libraries to purchase are assigned a PCN, whereas traditionally published books that are likely to be acquired by libraries are assigned a CIP. Unfortunately, this puts your print-on-demand paperback at a disadvantage when it comes to library purchases: The PCN (instead of a CIP) is a clear signal to the librarian that your book is printed on demand, and not traditionally published. Nonetheless, books with a CIP or PCN are included in the Library of Congress database and may be purchased by libraries. You can find more information about the CIP, PCN, and LCCN at http://booksandtales.com/pod/aloc.php or by using a search engine.

Whether you have a CIP or PCN, your book is just one fish in a vast ocean. So the fact that your POD book will have a PCN is not the real obstacle: Rather, if your goal is to get your book into libraries, you need to help librarians learn about your book. Librarians are familiar with specific titles and types of books that readers ask for when they speak with the librarians. When a book becomes popular through marketing (described in Chapter 8), sometimes several people go to the library to search for it. If you are highly effective at marketing, this is a possibility. Alternatively, you can visit libraries and show the librarian your book. Your local library may have an interest in having your book – especially, as many local people may know you and want to read your book. So the libraries in your city are the best places to start. Generally, librarians are friendly and very interested in getting people to read and helping them find what they want to read.

---

[49] Don't confuse the ISBN with the LCCN. The ISBN is a book identifier that every book has; the LCCN is a different number used for library catalogs.

Libraries are more apt to purchase books that are likely to be read and of interest to local readers. It may help if you can make the case that your book fits this criteria. Useful data may help – such as a good sales rank, favorable reviews, or official book reviews.

Authors who draw a significant royalty from sales to libraries often get a corporation to purchase a large quantity of their books and donate them to libraries across the country. Every business has a portion of their budget allocated toward donations because there is a tax incentive for doing this. Many businesses already have their annual donations lined up, but some are flexible. You can search for business who may be willing to make donations online, but anyone else who found their information online will also be approaching them – and for many other causes besides donating books to libraries. You may have a better chance with local businesses. When you contact the business, ask for the opportunity to make a presentation. You want to outline the benefits of donating your books to libraries, keeping in mind the many other charitable causes that the business could otherwise support. If your book spreads awareness of a disease or if the intended audience largely includes very low income families, for example, this will help make your cause stronger. Think about whether or not there may be great value to the community in making it possible for thousands of people to read your book for free at libraries. Will your book improve literacy, help train people for a job, or spread cultural awareness, for example? Businesses understand selling points and value, so this is what they will be looking for. Also, remember that you can offer your book for a substantially discounted price: For one, you can purchase your book at the author's cost directly from CreateSpace and pass a portion of this savings onto the potential business investor (if so, highlight the savings that you are passing on in your presentation); or you can offer a discount code so that the business can purchase your book directly from your CreateSpace eStore (that might seem more professional than paying you directly).

If you are successful in getting any libraries to buy a copy of your book – especially, your local library – encourage people to visit the library to read or check out your book. If your book just collects dust on a shelf and you write a second book, the library probably will not be interested in purchasing another dust collector; but if your book is frequently read, asked for, and checked out, the library is more likely to be interested in subsequent books that you write.

Finally, let's consider how you might get copies of your book in physical bookstores. If the only thing you do is opt for Expanded Distribution, your book will just be one of millions of books listed in a very extensive database. Bookstores will be happy to order your book for any customer who specifically asks for it, but isn't likely to spot your book in the database and order it to stock on their shelves. It's up to you to spread awareness of your book, market your book, and approach bookstores.

First approach small local bookstores and other small businesses that sell books (antique stores, for example). They like to support local talent, like to stock books that major bookstores (i.e. their competition) don't have on their shelves, and they know that local authors have relatives, friends, and acquaintances who live nearby and may very well come inside to purchase their books.

Next approach major bookstores in your city. You *might* have a positive experience with your effort, so it's worth trying – you won't know until you try. They might be happy to support a local author – again, they realize that a local author is likely to have a local following, and hence many potential customers. They might even offer you a chance to sit down for a couple of hours and sign copies of your book that customers purchase (if so, you really need to spread the word and get relatives, friends, and acquaintances to show up for your appearance). On the other side, the worst they can do is say, "No thank you," and it won't be the end of the world. They are more likely to direct you to a bureaucratic process for how to get our book considered for possible purchase than to tell you 'No.' If so, they might give you some useful advice – and it doesn't hurt to ask questions or ask for advice.

If you feel strongly that your book would be a great fit for a major bookstore chain to stock, you should browse their website. For example, you can find Barnes & Noble at www.barnesandnoble.com. Once there, find a link to Publisher & Author Guidelines at the bottom of the page. You'll see that Barnes & Noble orders books from publishing companies. If you use your own imprint (see Sec. 4.1.6), you are essentially your own publishing company, but you may also need to do more to be your own publishing business – like having a corresponding tax ID number (you can learn about starting a business and getting such a number in your state by searching online). In addition, the publishing company has to submit a catalog of books; you can see that a catalog with few entries or that features mainly or a few authors won't seem as serious as the extensive catalogs that traditional publishers will submit. There are also other requirements, like having the title and author printed on the spine and a cover price listed on the book that is the same as the published list price (and the published list price has to be the same for Barnes & Noble, Amazon, and everyone else). Also, as with libraries, the bookstore database may make a distinction between traditionally published books and print-on-demand books.

Barnes & Noble is likely to include your paperback book on their website if you simply opt for the Expanded Distribution with CreateSpace, is likely to order your paperback book for any customer who walks into their store and asks for it (provided that they can find it in their catalog, which means that you need to select the Expanded Distribution), and allows authors to self-publish eBooks for Nook. However, getting your paperback book stocked in their bookstores will not be an easy prospect. There is no harm in trying, though. You might get some helpful advice by talking to employees or management at your nearest store. Remember, businesses do want to stock products that will sell well. If you're able to meet with a person with the authority to make or influence purchase decisions and, after showing that person your book, the person predicts that your book will be a hot seller – chances are, they will want to stock your book and find a way to get it done. If you're getting the runaround or not getting interest – and your book idea has been considered – it may be because they don't predict much success from stocking your book. If you get the opportunity to pitch your book, you need to demonstrate your own belief in your book; and it will help to have any supporting data and information – like your marketing plan, sales rank, and book reviews.

Barnes & Noble is not the only major bookstore. Not all bookstores have the same policies. Search for other bookstores and research their policies (start by visiting their websites). If you are determined to get your book onto some bookshelves, your motivation and perseverance are likely to make the difference.

If a bookstore does show interest in ordering your book, be prepared to help them find your title. You can tell them that your book is listed with Ingram and NACSCORP if you selected the Expanded Distribution or if you purchased your ISBN directly from Bowker. You can also tell them that bookstores can purchase your book directly from CreateSpace Direct. There are two ways for bookstores to sign up with CreateSpace Direct and view their catalog: One is to visit https://www.createspace.com/pub/l/createspacedirect.do?rewrite=true directly; the other is to visit CreateSpace's home page, click Contact Us at the bottom of the page, and click CreateSpace Direct under Are You a Reseller?

If you are successful in getting any bookstores to stock your book, encourage customers to shop in those bookstores. If you write subsequent books, whether or not bookstores are willing to purchase your latest book to stock on their shelves will very much depend on how well or poorly your first book sold in their store.

4.1.8 How to Convert Your Interior and Cover Files to PDF

You will probably need to convert your interior and cover files to PDF format in order to publish your book. Why 'probably'? CreateSpace now allows you to submit a Word document (with .doc or .docx extension) or rich text file (with .rtf extension) instead of a PDF for the interior file, if you prefer (if you use the Guided Setup option – see Sec. 4.1.9). Also, if you use CreateSpace's free Cover Creator tool (Sec. 4.1.9), you won't need to submit a PDF file for your cover. So it's actually possible to avoid having to convert your files to PDF.

However, formatting may change significantly if you upload a Word document. Also, I recommend designing and making your own cover, as described in Chapter 3, instead of using the Cover Creator tool. This gives you the greatest flexibility in your cover design. If you make your own cover, you will need to convert the file to PDF format before you submit it.

The simplest way to convert a Word document to PDF format is to open the file in Microsoft Word, go to the File tab, choose Save As, change Save As Type to PDF, and select Standard (instead of Minimum). If the PDF for your cover doesn't look the same as your Word file, try selecting pictures and grouping them together (to learn how to select and group objects, in Sec. 3.1.8 find the third group of numbered steps and then find Step 7).

For most purposes, Word's built-in[50] PDF converter is satisfactory for converting Word documents to PDF format. However, if you have images, Word will reduce the DPI with the Save As feature, so a free converter is better. If you have a very richly formatted file that you had to split up into separate Word documents, you can combine all of the files together into a single PDF file using a more sophisticated PDF converter. If you have an advanced need for a PDF converter with more options – like being able to flatten figures (you may receive a note about this, which CreateSpace will do for you, when you submit your PDF files) – there are a variety of PDF converters to choose from. You can find many free PDF converters online. Adobe has a wide range of PDF software programs, many of which are quite expensive; there are several less expensive alternatives, such as Nuance PDF Converter Professional.

If your PDF converter has the option to embed the fonts, select this option. (In Word, when you Save As, click Tools, then Save Options, and check the box to Embed Fonts In The File.) Also, if not using Word's built-in PDF converter, check to see if there is an option to flatten the figures – that way, they won't be manually flattened by the publisher.

I recommend that you perform your own PDF conversion (with Microsoft Word's Save As feature, at least) rather than submitting a Word document and having CreateSpace convert the file to PDF for you (an option that's available with CreateSpace's Guided Setup). CreateSpace's PDF conversion may make changes to the layout of your document. For example, if you have floating pictures (i.e. not in line with the text), the pictures may move if you submit a Word document and have CreateSpace's software convert it to PDF for you.

4.1.9 How to Publish Your Paperback Book with CreateSpace

If you're still undecided about whether or not to use CreateSpace as your publishing service, consider contacting a representative. I contacted CreateSpace both by email and by telephone before I published my first book with them. They answered my questions, were courteous and professional, and did <u>not</u> pressure me to get started. If you simply sign up for a free account (signing up for a free account does not commit you to anything), after you login, from your Member Dashboard you can click Contact Support (in a gray bar at the left side of the screen, with a small triangle to the right of Support). If you choose the telephone method and it's during the specified hours, your phone will ring soon; if you prefer to email your questions, you may need to wait a business day or more for a response (you may also receive an automatic email promptly, telling you that your support request has been received).

Following are step-by-step directions for how to publish your paperback book with CreateSpace once you have completed your interior and cover book files (for help with that, see the previous chapters):

---

[50] You may be directed to Microsoft Office's website for a free download of the PDF converter. It's quick and easy – just follow the on-screen instructions. **For optimal pictures, use a different PDF converter instead.**

1. If you haven't already done so, sign up for an account with CreateSpace. It's free, with no strings attached. Visit their homepage (www.createspace.com) and click Sign Up.

2. When you login, the screen that you see is called your Member Dashboard. Click the Add New Title button in your Member Dashboard.

3. Open your interior book file (in the native program – like Microsoft Word – not the PDF file). Go to the copyright page. Check your title carefully to make sure that everything is spelled correctly. Highlight the title on your copyright page and copy the title (hold Ctrl and press C if your interior file is in Microsoft Word). Return to your internet browser. Paste (press Ctrl + V) the title into the field for "Tell us the name of your project." (You could just type it into the field, but copy/paste helps you avoid making a typo in the title.)

4. Click paperback. A dot will appear next to it if it recognized your click. A link will appear called Setup Instructions if you want to read more about the process before going on. Click one of the Get Started buttons – Guided breaks it up into steps and is intended for newbies, while Expert presents everything at once and is intended for those who have some experience with the process.

5. Click on any of the 'What's this?' links to learn more about that feature.

6. At any point, you may click the Save button at the bottom of the page to save your progress. When you complete a page, click Save & Continue to go on.

7. You will see the title entered. If you have a lengthy title, you may want to place your cursor inside the title field and press End on your keyboard to see if the entire title is present. If you want to shorten your title, keep in mind that there is also a subtitle option. The title that you enter in the title field must be exactly the same as the title on your book cover file and the title on the first page of your interior book file. So if you revise your title, be sure to change it in the cover and interior files for your book, too. The subtitle does not need to appear on the cover or the title page of your book.[51] (We discussed titles and subtitles in Sec. 4.1.3.)

8. Enter the name of the primary author in the author field. The author must have a last name or a surname, but you're not required to include the first name or middle name. You may add a prefix (e.g. a medical doctor might include the prefix Dr.) or a suffix (like III, as in John Henry III, or like Ph.D. if you have an advanced degree for a nonfiction book that relates to your area of expertise). Think about how you want your name to appear. The author's name(s) entered here must exactly match the name(s) from the cover and title page. Do not write the author's name in CAPS. If the author's name uses consecutive initials, like C.D. McMullen, enter the initials separately in the First Name and Middle Name fields (do not enter them together in the same field).

---

[51] Words in the title will show up in searches on Amazon US, Amazon websites for other countries, and other booksellers' websites (if you select the Expanded Distribution). Words in the subtitle will show up in searches on Amazon US, but may not show up on other websites (they may on some, but not others).

9. Consider whether or not you want to publish your book in your own name or in a pen name. There are many advantages of using your own name. Especially, friends, family, and acquaintances – anyone who recognizes your name – is a potential customer. People enjoy the rare occasion where they can read a book and know personally who the author is. If you use a pen name, you lose your name recognition. If you have expertise in your field or popularity (even having thousands of friends on FaceBook gives you some popularity), name recognition is an even greater advantage. Traditional authors often use a pen name when they write in two or more genres – e.g. using their real name for literary works and a pen name for juvenile fiction. There may be some legal issues involved in use of a pen name; if you would like legal advice, consult an attorney.

10. Did anyone else help with your book, such as a coauthor or illustrator? You can add other authors and contributors by selecting the type of contributor from the drop-down menu beside Add Contributors and then click the Add button. There are many options here, such as "Edited by" or "From an Idea by." Be sure to credit everybody who contributed toward your book; there may be legal ramifications if anyone is left out. You may need to hire an attorney to make legal contracts regarding how royalties are to be distributed, or to inquire about "works for hire."

11. If you have a subtitle, enter it in the Subtitle field. Your subtitle may include up to 255 characters (that includes spaces, too). Your title and subtitle will appear together, separated by a colon (:), in Amazon search results. Think about how this will look when a potential customers sees your book in the search results. A longer subtitle provides more information up front and may add more keywords, but a very long title/subtitle can also deter customers. Try doing some searches on Amazon and see how you feel (and you can poll friends and family) about search results that are short or long. A short title/subtitle is less informative and uses fewer keywords, but sometimes effectively intrigues potential customers.

12. Choose the volume number in the Volume drop-down menu if your book is (or will be) part of a series and you want your volumes to be numbered. If you add this, the volume number will appear in parentheses in the form (Volume 2) at the end of your title and subtitle in Amazon search results.

13. Add the description of your book in the Description field (see Sec. 4.1.2). I recommend copying and pasting your description from a Word file instead of typing it directly into the Description field. For one, you can use Word's spellcheck feature to help catch any typos. Secondly, in Word, if you click the word count box at the bottom left of the screen it will tell you how many characters (with spaces) you have used in the description. There is a limit of 4,000 characters, including spaces. You can find Amazon's policy for the description by clicking the 'What's this?' link and then clicking the link to Amazon's guidelines. Note that limited, simple HTML is permitted.

14. If you selected Guided Setup, click the Save and Continue button to advance onto the next step. In subsequent steps, you will see Next and Back buttons at the top of the page. If you selected Expert Setup, all of the steps instead appear on a single page.

15. Select your ISBN option. In Guided Setup, there are helpful links at the bottom of the ISBN selection page to help you learn more about this and to help you make an informed decision. This was also discussed in Sec. 4.1.6. Once you choose your ISBN option, it can't be changed. Also, ensure that you are happy with your title and author fields before selecting your ISBN option.

16. If CreateSpace provided you with an ISBN, you will now see your ISBN-13 and ISBN-10 on the screen. If you want these to appear on your copyright page, now is the time to copy and paste them into the interior file for your book (before converting the file to PDF). When you go to paste these numbers in Word, click the arrow on the bottom of the Paste button in the Home tab (instead of using Ctrl + V) and choose the Keep Text Only option (otherwise, you may have to wait for a long delay).

17. If you are using Guided Setup, click the Continue button.

18. At some point you may choose to Save your progress and exit the process of publishing your book. If so, when you want to resume your progress, login to your Member Dashboard and open your title.

19. Choose your Interior settings: Click Black & White or Full Color for Interior Type and also select White or Cream for Paper Color.

20. Select the Trim Size for your book. The default size is 6" x 9". To choose a different trim size, click the Choose a Different Size button. The industry-standard trim sizes (which includes the popular trim sizes shown at the top) offer the widest distribution options. If you click the More Sizes button, you can find custom trim sizes. However, custom trim sizes aren't eligible for some distribution channels within the Expanded Distribution option. There is even an option to enter your own trim size (but note that the maximum size is 8.5" x 11.69"). If you click the Compare All Sizes link (in the trim size selection window), you can download a file that lets you compare the various options available.

21. I recommend selecting Upload Your Book File and submitting your interior book file directly. CreateSpace offers Professional Design Services starting at $249. If you invest hundreds of dollars on design services, you are taking a large risk. If your royalty is $3, for example, it takes 83 sales just to recover your investment; if you also sell 10 books a month on average, that means you won't make any profit for 8 months. That's a big risk to take without having already published a book to get a feel for how successful your venture might be. However, it's very important to remove any typographical, spelling, grammatical, and formatting mistakes from your book. If spelling and grammar happen to be your weakness, I do recommend exploring the possibility of seeking help with this (such as CreateSpace's basic copyediting service).

22. The Guided Setup option now allows you to submit a .pdf, .doc, .docx, or .rtf file, but PDF is recommended (others often cause formatting problems). Look it over before submitting the file to CreateSpace.[52] In Microsoft Word 2010, open your Word document, go to the File tab, choose Save As, change Save As Type to PDF, check the box for Standard, explore the Options, and click Save (if you have images, use a free PDF converter instead). Once you are happy with the PDF for your interior book file, click Upload Your Book File at CreateSpace, click the Browse button, find your book on your computer (or jump drive, perhaps), click Open, and then click Save.

23. When you submit your interior book file, I recommend that you click the box entitled, "Run automated print checks and view formatting issues online." In Expert Setup, also check the appropriate box for how you want your pages to bleed (see Sec. 2.1.5).

24. If you have trouble uploading files or viewing instructions, try visiting the community forum (click the Community link at the top right of the screen). You may be able to correct some common issues as follows: Make sure that your internet browser is up-to-date; try a different browser (many are free), like Mozilla Firefox (usually works best) or Internet Explorer; and change the settings to (temporarily) allow popups.

25. On the next page – submitting your book cover – you can find some helpful links at the bottom of the page. If you want to spend $384 or more for professional cover help, you can explore the crowdSPRING options. I recommend keeping your investment as low as possible by designing your own cover for your first self-published book. If your royalty is $3, for example, you have to sell 128 books just to recover your $384; if you also sell 10 books a month on average, you won't make any profit for one year. CreateSpace also offers professional cover design help starting at $149. Again, I recommend at least trying to design your own cover and seeing how it looks when you get your first proof. You will be able to change your mind later if you want.

26. There are two ways to make a free cover. I recommend clicking Upload a Print-Ready PDF Cover and following the instructions in Chapter 3 for how to design and make your own book cover. (For the alternative, see Step 27.) This gives you the greatest flexibility in customizing your own cover exactly the way you want it. Once you have made your own book cover file in Word, open your Word document, go to the File tab, choose Save As, change Save As Type to PDF, check the box for Standard, explore the Options, and click Save. Check your PDF carefully. Once you are happy with the PDF for your cover book file, click Upload Your Book File, click the Browse button, find your book on your computer (or jump drive, perhaps), click Open, and then click Save. Be sure to remove the guides before saving your final PDF if you added the cover guides described in Sec. 3.1.5.

---

[52] They sometimes need to make slight revisions to the PDF file that you submit – e.g. to manually 'flatten' images. If so, they will tell you which changes – if any – have been made, and you will have a chance to preview those changes (as well as the entire book, even if there are no changes made) before you approve your proof.

27. The second way to make a free cover is to use the Cover Creator tool provided by CreateSpace. Click Build Your Cover Online to explore the Cover Creator options. If you check out the Cover Creator, follow CreateSpace's step-by-step instructions for how to use it. It's convenient and automated, but does not provide for as much flexibility and customization as designing it from scratch as described in Chapter 3.

28. In Guided Setup, the next page is called Complete Setup. If you click the Submit Files for Review button, CreateSpace will check that your book interior and cover files follow their publishing guidelines. Note that they will <u>not</u> edit or revise your files; they will <u>not</u> proofread your book; they will <u>not</u> check for most formatting or other mistakes. Your book will print straight from the files that you submit.

29. There are still more options to explore. In Expert Setup, these other options are visible before you submit your files for review.[53] In Guided Setup, you can find these other options by clicking the Return to Project Homepage button and then looking in the Distribute tab. You may select your Distribute options before submitting your files for review (although you may need to submit your book files before all features – like pricing – become available; they read your page count from the interior file, for example, and your page count is needed to determine your royalty).

30. In Channels, you can presently select up to six distribution channels. Three channels are free: Amazon US, Amazon Europe, and your CreateSpace eStore. Simply click the buttons to add or remove channels. The other three channels – Bookstores and Online Retailers, Libraries & Academic Institutions, and CreateSpace Direct – are available with the Expanded Distribution option. If you want to add the Expanded Distribution option (see Sec. 4.1.7), it is now free (it used to cost $25). Use the royalty calculator to see what your Expanded Distribution royalty would be before you commit to this option.[54] Note the links at the bottom of this webpage that tell you more about the distribution channels.

31. On the Pricing page, you set your list price in US dollars, Great Britain pounds, and European euro. You will also be able to see your royalty for Amazon US, Amazon UK, Amazon continental Europe, and Expanded Distribution as you set or change your list price. Take some time to play with the list price and see the possible royalty scenarios. If you have your list price on your cover, you may want to make sure that the list price and cover price match (and if you change your mind about the list price, you might want to revise your cover file). See Sec.'s 4.1.4-5 regarding the list price and royalty.

---

[53] You get a different experience with Expert Setup than Guided Setup. All of the ISBN choices are presented up front in Guided Setup, for example, while the biography and category options are presented up front in the Expert Setup. Also, keep in mind that website features frequently change: What was true when this book was first published is apt to change with time.

[54] See Sec. 4.1.5 to see how royalties are calculated. When you get to the pricing page, CreateSpace will have a royalty calculator that displays your royalty for each sales channel when you enter your list price. You can always return to the sales channel page and disable the Expanded Distribution channel if you change your mind.

32. There are several important features to explore on the Description page in the distribution options: Choose your BISAC category, add keywords for Amazon searches, add an author biography, and enter publication details on this page.

33. Click the Choose button next to BISAC Category to find the most appropriate category (see Sec. 4.1.3) for your book. There are often multiple categories that seem to fit, but you can only select one from the drop-down menu. You might browse through categories on Amazon to help determine which category is best: Find other books that are similar to yours, see which browse categories they are listed in (open their Amazon page and scroll down near the bottom to find this), and also compare sales rank (the lower the number, the more frequent the sales, in general – but see Chapter 7). Note, however, that the BISAC categories are not quite the same as Amazon categories.

34. Click the Add button next to Author Biography if you would like to add an optional biography (see Sec. 4.1.2) to your book's page. You can also join Author Central at Amazon to add an Author Page, which you can link to your book. If so, your Author Page link will show your photo and the beginning of your biography on your book's page. I have both an author biography added from CreateSpace and a link to my Author Page with a different biography on some of my Amazon books' detail pages: The author biography that I added from CreateSpace is shorter, varies from book to book, and relates specifically to each book; my Author Page has a much longer biography. You might not want to double up – if you want to choose just one, pick the Author Page (see Chapter 6).

35. I highly recommend adding five keywords in the Search Keywords field (see Sec. 4.1.3), separated by commas (like "mystery, thriller, suspense, detective novel, police chase"). Remember, don't duplicate combinations of words from your title or subtitle – since those combinations already function as keywords. For example, if your subtitle is A Spy Novel Set in World War II, it would be a waste to use "spy novel" or "war novel" as keywords – since your book will already be searchable with those keywords. For more advice on choosing keywords, review Sec. 4.1.3. Note that there is a 25-character limit (including spaces) on keywords. If you type your keywords in Word, you can check the character count there – and also use the spellcheck feature to help avoid typos.

36. You may also specify the book's country of publication, language, and date of publication. If you enter a publication date (which can't be in the future), note that your book's eligibility to be in the 30-day and 90-day new release categories may be based on this date. So if you enter a date from a month ago – or if you enter today's date, but don't approve your proof for a month – then your book might not show up when potential customers filter their searches by clicking the Last 30 Days link under New Releases when performing searches at Amazon. The New Release feature helps customers find books that were recently published. **Tip**: Leave the publication date blank. This way, the publication date will be the day that you click Approve Proof.

37. If your book is written in large print (or if you make a special large print edition of your book), you may check the Large Print box. Generally, the font size must be 16 points or higher for most font styles in order to qualify as large print. It is generally better to have a separate large print edition (if so, you might add "Large Print Edition" to your title or subtitle) rather than to make your only edition large print, since many people may prefer regular print.

38. Check the appropriate box if your book contains adult content. If your book is not suitable for minors – i.e. anyone who is under the age of 18 – you must check this box. Click the "What's This?" link to explore Amazon's content guidelines.

39. When you are ready to submit your files for review, from your project's homepage (click the Return to Project Homepage button), click the Complete Setup link and look for the Submit Files for Review button at the bottom of the page. If this button is not available, scroll through all of the pages and look for red writing – there may be a message telling you that there is some issue that you must resolve before you can submit your book for publication.

Following are a variety of other useful notes, tips, and tidbits, such as how to add a second browse category at Amazon, what you need to do before you can be paid for royalties, content guidelines, discount codes, and other information:

❖ If you strongly feel that your book should be included in a second browse category at Amazon, first wait a week or more to see which category or categories your book is included in. Check this by scrolling toward the bottom of your book's detail page at Amazon once it becomes available. Your detail page will be updated several times over the course of time – several times during the first month, and occasionally thereafter – so don't be surprised if it initially seems rather incomplete. You have to wait patiently and see how it progresses. If the category that you would like to add doesn't appear on its own, from your CreateSpace Member Dashboard, click the Contact Support button. Mention that you have recently published a book with CreateSpace, provide the title and title id (you can find this number on your Member Dashboard), and politely ask if it would be possible to have your book included with a second browse category at Amazon. Include your suggested browse category with your request – e.g. Books > Business & Investing > Small Business & Entrepreneurship > Entrepreneurship. Browse through the categories from Amazon's homepage to make sure that you have your browse path listed exactly the same way as you see the category listed below Department on the left-hand side of the screen.

❖ You can't add your book to a children's category (such as juvenile, teen, or baby) unless your original category was listed in a children's category. For example, if you want your book listed both in mystery and juvenile mystery, you must select the juvenile BISAC category and then request (if necessary) inclusion with mystery.

❖ Ensure that your title, subtitle, and author name (especially, a pen name) do not infringe upon any copyrights or trademarks. For example, you can't write a *Chicken Soup* book or a book *for Dummies* – so be sure not to include these words (and other phrases that are part of popular series) in the title or subtitle of your book. Once again, I must advise you to bring your copyright, trademark, and any other legal questions to an attorney.

❖ If you select the Amazon UK or continental Europe[55] distribution channels, any books that you sell directly through these Amazon websites will be manufactured in the UK or continental Europe and shipped from there, which greatly reduces shipping time and allows customers to potentially buy your book with free shipping incentives. Keep in mind that there are language differences: Even in the United Kingdom, British English has some important differences from American English; and in other countries, English is not the native language. Of course, there are people in continental Europe who speak English, who will serve as your customer base for sales for Amazon Europe. However, if you are fluent in another language or can find an inexpensive, but good, translation service, you may be able to attract Spanish- or French-speaking customers, for example (not just in Europe, but even in Mexico, South America, or Canada, for example). Foreign language books can be sold from Amazon US as well as from Amazon Europe. Although books sold through Amazon UK and Amazon Europe have the list price and royalty figured in pounds or euro, you may choose to have your royalties deposited in US dollars in a US bank account.

❖ There is a minimum royalty accumulation needed before your royalties can be paid: It is $10 for Amazon US royalties, 10£ for Amazon GBP, and 10€ for Amazon Europe. Your cumulated royalties for a given month are paid close to the end of the following month. However, if your royalty balance is below these minimum values, it will carry over to the next month and you will be paid when your cumulated unpaid royalties finally exceed these minimum values.

❖ You must enter some information in your account before you can receive royalty payments. This includes a social security number for income tax reporting. From your Member Dashboard, click the Edit Account Settings link on the left-hand side of the screen to enter or update your account information.

❖ You can delete your book anytime up until the moment when you click Approve Proof – simply by clicking the trash can icon from your Member Dashboard (afterward, you can retire it, but not delete it). Make sure that you are happy with your book – and have reviewed your proof carefully – before clicking Approve Proof. We will discuss what to look for when proofing your book and how to make revisions in Chapter 5.

---

[55] Yes, the United Kingdom (UK) is part of Europe: The distinction here is whether your book will be manufactured in and shipped within the UK or whether it will be manufactured in and shipped to continental Europe. Amazon has multiple European websites, including the UK, France, Germany, Spain, and Italy.

❖ We will discuss how to order a proof, how to edit your proof, what to look for when you review your proof, how to revise your proof, and how to solve common problems in Chapter 5.

❖ Your title and author information will be locked once you select your ISBN option. If you want to change your title, author, or your ISBN option, you must delete your book and start over. Once you click Approve Proof, you can't delete your book.

❖ Once you publish your book, customers can buy it. It may take a day or a few days before your book appears on Amazon. It will take weeks before some features are activated, such as the Search Inside feature. It will take time for your book to become more visible in searches on Amazon. It will take many sales before your book is linked with other books – e.g. for Amazon to list your book on other books' detail pages where it says, "Customers Who Bought This Item Also Bought." Sales may start out slow; if so, they may gradually build up. The best thing you can do to improve sales is develop an effective marketing plan. We will discuss marketing ideas in Chapter 8. Most books do <u>not</u> sell well all on their own. A new book is buried down in search results. Sales help to build sales, and to spread awareness of your book. Most books that succeed do so because of a good marketing strategy: Marketing helps to make customers aware of your book and to drive sales. There are millions of books for sale. Authors who succeed in getting their books to be in the top 200,000 (or better) out of millions of books almost always achieve this through some form of marketing. As we will see in Chapter 8, there are a variety of free or cheap marketing strategies that authors can use to help improve their sales.

❖ If you opt for the Expanded Distribution, some books sold through the Expanded Distribution channel may be printed with some other print-on-demand service (i.e. other than CreateSpace). Therefore, there may be slight printing variations for books sold through the Expanded Distribution channel. A third-party may use different paper, so the paper thickness may vary slightly; similarly, the colors may vary slightly.

❖ I once inquired about hardcover and was told – at the time, anyway – that there actually was a hardcover option. However, there was an upfront fee (a couple hundred dollars), and hardcover editions were <u>not</u> available for print-on-demand sale from Amazon. Hardcover books are also more expensive. After paying the upfront fee, you buy as many copies as you would like and they ship them directly to you. So hardcover may be available, but it's expensive and it's like traditional self-publishing, not like the modern print-on-demand publishing of paperbacks. If you really want hardcover books, this is one way to do it. Once you have the hardcover books, you can sell them on Amazon as a Marketplace seller (or through Amazon Advantage). It may even be possible, acting as your own publisher, to distribute copies to Amazon (or other bookstores) to stock and sell – if you have business or sales skills. However, paperback is cheaper and available in print-on-demand from Amazon.

❖ You can find your CreateSpace eStore options by clicking on the title from your Member Dashboard to get to your Project Homepage, and then selecting Channels under Distribute. Below CreateSpace eStore, you can find one link called eStore Setup and another link called Discount Codes. Click on the eStore Setup link to find the url for your eStore – it will have the form https://www.createspace.com/3762151, where the final number is your title id. Explore the options on this page to customize your eStore. Customers will only find your eStore if you include the url for your eStore through marketing. You earn higher royalties when customers purchase your book through your eStore, although there are some other advantages to selling on Amazon instead – e.g. every sale on Amazon improves your sales rank. If you click the Discount Codes link,[56] you can make a discount code and offer the discount to potential customers who purchase your book from your eStore. A discount code can be a handy incentive for customers to buy your book. If you have your own website and don't want to sell and ship books directly, you can instead provide a link to your CreateSpace eStore. (Alternatively, you can link to your Amazon detail page – and earn a commission from any sales through Amazon Associates. See Chapter 6.)

❖ Once you approve your proof and your book begins to sell at Amazon (assuming that you selected Amazon as one of your distribution channels), you can track the progress of sales by viewing reports. (We will discuss how to order your proof, what to look for when you order your proof, and common issues in Chapter 5.) When you login to your CreateSpace account, your Member Dashboard will show how many units of each title you have sold for the month.[57] You can find more sales and royalty data by clicking the View Reports link at the left-hand side of your Member Dashboard. Royalty Details will show you all of your sales in the order in which they were sold (unless you click the heading at the top of one of the columns). Royalty by Title shows you how many of each book you sold and also the royalty that you made in the US, GB, and Europe for each book. In any of the tabs, click Run New Report to modify the reports – e.g. you can show a report for the entire year by changing the dates.

❖ You can have daily, weekly, or monthly sales/royalty reports emailed to you by clicking View Reports from your Member Dashboard and then selecting E-Mail Report Settings near the bottom of the page. Check the boxes you want and then click the Save Settings button.

---

[56] Unfortunately, the discount code only works in your CreateSpace eStore. You can't make discount codes for Amazon. You can change the list price of your book, but dropping the list price will not appear as a discount. Amazon discounts some books from the list price, but does not discount others, solely at their own discretion; books with a higher list price (like $15.99) might be more apt to have their prices discounted by booksellers.

[57] If you have more than 10 titles, then only 10 titles will show on your Member Dashboard – use the Sort By dropdown menu to order them based on number of sales or some other criteria. You can find and edit all of your books by clicking the View All Titles link at the bottom; but if you want to see sales data for all of your titles, instead click the View Reports link at the left.

❖ When you sell a book on Amazon, the royalty is reported when CreateSpace manufactures the book – which could be a matter of hours. Your cumulated royalties for a given month are paid at the end of the following month.

❖ When a book sells through the Expanded Distribution, it can be several weeks before the royalty is reported. Most Expanded Distribution royalties are currently reported at the end of the month – and these royalties may be for books that sold in a previous month. So it might be a few months before you can tell if your books are selling through the Expanded Distribution. Remember, sales may be a growing process – it takes time for all of the features to work on Amazon, for your book to get noticed, etc. If sales are slow starting out, there is the potential for growth. The best way to help grow sales is through marketing (see Chapter 8).

❖ If you have multiple editions of the same book, they will probably be linked together – and just one of the editions may show up in Amazon search results. For example, if you make a large print edition of your book, potential buyers can find your large print edition by opening the detail page for your primary edition and clicking the plus (+) sign under Formats. For example, if you search for my chemistry book, *Understand Basic Chemistry Concepts*, after you open the Kindle edition detail page for this book, under Formats (in a rectangle near the top of the page) you will see that it is available in Kindle and Paperback. Find the little + next to paperback. If you click on the +, you will learn that there are two paperback editions available. I can't imagine how anyone who wants the large print edition is going to think of looking for this tiny + sign (hopefully, you see the irony here), but that's the way Amazon links regular print and large print editions together. If you search for "basic chemistry concepts" on Amazon, only the paperback and Kindle editions will be visible in the search. However, if you search for "chemistry large print" on Amazon then the large print edition will show up.

❖ If you have both paperback and Kindle editions of the same book, the Kindle edition will show up in Kindle searches and the paperback edition will show up in book searches even if the two editions are linked together – both books are much more visible than my large print example in the previous bullet. If someone opens your paperback edition, it will be very clear that you also have a Kindle edition, and vice-versa (unless, of course, they open your eBook from an eReader). You should also be aware that if your paperback and Kindle editions get linked together, reviews from both editions are collected together. So, for example, if someone leaves a negative review to complain about the formatting of your eBook, this review will be included with the reviews for your paperback book. You might not like it, but that's the way it is. Therefore, if you have an eBook edition of your paperback book, it's very important to have good formatting – since a negative review will affect the sale of both editions of your book. On the other hand, if a customer leaves a positive review for either edition, that will help the sale of both books. At least, it works both ways.

❖ If you would like professional help with design, editing, or marketing, for example, you can search for services locally or online (or ask friends, family, acquaintances, or fellow authors) for advice. You can also explore CreateSpace's full range of services by going to their homepage, clicking Books, selecting Publish a Trade Paperback, and then clicking the Everyday Low Prices link near the top right of the page. My advice is to publish your first book with less than $50 expense, total, so that you don't need to sell too many books just to recover your investment (unless your book is highly marketable as described in Sec. 5.1). Once you've achieved some success with one book, you will know how much you can afford to invest in a subsequent book; and if your first book isn't as successful as you'd like, you might be glad that you didn't invest too much money in it (in addition to your valuable time and effort).

If you need help, have questions, or come across specific problems, read the paragraph at the end of Sec. 4.1.1, which describes how you can ask questions to CreateSpace representatives and how you can get help from fellow authors.

Be sure to follow the content guidelines:

https://www.createspace.com/Help/Rights/ContentGuidelines.jsp

These guidelines will also tell you what is not allowed in the product title, description, biography, images, and reviews at Amazon US and other Amazon websites. You can find a comprehensive list at the above link. The list below is not comprehensive, but may include a few things that you might want to be aware of:

⊗ Obviously, pornographic, obscene, or offensive material is <u>not</u> allowed.

⊗ <u>Don't</u> give out any personal information in your book description, the title of your book, a review, or your biography. This includes phone numbers, addresses, email addresses, and webpages. You can include contact information inside your book if you want readers to potentially contact you. If you have an author page (see Chapter 6), you can include the webpage url for it in your copyright page and/or an About the Author section at the end of your book, for example.

⊗ <u>Don't</u> mention the price in the description.

⊗ <u>Don't</u> spoil the plot in your description.

⊗ <u>Don't</u> include reviews, quotes, or testimonials in your description or biography.

⊗ <u>Don't</u> ask customers to review your book in your description or biography.

⊗ Advertisement and promotion is <u>not</u> allowed in your description or biography.

4.2 Publishing Your eBook Online

4.2.1 Where to Publish Your eBook

You can publish your eBook with a variety of eReaders – including Amazon's Kindle, Barnes & Noble's Nook, Sony's eReader,[58] and more – all for <u>free</u>. Some authors publish their eBooks with all of the major eReaders, while some publish their eBooks exclusively with Amazon's Kindle. The reason that some authors choose to publish their eBooks only with Kindle is because Amazon's KDP Select program provides an incentive to authors for doing so. I suggest that you read Sec. 4.2.7, which discusses both the pros and cons of the KDP Select program, before you commit to where you will publish your eBooks. If you decide not to enroll your eBook in the KDP Select program, then I highly recommend publishing your eBook with all of the major eReaders (at a minimum).

There is a third alternative: A commitment to the KDP Select program is not permanent, but comes in 90-day intervals. Some authors initially enroll their eBooks in the KDP Select program, and then opt out after the 90-day period ends. In this way, they enjoy the benefits of the program for a few months, and then publish their eBooks will all of the major eReaders after this period. This 90-days period gives you a chance to test the program out and see if you like the benefits enough to keep your eBook enrolled in it. This also gives you time to revise your eBook's formatting specifically for other eReaders.

Regardless of where you choose to publish your eBook, I highly recommend publishing your eBook directly with each eReader company that you choose. For example, publish a Kindle eBook directly from Amazon's website (as described in Sec. 4.2.8) and publish a Nook eBook directly from Nook Press, which is Barnes & Noble's eBook publishing website (as described in Sec. 4.2.9). Since there are formatting differences between Kindle, Nook, and other eReaders – there are even formatting differences between the different types of Kindles, like eInk and Fire, for example – you will be able to preview exactly how your eBook will look on each eReader by publishing your eBook directly with each company. Amazon's preview tool for Kindle will even show you how your book will look on an iPhone and an iPad when customers with those devices purchase your Kindle eBook from Amazon.

Some authors choose to publish their eBook with a company like Smashwords, which publishes your eBook on most of the major eReaders for you (note that you still have the option to select whichever eReaders you want to publish with). The formatting may be better if you adapt your eBook to best fit the different types of eReaders, since formatting features

---

[58] Kindle and Amazon are trademarks of Amazon.com, Inc. Nook and Barnes & Noble are trademarks of Barnes & Noble, Inc. Sony is a registered trademark of Sony Corporation. These trademarks and brands are the property of their respective owners.

may vary from one eReader to another. This is especially true if you have large pictures or rich formatting, equations, or tables. When you publish directly with the eReader company, you can use the eReader's preview tool to see exactly how your eBook will appear on that company's eReaders. If you don't elect to publish your eBook with Kindle Select, then I do recommend publishing your eBook on Smashwords (as described in Sec. 4.2.10); Smashwords does provide some free benefits, like a free ISBN and the option of publishing with Apple. However, you should also consider publishing directly with Nook and other eReaders, when possible, instead of having Smashwords publish your eBook with them for you. At the very least, I suggest beginning the publishing process with Nook in order to use their preview tool – this way, you can see if the same eBook file will format well on Nook.

I also recommend that you convert your paperback interior file to an eBook file as described in Sec. 2.2. I do not recommend using the eBook files that CreateSpace generates from your submitted PDF for the reasons summarized in Sec. 2.2.2.

If you do publish your eBook with multiple eReaders, you should be aware that some eReader companies, like Barnes & Noble, require the list price to be no higher than the list price anywhere else (and also no higher than the paperback edition of the same book). Other companies may choose to pricematch a competitor's price for your eBook (and, depending on their terms and conditions, they may pay you a royalty based on the matched price instead of the list price that you set with them). This is important to keep in mind if you make your eBook temporarily free with one eReader service – since a competing eReader may, if you published with them, too, also offer your eBook for free during the same period.

Note that eReaders impose different memory limits on your content file size. The content file size limits of the three major eReaders are summarized in the following table; the file for the interior of your eBook file must be below these limits. If you want to find out what the file size is for your eBook, find your file in the Documents or Computer folder on your computer, right-click in the white space where the files are shown in the folder and change View to Details, and then look for the file size in kilobytes (KB) – or right-click on the filename, click Properties, and look for the file size in the General tab. See Sec. 4.2.4 to learn ways that you might decrease the memory size of your file; even if the file size doesn't exceed the maximum limit, decreasing the file size might also increase your royalty (see Sec. 4.2.5).

eReader	Maximum Content File Size
Amazon's Kindle	50 MB (50,000 KB)
Barnes & Noble's Nook	20 MB (20,000 KB)
Sony Reader	5 MB (5,000 KB)[59]

---

[59] This is the file size limit if you use Smashwords to publish your eBook with the Sony Reader (see Sec. 4.2.10).

Amazon's Kindle, Barnes & Noble's Nook, Sony's Reader, and the Kobo[60] eReader are the major eReaders. Customers can also purchase eBooks for tablets (like the Apple iPad, Microsoft Surface, Google Nexus, and Samsung Galaxy Tab), laptops, PC's, and even their cell phones. One way to read an eBook on a laptop or PC is to download Kindle's or Nook's software for the PC – which allows customers to purchase Kindle or Nook eBooks and read the eBook on their laptop or PC. We will discuss how to publish directly with Kindle in Sec. 4.2.8, and directly with Nook in Sec. 4.2.9. You can't publish directly with Sony's Reader, but you can make your eBook available for Sony's Reader using Kobo or Smashwords, as we will describe in Sec. 4.2.10. If you publish an eBook with Smashwords, you can also make it available for other eReaders, as we will see in Sec. 4.2.10.

4.2.2 Perfecting Large Pictures for a Variety of eReaders

Different eReaders – even those offered by a single company – come in a variety of aspect ratios. This makes it <u>impossible</u> to create full-page pictures that completely fill the screen on every eReader (and still preserve the original aspect ratio of your pictures). The best that you can do is target a couple of specific eReaders – like the Kindle Fire and Nook Color – and design full-screen pictures around those devices.

Let me illustrate the underlying problem with an example. Suppose, for example, that you plan to take advantage of KDP Select and publish exclusively with Kindle: In this case, if you are designing a full-color picture book, you might choose to target the Kindle Fire. The problem is that many customers may buy the eBook for their cell phones, other brand tablets, laptops, and PC's. An eBook that is published exclusively with Kindle may still be read on a variety of devices. The Kindle Fire is long and skinny. If you make long, skinny pictures that completely fill the screen of the Kindle Fire, there will be noticeable gaps at the sides of the picture when the same eBook is read on other devices – and these gaps will be more pronounced when the eBook is read on a device that has a screen that is much more square. In the other extreme, if your pictures are nearly square, when a customer reads your eBook on the Kindle Fire, there will be a large gap underneath the picture. Obviously, it will be easiest to make out the details of a picture that completely fills the screen; when the picture's

---

[60] Kindle and Amazon are trademarks of Amazon.com, Inc. Nook and Barnes & Noble are trademarks of Barnes & Noble, Inc. Sony is a registered trademark of Sony Corporation. Kobo is a registered trademark of Kobo, Inc. These trademarks and brands are the property of their respective owners.

aspect ratio doesn't match the device's aspect ratio, there will be a gap below or gaps beside the picture. Apps that automatically adjust the aspect ratio don't solve the problem: This fills the screen on each device, but may greatly distort the picture to accomplish this.

To make matters worse, customers have a choice of holding the device in portrait mode or landscape mode. If you design pictures for the Kindle Fire, for example, which is long and skinny, if the customer holds the Kindle Fire in portrait mode and your picture fills the screen, the picture will be very small with very large gaps when another customer holds the Kindle Fire in landscape mode. Some customers have such a strong tendency to hold the device in a particular orientation that they may not try the other. (You can always include a note suggesting which orientation is best for viewing your book, but a few customers will still do as they please. Remember the age-old adage, "The customer is always right.") A square picture will have a very significant gap regardless of how the customer holds a device with a long, skinny screen, but will look about the same regardless of whether the customer holds the device in portrait or landscape mode.

Since an eReader can be held in portrait or landscape mode (controlled by turning the eReader 90°, so that the device can sense, via gravity, the distinction between 'top' and 'bottom'), it's important to design the orientation of your pictures with your intended mode in mind. The 'bottom' of your picture (as you see it on your screen when you submit your eBook file) will always match the 'bottom' of the eReader. Thus, when the customer switches between portrait and landscape mode, the picture rotates with the device. If you submit a picture that looks sideways to you when you view your eBook on your PC, it will <u>always</u> look sideways to the customer no matter which mode the customer chooses. Therefore, you should avoid submitting any pictures that look sideways when you proofread your eBook.

To make matters worse, every eReader has built-in margins (these are in addition to any margins that you may add using the Paragraph tab in Microsoft Word). The margins apply whether the eReader is showing text or images. You <u>can't</u> make a full-screen picture because of these automatic margins. Furthermore, the aspect ratio of the usable screen space is different from the aspect ratio of the actual screen size. As a result, if you make a picture with the same aspect ratio as the screen size, it won't quite fill the usable screen space. If you want a picture to fill the usable screen space of a specific device, you must figure out the new aspect ratio that is created by the automatic margins.

Amazon eReaders	Screen Aspect Ratio
Kindle Fire HD 8.9"	1200 x 1920 (5:8)
Kindle Fire HD 7"	800 x 1280 (5:8)
Kindle Fire	600 x 1024 (≈3:5)
Kindle Paperwhite	758 x 1024 (≈3:4)
Kindle Keyboard	600 x 800 (3:4)
Kindle DX	824 x 1200 (≈2:3)
Kindle Touch	600 x 800 (3:4)
Kindle 6"	600 x 800 (3:4)

Barnes & Noble eReaders	Screen Aspect Ratio
Nook HD+	1280 x 1920 (2:3)
Nook HD	900 x 1440 (5:8)
Nook Tablet	600 x 1024 (≈3:5)
Nook Color	600 x 1024 (≈3:5)
Nook Simple Touch	600 x 800 (3:4)
Nook Classic	600 x 800 (3:4)

Sony Readers	Screen Aspect Ratio
Sony Reader	600 x 800 (3:4)
Sony Pocket	600 x 800 (3:4)
Sony Touch	600 x 800 (3:4)
Sony Daily	600 x 1024 (≈3:5)
Sony PRS	600 x 800 (3:4)

Other eReader Devices	Screen Aspect Ratio
Kobo Inc.	600 x 800 (3:4)
Kobo Touch	600 x 1024 (≈3:5)
Samsung Papyrus	600 x 800 (3:4)
Microsoft Surface	768 x 1366 (≈4:7)
Apple iPad 3rd Gen.	1536 x 2048 (3:4)
Apple iPad	768 x 1024 (3:4)
Apple iPhone 5	640 x 1136 (≈4:7)
Apple iPhone 4	640 x 960 (2:3)

Most other brands of basic eReaders are presently 600 x 800 (3:4), but trends are changing. The ≈ symbol means that the aspect ratio is approximate (rather than exact).

The aspect ratios of the vast majority of eReaders range from 4:7 (where the width is just 57% of the height) to 3:4 (where the width is 75% of the height) in portrait mode. In landscape mode, the range is from 4:3 (where the width equals 133% of the height) to 7:4 (where the width equals 175% of the height). Keep in mind that a few screens, like the monitor of a PC, can only be viewed in portrait mode. The 3:4 aspect ratio is very common among classic-style eReaders. Although this aspect ratio is the most common aspect ratio on the table shown on the previous page, the latest round of eReaders are the tablet size – like the Kindle Fire HD and Nook HD – which have aspect ratios of 3:5 and 5:8. This is the aspect ratio that customers with the latest technology will have. It's tempting to gear full-color, full-page eBooks toward this tablet size – but then the iPad is 3:4 and many cell phones, like the iPhone 5, are 2:3.

Many authors size their pictures with a 3:4 aspect ratio, using 600 pixels x 800 pixels, which matches the display size of most eReaders. This aspect ratio will look reasonably good on a variety of devices. The 3:4 aspect ratio looks okay on long, skinny devices like the original Kindle Fire. The 3:4 aspect ratio also looks okay even if customers use landscape mode for a picture that was designed with portrait mode in mind, for example. On the other hand, if you make a long, skinny picture specifically with the traditional Kindle Fire, which is 3:5, or the new Microsoft Surface, which is 4:7, in mind, for example, these may not look as good on an eReader that is 3:4 – especially, on a small device like a cell phone. Thus, if you want to accommodate the greatest variety of eReaders, 3:4 may be a good fit.

Note that pictures with 600 pixels by 800 pixels will not perfectly match 3:4 devices because of the internal margins that every device has. For example, suppose that the display screen has a size of 3.6 inches by 4.8 inches (the diagonal is then 6 inches, corresponding to a 6" display size, which is common among 3:4 eReaders). If the internal left and right margins are each 0.1875 inches (that's 3/16") and the top and bottom margins are each 0.375 inches (that's 3/8")[61], then the usable screen size is 3.225 inches by 4.05 inches. In this case, a picture size of 637 pixels by 800 pixels will match the aspect ratio of the usable screen size, and best fill the screen. On some devices, the customer can actually choose from a few different margin settings – which makes it impossible to precisely plan for the actual margin size. One disadvantage of 640 pixels by 800 pixels (which is equivalent to 600 pixels by 750 pixels, except that 640 x 800 is slightly higher resolution) is that 600 x 800 may look somewhat better than 640 x 800 on skinnier devices like the Kindle Fire.

Similarly, if you make your pictures 600 x 1024 with the Kindle Fire in mind, if you account for the internal margins, 610 x 1024 may fit the usable area of the display better – depending upon the customer's choice of the internal margin size.

Perhaps the common 600 x 800 is the best fit for a variety of devices.

---

[61] The top margin may be slightly thicker than the bottom margin due to the presence of the heading (i.e. the title of the eBook that appears on a small line at the top of the screen).

Some programmers have actually developed applications to help adapt the picture size for various eReaders. Some applications allow you to set one dimension to 100% and the other dimension to Auto. This way, the picture fills the screen; but the disadvantage is that the aspect ratio is not fixed – so the image may be stretched horizontally or vertically, as needed to fill the screen. Some images will look funny if stretched; in that case, automatically stretching the image to fill the screen may not be a good idea. There are other applications that include two different sets of images for two different types of devices. If you're interested in checking out the latest applications that may be available to help adapt your images to a given device, try searching for them on your favorite search engine (there are always new applications coming out) or try asking fellow authors about this on community help forums (see Sec. 4.2.12). For example, check out Kindlegen (you can find a link for it at http://www.amazon.com/gp/feature.html?docId=1000729511), which is an Amazon tool, and Mobipocket Creator (you can find it by clicking the Software tab from their homepage at http://www.mobipocket.com/en/HomePage/default.asp?Language=EN) – when you upload an eBook for publishing with Kindle, Amazon automatically converts it to Mobipocket format (with a .mobi file exteion), so Mobipocket is actually a tool that is used by Amazon.

There are two other properties of your images that you need to consider besides the aspect ratio: One is the pixel count, which affects both the resolution of your images and the memory size of your file; the other is picture size – i.e. how large the picture looks.

Your picture won't show in higher resolution than the display size. For example, if you make pictures that are 900 pixels by 1200 pixels, they will only show with a resolution of 600 x 800 on an eReader with a 600 x 800 display. On the other hand, if an eReader has a higher resolution display than the images that you submit, your full-screen pictures will not appear as sharp as the full-screen pictures of eBooks that use the optimal resolution. For example, a third-generation iPad has a 1536 x 2048 display: A picture that is 1536 x 2048 will appear 2.5 times sharper than a 600 x 800 image viewed with this device. Higher resolution images appear sharper, but they also increase the memory of the content file size. We will discuss the problem of memory in Sec. 4.2.4, and we will see how this may affect the possible list price and your royalty in Sec. 4.2.5.

You lose resolution when you decrease the pixel size of your image, but you don't increase the sharpness when you increase the pixel size. For example, if you begin with a 150 x 200 image and resize it to 600 x 800, the image will not appear sharper. If you want sharp, high-resolution pictures, the original picture must already have high resolution. If you started with a 1500 x 2000 image, resized it to 300 x 400, and then change your mind about it – go back to the original 1500 x 2000 image and then resize it as needed (don't increase the size of the 300 x 400 image). Similarly, if you draw a small image in Word, copy/paste the image into Paint, and then increase the pixel size, your image won't look nearly as sharp as if you first create a very large image in Word (the page size can be as large as 20" x 20", so you can make a 20" x 20" image) and then decrease the pixel size to the desired amount (see Sec. 2.2.5).

The size of the image affects how large it appears on the eReader screen. If you don't want a picture to fill the screen, make it smaller. The physical dimensions of the picture correspond to the picture's size, and the pixel count corresponds to the picture's resolution. If you make full-page pictures 600 x 800, then a picture with half the width and half the height should have a resolution of 300 x 400, for example (don't waste memory by making smaller images have more resolution than needed).

If you want to get the size of your pictures and the resolution right, what you should do is make a small sample of a variety of pictures – I mean a variety of sizes and resolutions – and then go through the minimal steps of the publishing process (see Sec.'s 4.2.8-4.2.11) needed to upload a content file (not the entire book – just a few pages with sample images). Then view the images with the publisher's previewer. If you are dissatisfied with the images, make some changes to the images and resubmit them. Perfect your technique before you make the pictures for your entire eBook. Authors who draw dozens of pictures first and then proceed to publish their eBooks often become very frustrated; the less frustrating way to proceed is to draw only a few sample pictures, learn how to draw them so that they format to your satisfaction, and then draw the remaining pictures.

Amazon's Kindle won't display an image larger than the screen size. Therefore, if you submit a picture that is larger than the display size, it will automatically reduce the size of the image so that it fits on the screen. However, not all eReaders may do this. For example, with Barnes & Noble's Nook, if your picture has a higher pixel count than the eReader can display, your picture may overfill the display and be cut off. If your pictures are 600 x 800, you should not experience this problem. For pictures with higher resolution, you may want to resize them for any eReaders where this may be a problem. Remember, you can easily preview the pictures for your eBook on any eReader by going to the publisher's website, uploading your content file, and using the publisher's preview too (see Sec.'s 4.2.8-4.2.11).

Note that this section has been devoted solely to pictures that appear in your eBook's content file. The cover picture is a different matter – you should make it as high resolution as the publisher allows (see Sec.'s 4.2.8-4.2.11).

Want or need help or advice? See Sec. 4.2.12 and Sec.'s 4.2.8 thru 4.2.11.

4.2.3 Revising Your Paperback Book Description for Your eBook

Since your eBook may be somewhat different from your paperback book – due to differences in formatting features, pictures, equations, etc. – if you have already written a description for your paperback (as described in Sec. 4.1.2), you may want to revise it for your eBook.

One important difference between an eBook and a physical book is that eBooks don't have definite page sizes. Instead, the eBook's size is based on memory (in kilobytes). The memory itself doesn't really tell a customer how long the eBook is though – since pictures, tables, equations, and rich formatting (that which the eBook's publisher allows) take up memory. For example, an eBook can have a huge file size, yet be very short because it mostly consists of full-screen, high-resolution images.

The description of your eBook should make the length of your eBook very clear. This way, a customer will be less likely to complain that the eBook is shorter than expected. For example, for fiction, is your book a collection of short stories (each less than about 10,000 words), a novelette (about 10,000 to 20,000 words), a novella (about 20,000 to 50,000 words), or a novel (about 50,000 to 100,000 words)? A customer who purchases an eBook expecting a typical 'book' will be disappointed if it turns out to be a novella, for example.

It may be helpful to include the word count in your description. In Microsoft Word, when you open your eBook file you can find the word count in the bottom left corner. You can also use this to check the word count of your eBook description if you type it in Word: There is a 4000 word limit for Kindle descriptions, for example.

If your book includes color pictures, state this in your description. Customers who have color eReaders like to take advantage of this. Does your eBook have any special features, such as an active table of contents (see Sec. 2.2.8)? If your eBook has features that many eBooks lack, this may be a selling point for potential customers.

As with your paperback book, eBook customers primarily want to know what your book is about. So don't get carried away with word count, pictures, and other eBook features to the point that it's difficult for customers to determine if your content suits them.

Since Amazon, Kindle, Barnes & Noble, Nook, Sony, etc. are trademarks of their respective owners, the eBook publisher may choose not to allow you to use these brands and names in the description of your eBook. The main problem that most eBook authors run into is wanting to specifically declare that the eBook is a Kindle edition or a Nook edition, for example, in the title or description. The eBook publisher may not want to give any implication that your eBook may be 'endorsed' by the publisher, and so the publisher probably will not allow you to make such declaration. If you're writing an eBook that helps customers make the most of their Kindle Fire or helps customers publish games on the Kindle Fire, for example, then you may be able to include 'Kindle Fire' in your title; if so, be sure to provide a declaration of the actual company that owns the brand name and trademark (and speak to an attorney to see if this will suffice). Consult an attorney for legal advice on this matter; I'm only suggesting that the publisher or brand might not allow you to do this – only an attorney will be qualified to advise you on what you should or should not do.

It's not really necessary to declare that your eBook is a Kindle edition, for example. Amazon will include the words 'Kindle Edition' after your title on your Amazon detail page, so it will be clear that this edition of your book is a Kindle eBook, even if this is not in the title.

You can include a brief biography at the end of your description if you want. Unlike CreateSpace, Kindle does not have a separate section for an author biography in addition to the description. However, Amazon does have an About the Author feature for the latest

Kindle devices (such as the Kindle Fire HD), which ties into the author's Amazon page at Author Central (see Chapter 6). It's probably worth mentioning pertinent qualifications in the eBook description, but otherwise I would avoid including most biographical information in the description. Most eBook publishers do have some means of posting an author biography – either by linking to an author page or having a separate paragraph for it.

Some eBook publishers allow linespaces in the description in order to help divide the description into paragraphs; but they will probably not respect tab spacing for indentations.

Following is a sample description for my eBook, *An Introduction to Basic Astronomy Concepts (with Space Photos)*:

This eBook provides a highly visual and colorful introduction to a variety of basic astronomy concepts: (1) Overview of the Solar System (2) Understanding the Lunar Phases (3) Understanding Solar and Lunar Eclipses (4) Understanding the Seasons (5) Evidence that the Earth is Round (6) Models of Our Solar System (7) Laws of Motion in Astronomy (8) Beyond Our Solar System. This eBook features numerous NASA space photos. (NASA did not participate in the writing or publication of this eBook.) Many diagrams, like the heliocentric and geocentric models or explaining the phases of the moon, were constructed by combining together NASA space photos instead of simply drawing circles. Educators may use this material for the purpose of teaching astronomy concepts to their students. The content is suitable for a general interest audience, as well as those who may be learning astronomy and are looking for some supplemental instruction that is highly visual and focused on a variety of fundamental concepts.

There are about 17,000 words in this eBook and over 100 color images. (The paperback edition of this eBook has 186 pages.)

4.2.4 Managing the Cover and Content File Sizes

There are three important reasons for managing the size of your content file:
1. First, if your file size exceeds the limits tabulated in Sec. 4.2.1, you won't be able to publish your eBook with each eReader unless you are able to reduce the content file's memory below that eReader's file size limit.
2. Secondly, the size of your file may impact your royalties, as described in Sec. 4.2.5.
3. Also, the file size impacts the customer. A larger file uses up more of the customer's available memory, and on an older device can take a long time to download.

Remember, you can find out what the size of your content file is by finding it in the Documents or Computer folder on your computer, right-clicking on the filename, clicking Properties, and looking for the file size in the General tab.

Pictures, equations, and tables hog most of the file's memory. You may be able to reduce the size of your file by compressing the pictures. In Microsoft Word, select a picture (just click on it) in your file, go to the Format tab that appears after you select it, click Compress Pictures, uncheck the Apply Only To This Picture box, and select a Target Output. E-mail resolution (96 ppi – pixels per inch) will give you the minimum possible file size. Before you try this, save the original version of your file, then save a new version of your file (with a different filename) with the revised Target Output. This way, you will still have the original.

If you need to shrink your file size further, there are other changes that you can make to achieve this, such as:

❖ Try changing the file format between .doc, .docx, .html, and .pdf, for example (also, check which file formats each publisher accepts – see Sec.'s 4.2.8-11). In Word, click the File tab and choose Save As to resave the file with a different format. After you change the file format, first check to see if the file size decreased – if so, then view the file carefully (some features may not look the same after the change). Also, a file that looked fine on the publisher's preview in one file format may look different after the change, so be sure to check the preview. The file format with the least memory might have several formatting problems – so check this carefully in the preview.

❖ Did you use an application, like Kindlegen or Mobipocket Creator? Some applications that provide helpful picture formatting options significantly increase the file size. If you used an application such as these, compare your eBook file to the original file (i.e. before you used the application) to see if it increased the file size. If so, weigh the benefits of the improved picture formatting with the effect that it has on your royalty.

❖ Decreasing the resolution of your pictures may reduce your file size. You want to find the best compromise between sharp images and a reasonable file size.

❖ If you have a lot of content, consider splitting your eBook into multiple volumes. In order to do this successfully, there must be enough content in each volume that the customers will feel that the content that they receive in each volume is worth the price of the volume. Customers won't be happy if you have a short eBook that they feel is worth $3.99 and split it up into two $2.99 eBooks, for example; but if you have a long novel, for example, that customers would value at $9.99, they should not mind spending $4.99 for each of two separate volumes.

❖ If you really need to cut your file size and you've already implemented the other suggestions that apply, consider whether or not there is any memory-hogging content (like a picture or table) that you are willing to part with or that you are willing to recast in a plain form (e.g. putting the same information in plain text).

❖ If you have equations, see the suggestion in Sec. 2.2.7.

Go through the minimum publishing steps required (see Sec.'s 4.2.8-4.2.11) to upload your content file and view a preview of your eBook to see how the pictures look after resizing them. You want to find the right compromise for your eBook between the royalty that you earn (which may depend on the file size, as explained in Sec. 4.2.5) and the quality of your pictures.

Some eReader publishers have maximum file size limits on the cover, too. Nook Press, for example, the publisher for Barnes & Noble's Nook, places a limit of 2 MB (2000 KB) on the size of the cover file. Since the cover is a JPEG file, if your picture exceeds this limit, one way to reduce the cover file's memory is to open the file in Paint and resize it with a lower pixel count.

4.2.5 List Price and Royalties for Your eBook

Your royalty will depend on the publisher of your eBook. Amazon has two options for royalties of Kindle eBooks: One option is a flat 35% of the list price; the other option is 70% of the adjusted price (after subtracting the delivery cost from the list price) for eligible eBooks sold in qualifying countries (and a flat 35% otherwise). The main eligibility criteria is that your eBook does not contain public domain content. In the US, the delivery cost is 15 cents per megabyte (MB) of the content file size after Amazon automatically converts your book to Mobipocket (.mobi) format. In the UK, the delivery cost is £0.10 per MB and in Europe it is €0.12 per MB. If you have a large file size, the flat 35% royalty rate could actually be higher than the 70% royalty option, so it's worth checking both options. After you upload your book for publishing with Amazon Kindle, you will be able to use Amazon's royalty calculator to check the royalty for your eBook with each method. If your book is available for less – e.g. if the paperback edition is selling for less than your eBook through some channel or if your eBook is available for a free promotion through some other channel, then Amazon will pricematch your eBook and pay your royalty based on the lower price.

You set the list price for your eBook. The maximum list price for a Kindle eBook is $200 for the 35% royalty rate and $9.99 for the 70% royalty option. The minimum list price depends on your converted content file size. For the 35% royalty option, if your converted content file size is not greater than 3 MB, you may price your Kindle eBook as low as 99 cents; if it is greater than 3 MB, but not greater than 10 MB, you may price your Kindle eBook as low as $1.99; and if it is greater than 10 MB, the minimum price is $2.99. Visit https://kdp.amazon.com/self-publishing/help?topicId=A301WJ6XCJ8KW0 to find the pricing limits for other countries. For the 70% royalty option, the minimum list price is $2.99. Customers who purchase your eBook in other countries may also pay a value-added tax (VAT) – see Sec. 4.1.7.

The 70% royalty option provides an incentive for publishers and authors to price their Kindle eBooks between $2.99 and $9.99 – Kindle eBooks priced below $2.99 or above $9.99 are only eligible for the 35% royalty rate. It also provides an incentive to keep your content file size down – since every MB of memory subtracts 15 cents per sale from your royalties. If it qualifies for the 70% royalty, don't price your eBook between $10.00 and $20.00 – since you would actually make more money by pricing your eBook $9.99 and choosing the 70% royalty.

If you want to price your book under $2.99 – and are therefore willing to accept the 35% royalty rate – there is an incentive to keep your content file size under 3 MB (since you are then eligible for a 99 cents list price) or under 10 MB (which qualifies you for a $1.99 list price). If the file size exceeds 10 MB, then the minimum list price is $2.99.

We will now consider a few examples to see how the royalty rates are calculated for Kindle – but remember, Amazon will also have a royalty calculator available when you go to publish your eBook. Suppose, for example, that your eBook has a file size of 5 MB. If you price your eBook at $1.99 (the lowest possible in this example), your royalty will be 70 cents (since only the 35% option applies) – since $1.99 x 0.35 = $0.70 (your actual royalty could be a penny less than this). If you price your eBook at $2.99, your royalty will be $1.05 with the 35% option – since $2.99 x 0.35 = $1.05 – and $1.57 with the 70% option – since ($2.99 – 5 x $0.15) x 0.7 = ($2.99 – $0.75) x 0.7 = ($2.24) x 0.7 = $1.57. In this example, you would have to sell more than twice as many eBooks at $1.99 than you would at $2.99 with the 70% option in order for the $1.00 discount in the list price to increase your overall royalties.

Let's look at another example where the file size is 2 MB. In this case, your eBook is eligible for a list price of 99 cents. If you price your eBook at 99 cents, your royalty will be 34 cents – since $0.99 x 35 = $0.34. If instead you price your eBook at $2.99, your royalty will be $1.88 with the 70% option – since ($2.99 – 2 x $0.15) x 0.7 = $1.88. You have to sell 6 times as many eBooks at 99 cents as you would at $2.99 in order for the 99 cents list price to increase your overall royalties. For example, if you sell 20 eBooks in the month at $2.99, your royalty would be $37.60, whereas you would need to sell 111 eBooks at $2.99 just to make the same royalty. Some eBooks do sell well at 99 cents or $1.99, but some eBooks don't.

The list price should reflect the quantity and quality of the content. If your eBook has only a little content – like a novella or a short picture book – you might not sell *any* books for $2.99; in that case, a lower price of 99 cents could make a huge difference.

I highly recommend searching for eBooks that are similar to yours and noting their list prices. Also, look for important differences between each eBook and yours – such as the use of a traditional publisher, well-known author, approximate page count, and substantial differences in content. Check the sales ranks, too, to see how well similar eBooks are selling, and note the visibility of each eBook in the search results. Pricing similar titles will help you establish what price range is appropriate for your eBook.

If your eBook is also available in paperback, the list price of your eBook should probably offer customers a discount compared to your paperback selling price (which could be less than its list price, especially if it is on sale). If it does, Amazon will highlight the savings of the Kindle edition compared to the paperback edition so that potential customers see this as a clear discount – that's a nice incentive for doing this. As with paperback books, an eBook with a lower list price does not always (although it sometimes does) increase sales (see Sec. 4.1.5 for a discussion of pricing and royalties).

If you have the rights to sell your eBook in other countries, you also need to set the list price of your eBook for those countries. You can have Amazon automatically calculate a list price for your eBook in those countries based on your US list price. If you prefer to set your list prices manually, you should first visit the websites for Amazon in other countries (such as Amazon UK) in order to establish the price range of similar titles in those countries. If you set a different list price for each European country, Amazon may occasionally need to match the price (e.g. when a customer in one country has a choice of buying your eBook from two different countries, that customer is entitled to the lower price).

I priced this eBook at $4.99 for US sales, which offers a 50% discount compared to the paperback edition. I felt that the paperback price was already a great value (as I explained in Sec. 4.1.5, I found similar paperback titles selling for $14.99 to $24.99; and I also believe[62] that you get a great deal of detailed and helpful information for both paperback and eBook publishing in my book, and it has the advantage of being self-published – compared to a traditionally published author trying to teach you how to self-publish). Even so, I feel rather strongly that eBooks should provide a healthy discount compared to paperback books – after all, look at all the printing, paper, and shipping/handling that is not involved in the purchase of an eBook – which is why I priced the eBook edition 50% less than the paperback edition of this book.

If you choose to enroll your Kindle eBook in the KDP Select program, you also earn royalties when your eBook is borrowed by customers. We will discuss the KDP Select Program, including how the royalty is determined for borrows, in Sec. 4.2.7.

I recommend using the same list price for your eBook regardless of where you publish it. Some publishers, like Barnes & Noble's Nook, require your list price to be no higher than any other sales channel.

Nook Press – the publisher for Barnes & Noble's Nook – pays 65% if your list price is between $2.99 and $9.99 and 40% if your list price is between 99 cents and $2.98 or between $10.00 and $199.99. It would be foolish to price your Nook eBook between $10.00 and $16.23 – since you would actually make a higher royalty with a list price of $9.99! The royalty for Nook eSales is often better than the royalty for Kindle eSales since Nook Press does not charge a delivery fee (instead, Nook Press simply imposes a maximum file size of 10 Mb) – such that 65% with no delivery fee may be better than 70% after a delivery fee; and, of course, for other price ranges, 40% is better than 35%.

---

[62] But please form your own opinion (if you haven't already).

If you publish your eBook with Smashwords, you can make it available for Kobo, Sony, and other eReaders. Sony used to have a store specifically for Sony Reader books, but is now using Kobo books. Make your eBook available with Kobo to reach Sony customers.

Kobo pays a 70% royalty for a wider range of list prices than Kindle or Nook – a list price in the range of $1.99 thru $12.99 qualifies for the 70% royalty at Kobo. For list prices outside of this range, Kobo's royalty rate is 45%, which also beats both Kindle and Nook. However, Kobo does require the list price of your eBook to be at least 20% less than the price of your paperback edition (if you have a paperback edition of your eBook).

4.2.6 ISBN, Keywords, and Categories for Your eBook

Unfortunately, if you have a paperback book, you are **not** allowed to use the same ISBN for your eBook. If you would like to have an ISBN for your eBook, you must either purchase one from Bowker (as described in Sec. 4.1.6) or get one from an eBook publishing company like Smashwords (Sec. 4.2.10) that has a free ISBN option. You can publish an eBook for most eReaders without having an ISBN for it. The main exception is the Sony Reader, which requires the eBook to have an ISBN (remember, you can get a free ISBN from Smashwords).

Even if you don't purchase an ISBN for your eBook, you must still use exactly the same title and author information for both your eBook and your paperback one (if you have one). You are not supposed to add any extra words to the title of your eBook (Amazon, for example, states this very clearly next to the area where you enter the title for your eBook). There is generally not a separate place for the subtitle (but there are places to enter the name of a series and the volume number). If you have a subtitle, you might be allowed include it with the title, separated by a colon – provided that the combination of title and subtitle does not exceed any maximum character length. Note: KDP recently added a subtitle option.

You will have the opportunity to specify keywords associated with your eBook when you publish it. Most of what we discussed regarding how to select keywords in Sec. 4.1.3 also applies to eBooks; I suggest reviewing that section for some important advice. However, there are a few important differences:

- Kindle Direct Publishing with Amazon allows 7 keywords and does not impose a length restriction like CreateSpace. Beware that if you include several words in a single keyword (like "how to self-publish a book," your title will only show up in search results when a customer enters <u>all</u> of those words. So you can't make more than 7 keywords by grouping words together. When you publish an eBook for Nook, on the other hand, there is no limit on the number of keywords, but there is a limit of 100 characters overall.
- The common keyword searches on Amazon are different from common keyword searches on Kindle, for example. You just have to use a Kindle to see what's popular.

- If you publish both an eBook and a paperback book, you can choose to have the keywords of one edition supplement the keywords of the other – instead of doubling up and using the same keywords for both. This may increase your book's visibility.
- There are special keywords that apply to eBooks that don't apply to paperback books – like "Kindle for kids." However, keep in mind that customers who are actually using a Kindle probably won't include the word 'Kindle' when they search for eBooks – since only Kindle eBooks will show up in search results when the customer is holding a Kindle in his/her hands. On the other hand, a customer who discovers your eBook while doing a search on a PC might then go purchase your eBook on a Kindle.

You will also need to specify browse categories for your eBook. Review Sec. 4.1.3, which discusses how to select browse categories for your paperback book. Kindle Direct Publishing allows you to enter up to two browse categories for your eBook. If you find more than two categories, using different categories for your paperback book and your eBook is one way to have your books show up in more searches.

4.2.7 Amazon's KDP Select and KOLL Programs for Kindle eBooks (and MatchBook)

Amazon has two Kindle programs that you should be aware of: Kindle Direct Publishing (KDP) Select and the Kindle Owners' Lending Library (KOLL). Customers who own a Kindle can join the KOLL program by signing up for Amazon Prime membership. A customer enrolled in the KOLL program can borrow up to one eBook from the lending library per month for free; the customer must return one eBook before borrowing another. The KOLL program has incentives for both authors and readers.

It costs $79 per year for customers to sign up for Amazon Prime membership, and they must also own a Kindle device in order to join the KOLL program. If a customer borrows one eBook per month, the average price must be $6.58 per eBook for the customer just to 'break even' in terms of borrows. But there are other incentives for customers to join Amazon Prime besides just borrowing a free eBook every month:

$ Amazon Prime members get free two-day shipping on millions of eligible items (there is even a convenient way to filter search results on Amazon such that only Prime-eligible products show up).

$ Shipping on Prime-eligible items is not only faster than Free Super Saver Shipping, but there is no minimum purchase (whereas Free Super Saver Shipping requires a $35 minimum purchase).

$ Prime Instant Videos, which includes thousands of movies and television shows, can be streamed instantly for free.

$ Customers can try Amazon Prime for one month for free.

$79 is a lot of money to spend up front, but if you have a Kindle, read at least one book a month, make multiple purchases at Amazon each year, and like to watch videos, then it's a good value. I'm a Prime member myself, and so are many other self-published authors.

You must enroll your eBook in the KDP Select program in order for your eBook to be included in the KOLL program (if you publish multiple eBooks, you have this option for each individual eBook – i.e. you *don't* have to enroll *all* of your eBooks in the program). There are some good incentives for publishers and authors to enroll their eBooks in the KDP Select program – listed below – but you must also make a commitment if you do this: Any eBook enrolled in the KDP Select program must be available exclusively on Kindle during the enrollment period (which comes in 90-day intervals). You may have paperback editions of your book available with other publishers, but if you enroll your eBook in the KDP Select program, you may not publish that eBook with Nook, Sony, or any other channel besides Kindle (they do have software that automatically checks on this). Your list price must also be between $0.99 and $9.99 in order to be eligible for the KDP Select program. Also, keep in mind that customers are more likely to purchase a $0.99 eBook rather than borrow it.

Publishers and authors have the following incentives to enroll their eBooks in the KDP Select program:

$ Authors are paid royalties for eBooks that are borrowed for free in the KOLL program. The royalty for a borrowed eBook is a share of the KDP Select fund.

$ The KDP Select fund is $500,000 or more – e.g. it was $700,000 for November, 2013. Every time a customer borrows your eBook through the KOLL program, you receive one share of the KDP Select fund.

$ Your royalty for sales is still the same as described in Sec. 4.2.5. Your royalty for eBooks borrowed through the KOLL Program depends on how many eBooks are borrowed in the program during the month: One share equals the KDP Select Fund divided by the total number of borrows during the month. For example, if the KDP Select Fund is $700,000 for the month and there are 350,000 borrows during the month, then the royalty is $2.00 for every borrow. Thus far, the royalty for borrows has usually been a little over $2.00. Even if your royalty for sales is greater, the borrows help to increase your overall royalties for the month; and a customer who was willing to borrow your eBook might not have been willing to purchase it.

$ You can make your eBook free for up to 5 days in every 90-day enrollment period. You do not earn royalties when customers 'buy' your eBook for free. However, you can greatly increase your audience around the world using this free promotion opportunity. Customers who 'purchase' your eBook during the free promotion who like your eBook may tell friends and family about your eBook. Free promotion 'sales' also help to associate your eBook with other eBooks (so that your eBook will appear in the list of "Customers who bought this item also bought" eBooks), improve your sales rank if the promo is successful, and improve your chances of getting book reviews.

- $ If you have multiple eBooks available on Kindle and at least one is enrolled in the KDP Select program, when you make one eBook free, some customers who enjoyed your eBook might purchase one or more of your other eBooks in the future. If you have a series, periodically making the first volume free could be a helpful marketing strategy.
- $ A new alternative to the free promo is the Kindle **Countdown Deal**. You can't do both free promos and Countdown Deals in the same 90-day period. The Countdown Deal allows you to set a temporary price reduction that shows as a discount to customers and also shows when your sale will end.
- $ An eBook enrolled in the KDP Select program earns 70% royalties for sales in Japan, India, Brazil, and Mexico; otherwise, the royalty is 35% in these countries.
- $ At the end of the 90-day enrollment period, you may opt out of the KDP Select program. Enrolling for at least one 90-day period allows you to take advantage of the free promotion opportunity. This is a good incentive to at least test the program out.

Some authors like the KDP Select program; others don't. If you want to hear fellow authors discuss what they did and didn't like about the program, and how successful it was or wasn't for them, try asking about it on Kindle's community help forum (see Sec. 4.2.12). I have enrolled almost all of my eBooks in the KDP Select Program. Presently, the eBooks that I have published with other eReader brands were either prior to Amazon's KOLL program or were eBooks that I have published (mostly with Nook) on behalf of fellow authors.

Authors who feel that their eBooks are successful with the KDP Select program tend to love it. Those who don't receive many borrows or don't get as much out of the promotional tools tend to opt out of the KDP Select program and explore publishing with Nook, Sony, Kobo, Smashwords, and other eReaders in addition to Kindle. Your eBook will have greater availability if you publish it in more places, and some of the competition is removed from other eBook publishing platforms – i.e. any eBook enrolled in the KDP Select program won't be selling on Nook, Sony, Kobo, Smashwords, etc.

Don't confuse the KOLL program with Kindle Book Lending. Borrowing and lending have different meanings in these two programs. A customer may lend your eBook to friends and family through the Kindle Book Lending program. In the case of Kindle Book Lending (unlike the KOLL program), no royalty is paid. Customers can lend your eBook through Kindle Book Lending even if your book is not eligible for the KOLL program (but you may choose to opt out of Kindle Book Lending if your eBook is on the 35% royalty option). An eBook that is loaned through the Kindle Book Lending program is only available for 14 days (and during this period, it is not available to the lender).

Another new program is Kindle **MatchBook**. (This does <u>not</u> require enrollment in KDP Select.) MatchBook provides an incentive to customers to purchase your Kindle eBook together with your paperback edition. To participate in the MatchBook program, you must select the option to discount your eBook for any customer who purchases your paperback.

4.2.8 How to Publish Your eBook with Amazon's Kindle

This section will provide step-by-step instructions for how to publish an eBook with Kindle Direct Publishing (KDP), which is Amazon's Kindle publishing service.[63] It's very important to get the formatting right. If your eBook provides a "poor customer experience," your eBook may be unpublished. Also, if you have a paperback edition of your eBook, the two editions may get linked together – so that a negative review of your eBook due to poor formatting may adversely affect the sales of your paperback edition, too. See Sec. 2.2 regarding how to format your eBook; note that many standard features available in common word processors such as Microsoft Word do <u>not</u> work in eBooks (as explained in Sec. 2.2). For help making figures, see Chapter 3; for help formatting pictures specifically for an eBook, see Sec.'s 2.2.5 and 4.2.2. We discussed how to design a cover for your eBook in Chapter 3. If you are having trouble with the file size, see Sec. 4.2.4. Once your eBook content and cover files are ready for publishing, here are the directions for how to publish your eBook with KDP:

1. If you don't already have an account with Amazon (at www.amazon.com), sign up for one. You will use your same Amazon account to publish with KDP.
2. The website for KDP is https://kdp.amazon.com/self-publishing/dashboard; this will take you to your KDP dashboard.
3. From your KDP dashboard, click the Add New Title button.
4. If you want to enroll your eBook in the KDP Select program (described in Sec. 4.2.7), check the box at the top of the page. Be sure to read the terms and conditions before you sign up.
5. Enter the exact title of your eBook in the field below Book Name; check the spelling and wording carefully. Note that you are not permitted to enter additional words – such as Kindle Edition – in the Book Name field that are not included in the title of your eBook. If you have a paperback edition of the same book, both the title and subtitle need to match exactly (along with the author name, spelled and punctuated – e.g. if there are initials – exactly the same way) in order to get the two editions linked together on Amazon.
6. If your eBook is (or will be) part of a series, check the appropriate box and enter both the series name and volume number in the space provided.
7. You may enter the edition number of your eBook – it's optional.
8. Enter your eBook's description. I recommend typing your description in Microsoft Word and using copy/paste (with Ctrl + C and Ctrl + V). This way, you can take advantage of Word's spellcheck and word count features. **Note**: KDP now supports basic HTML in the description. See Sec. 6.1.4.

---

[63] Kindle and Amazon are trademarks of Amazon.com, Inc. These trademarks and brands are the property of their respective owners.

9. Click the Add Contributors button to identify everyone who contributed to the eBook. In addition to the author(s), you may also add editors, illustrators, and more. The name(s) of the author(s) must exactly match those of your copyright page and the paperback edition of your eBook, if you have one.

10. If your book is not written in English, select your eBook's language from the drop-down menu.

11. The publication date, publisher, and ISBN information are all optional. Leave the publication date blank. This way, the publication date will be the day that your actually published. This maximizes your visibility in the New Releases. You can act as your own publisher and make your own imprint (but **don't** enter CreateSpace), but, if so, do research to search for the name that you choose to avoid using the same imprint as another publisher and, especially, to avoid using any name that may be trademarked.

12. You may **not** use the same ISBN from your paperback book for your eBook. If you would like an ISBN for your eBook, you can purchase a separate ISBN for your eBook through Bowker (as described in Sec. 4.1.6). You can get a free ISBN with Smashwords, but that's intended for use when you publish directly through them (Sec. 4.2.10).

13. Click the appropriate choice to declare your publishing rights. If you're not sure about the distinction, click the "What's this?" link. (Note that just about every field has a "What's this?" link in case you would like more information.)

14. Select up to two categories and enter up to 7 keywords separated by commas.

15. Click the Browse For Image button. Find the JPEG or TIFF file for your eBook's cover on your computer, in your documents, or on your jump drive, for example. After you select your file, click the Upload Image button. If you have computer issues, check your internet browser to make sure that it's allowing popups, try upgrading to the newest version of your internet browser, try using a different internet browser (Internet Explorer, Mozilla Firefox, etc.), ask for help at the KDP community help forum, or contact Kindle for support (see Sec. 4.2.12).

16. Click your preference for digital rights management (the "What's this?" link will tell you more about it). Click the Browse For Book button. Find and select your eBook's content file (.docx, .doc, .zip, .htm, .html, .epub, .mobi, .pdf, .rtf, or .txt), then click the Upload Book button. Note the links that outline the KDP content guidelines and provide help with formatting.

17. It may take a while for KDP to upload your book and then convert it to Mobipocket (.mobi) format. You will either receive a message saying, "Upload and conversion successful," or an error message – e.g. if your file is not an acceptable format (accepted formats are Word .doc or .docx, HTML .zip, .html, or .htm, Mobipocket .mobi, ePub .epub, Text .txt or .rtf, and PDF .pdf) or if your file size exceeds 50 MB. If you encounter other problems or issues, see Sec. 4.2.12.

18. I have sometimes clicked the Save As Draft button, only to find later that some of the information has disappeared. If you save your work and return to it later, check all of the fields carefully to make sure that all of your work is still there.

19. Once the upload and conversion of your eBook are successful, click the Preview Book button. Use the Device drop-down menu to preview your eBook on Kindle, Kindle Fire, Kindle Fire HD, iPhone, and iPad – you want to ensure that your eBook formats well on each of these devices. You can also view the orientation in both portrait and landscape. It should look great one way, and at least satisfactory with the other orientation – since a few customers may use their preferred orientation instead of whichever appears better. The buttons on the bottom allow you to advance the page.

20. The formatting of your eBook may have a very significant impact on sales frequency and customer reviews, so it is well worth investing the time to preview your eBook thoroughly – and it is also well worth investing any time needed to make necessary revisions. I strongly recommend that you proof your eBook files carefully (Sec. 5.2).

21. **You should also download the free previewer along with your eBook preview file**, which allows you to preview how your eBook will look on Kindle DX and Touch.

22. Once you are happy with the formatting of your eBook and all of the other information on the first page is complete (you should double-check it), click Save and Continue.

23. Select the territories where you have the right to sell your eBook.

24. Choose a royalty option. These are described in Sec. 4.2.5.

25. Enter your list price for Amazon US. Either select the option for KDP to automatically calculate a list price for your eBook in other territories based on your US list price or enter those list prices manually. See Sec. 4.2.5. Beneath the pricing area you will find the size of your content file after conversion; if this seems rather large, see Sec. 4.2.4. You will also see a note about pricing in this area.

26. The Kindle Book Lending box will automatically be checked. You can only uncheck this box if you opt for the 35% royalty option.

27. Read the terms and conditions (there is a link for them), then there is one final box to check. Read this statement carefully before checking this box.

28. Click the Save and Publish button when you are ready. Amazon will send you an email when your eBook becomes available on Amazon US – usually about 12 hours.

29. I strongly recommend that you find a Kindle that you can use to purchase your eBook as soon as it becomes available. This way, you can see firsthand exactly how your Kindle eBook looks. If you find any problems, you may submit a revision (though your original may sell before the revised version becomes available).

30. If you revise your eBook to make significant corrections, you should visit https://kdp.amazon.com/self-publishing/help and click the Notify Customers of Book Updates link under Updating Your Published Book; also, note the Contact Us button at the bottom of the help pages. For more support options, see Sec. 4.2.12.

31. Use the reports tab at the top of your KDP dashboard to generate sales and royalty reports for sales of your eBooks.

Note that Amazon also has a Kindle Singles program, which is separate from publishing an eBook through KDP. To learn more about Kindle Singles and how to submit your eBook (if it qualifies) or to submit a proposal, visit Amazon's homepage, click Kindle and then Kindle Books under Shop By Department, select Kindle Singles under Browse, and click the Learn More link under "Want to Write a Kindle Single?" on the left-hand side of the page.

4.2.9 How to Publish Your eBook with Barnes & Noble's Nook

Nook Press is the eBook publishing service for Barnes & Noble's Nook.[64] Note that there are important differences between Kindle formatting and Nook formatting – e.g. Kindle provides some table support, and large, high-resolution images may overfill Nook's display screen (see the end of Sec. 4.2.2). Therefore, you will probably need to adapt your content eBook file for publishing with Nook. You will have the opportunity to preview how your content eBook file looks on different Nook devices, so if there are any problems, you can revise your files and resubmit them. Also, read the note about Nook figures near the end of Sec. 4.2.2.

Remember, you can't publish your eBook with Nook or any other channel if your eBook is enrolled in the KDP Select program (and if you start that program and later cancel it, you still can't publish your eBook elsewhere until the 90-day period expires).

If you publish with Smashwords (see Sec. 4.2.10), they can publish your eBook with a variety of eReaders for you, including Nook. However, there may be differences in formatting from one eReader to another. If you want to use Smashwords to publish with Nook, I recommend that you at least go through the initial steps of publishing your eBook with Nook Press so that you can use the free preview tool, which will show you exactly how your eBook will appear on Nook and Nook Color. This way, you can see if the same eBook file is suitable for Nook before you have Smashwords publish your eBook for Nook. You should also compare Smashwords' royalty for Nook sales (60%) to the Nook Press royalty (65%).

When you are ready to publish your eBook with Nook, follow the instructions below. Some of the notes that I included in Sec. 4.2.8 for KDP publishing also apply for Nook publishing (such as being sure to enter the exact title of your eBook and not to add extra words, like "Nook Edition") – in those cases, the information might not be repeated again here. Also, I'm not going to include all of the reminders again (like mentioning, "See Sec. 4.2.5 regarding how to set your list price"). **Note: Publt! is now Nook Press.**

1. Visit www.nookpress.com, the website for Nook Press. Sign up for an account.

---

[64] Nook, Publt!, and Barnes & Noble are trademarks of Barnes & Noble, Inc. These trademarks and brands are the property of their respective owners.

2. Login to your Nook Press account. Click the Create New Project button.
3. Enter the title of your eBook.
4. Browse for and upload the content file (.doc, .docx, .html, .rtf, or.txt) for your eBook. Remember, the maximum file size for the Nook content file is 20 MB. Click any of the links to see Nook's formatting guidelines (e.g. see the issue with **subscripts**).
5. Enter the list price (it can't be higher than the list price of your eBook through any other channel), the publication date, the publisher (this could be your own Imprint or your name, but it can't be CreateSpace), and up to 5 contributors.
6. Preview your eBook with Nook and Nook Color. If you encounter problems, see Sec. 4.2.12 (but if your images exceed the page size, see the note near the end of Sec. 4.2.2). I strongly recommend that you proof your eBook files carefully (Sec. 5.2). Note that page breaks may not show on the preview – a problem for some picture eBooks (see the page break tip in Sec. 2.1.8).
7. Browse for and upload the JPEG cover file for your Nook eBook. Note that the maximum dimension is 2000 pixels for a Nook cover, whereas it is 2500 pixels for Kindle. Nook has a maximum cover (not content) file size of 2 MB.
8. Enter the ISBN number if you purchased a separate ISBN from Bowker specifically for the eBook edition of your book (you can't use the paperback ISBN). Also, note that Smashwords has a free ISBN option if you publish an eBook with them (Sec. 4.2.10).
9. Check 'yes' and enter the series name and number if your eBook is part of a series.
10. Indicate if your eBook is also available in print and, if applicable, the page count.
11. Indicate whether or not your eBook includes public domain content.
12. Use the drop-down menu to select the appropriate age group for your audience.
13. If your eBook is not in English, change the language in the drop-down menu.
14. Select the territories where you have the rights to publish your eBook.
15. Select a digital rights management option.
16. Nook allows you to enter up to five categories, which is pretty cool (Amazon currently only allows up to two). ☺
17. Enter up to 100 characters worth of keywords (a counter will show you how many characters remain as you type) separated by commas. You should try searching on Nook – or at least on Barnes & Noble's website for Nook eBooks – to see which popular keyword searches may be relevant for your eBook. You can enter more keywords by choosing shorter keywords, whereas the number of search results is likely to be smaller for a longer keyword (but customers may also be more likely to search for shorter keywords than longer ones).
18. Your eBook description may have up to 5000 characters.
19. You may add an About the Author section of up to 2500 characters.
20. If you have a legitimate editorial book review, you may enter it. If you have a review, but don't know if it qualifies – ask first (click the Support tab at the top right).

21. Read the statement carefully, check the box, and click the Put On Sale button when you are ready to publish your eBook. At any time, you can click the Save button and come back to your eBook later.
22. You can track sales with the My Sales tab at the top of your dashboard.
23. If you have problems, issues, questions, concerns, or just want to meet fellow Nook authors, see Sec. 4.2.12.

4.2.10 How to Publish Your eBook on Sony's Reader and More with Smashwords

A self-published author can't publish an eBook directly with Sony,[65] but an eBook that is published with Smashwords can be made available for the Sony Reader (through Kobo) in addition to a variety of other eReaders, including Barnes & Noble's Nook and even libraries through Baker & Taylor. As mentioned previously, I recommend publishing your eBook with each eReader individually, when possible – or at least going through the initial steps of the publishing process with each eReader, like Nook, in order to see how your eBook looks on the publisher's previewer. Your royalty may be different if you publish your eBook with other eReaders using Smashwords compared to direct publishing (in some instances, though, it could actually be higher with Smashwords, so it's worth comparing). You can use Smashwords to publish your eBook with the following eReader companies:

✓ The Sony Reader Store (Reader), now through Kobo, Inc.
✓ The Apple iBookstore (iPhone and iPad)
✓ Barnes & Noble (Nook)
✓ Kobo, Inc. (Kobo)
✓ Baker & Taylor (public libraries)
✓ Smashwords' website
✓ Diesel, Aldiko, and more

Remember, Sony's Reader will not accept eBooks that do not have an ISBN specifically for the eBook edition. If you would like an ISBN for your eBook, Smashwords offers a free ISBN option; alternatively, you can purchase a separate ISBN for your eBook from Bowker (see Sec. 4.1.6). If you use Smashwords to publish your eBook with Kobo, you will also need an ISBN for that (you can also publish with Kobo directly, as described briefly in Sec. 4.2.11). Note that Sony no longer has a separate store: Publish with Kobo to reach Sony customers.

Publishing with Smashwords comes with some benefits, such as a free ISBN option for your eBook, distribution to libraries, and free marketing and selling tools (for example, Smashwords has a Coupon Manager).

---

[65] Sony is a registered trademark of Sony Corporation. Smashwords is a registered trademark of Smashwords. These trademarks and brands are the property of their respective owners.

Smashwords also provides some helpful literature for free. To find this, from the Smashwords homepage (www.smashwords.com), click the How To Publish On Smashwords link. I highly recommend that you read the <u>free</u> *Smashwords Style Guide* by Mark Coker (find it under, "Getting Started is Easy as 1-2-3"), which is also available for <u>free</u> on Amazon (you can read it with your Kindle or download the free Kindle for PC). If you scroll down to the bottom of the page (the same page you pulled up from the Smashwords homepage after clicking the How To Publish On Smashwords link), you can find more useful literature. This includes, the *Smashwords Book Marketing Guide* by Mark Coker (also free at Amazon), the *Secrets to Ebook Publishing Success* by Mark Coker (also free at Amazon), and a blog post, *How to Self-Publish an Ebook with Smashwords* with contributions from 31 veteran Smashwords authors. It is definitely worth investing the time to read these and follow the advice if you would like for your eBook to successful.

Follow the instructions below in order to publish your eBook with Smashwords. Some of the notes that I included in Sec. 4.2.8 for KDP publishing also apply to publishing with Smashwords – in those cases, the information might not be repeated again here. Also, I'm not going to include all of the reminders again (like mentioning, "See Sec. 4.2.5 regarding how to set your list price").

1. Visit the Smashwords homepage at www.smashwords.com.
2. Sign up for a new account and login to it.
3. Click the Dashboard link near the top of the page.
4. Click the Comments/Questions/Customer Support link at the top of the page. Explore the links above, which will answer several questions that you may have. I recommend clicking the Distribution FAQ link and the Earnings & Payment Schedules Link. From the latter, scroll down to "How are earnings calculated?" to learn how Smashwords royalties are computed for sales through a variety of eReaders.
5. When you're finished exploring the options in Step 4, scroll up to the top of the page and return to your dashboard (by clicking the Dashboard link).
6. Read the free *Smashwords Style Guide* and revise the formatting of your eBook, if necessary. This guide is actually short, although when you first open the file it might seem rather long. The guide also tells you how to avoid AutoVetter errors, which is very important because your eBook won't be included in the Smashwords catalog until all AutoVetter errors have been resolved. <u>Don't</u> stop reading when the guide you reach the Frequently Asked Questions – there are many useful notes beyond that section, such as formatting tips and requirements for the title and copyright pages.
7. The formatting of an eBook is a little different for SmashWords than other eBook publishing services. Here are a few examples:
    a. There is a 5 MB limit on the size of your content file (compare to 20 MB with Nook and 50 MB with Kindle).
    b. Save your content file as a Word document with a .doc (not .docx) extension.

c. Your cover file should be in JPEG format.

d. Your cover image must be at least 1400 pixels wide; 1600 x 2400 is the recommended cover image size. The exact title and author must appear on your cover image. The price may not appear on your cover image. You can't have a hyperlink or web address on your cover, or advertisements.

e. You must have a special note in the copyright page of your eBook. Either include "Smashwords Edition" or "Published by ___ at Smashwords" where you fill in the blank (___) with your name (don't underline your name, of course). Place this on its own line in the copyright page (without the quotes, of course).

f. You must use the bookmark method for creating an Active Table of Contents, and not Word's built-in table of contents tool (see Sec. 2.2.8). Also, you need to bookmark the Table of Contents heading (but <u>don't</u> add a hyperlink to it) and name this bookmark ref_TOC.

g. If you have any bookmarks that are not part of your Table of Contents, rename them with a ref_ at the beginning of the names of those bookmarks.

h. Smashwords does <u>not</u> support Word's cross-referencing tool. If you used any field codes, you must remove them (consult the *Smashwords Style Guide*).

i. Read the note near the end of Sec. 4.2.2 regarding pixel count (600 x 800) and full-screen images potentially appearing larger than the eReader screen.

j. Prices at Apple must end in .99 (like $2.99 or $3.99). If you want to have the same list price everywhere (some eReaders require their list price to be no higher than anywhere else), you should price your eBook with this in mind.

8. When you are prepared to publish your eBook with Smashwords, click the Publish link at the top of your dashboard.

9. Enter the information for your eBook. Upload the cover and content files.

10. Preview the Smashwords edition of your eBook very carefully in Word before you upload your files. When you press the Publish button, your eBook will show up on the Smashwords website. You want your eBook to be as nicely formatted as possible when you first publish it, since your eBook may be highly visible for 15 minutes or so on their homepage after you click the Publish button.

11. When you finish entering the information and uploading your files, read the publishing agreement carefully, and if you accept the agreement click the Publish button.

12. Read Step 27 of the *Smashwords Style Guide* to learn how to preview the various formats of your eBook file. Check these files carefully and revise any content issues.

13. You will receive an AutoVetter report regarding the formatting of your eBook (not as observed by a person, but based on criteria that a computer program is looking for). Read your AutoVetter report and correct any issues that are flagged. These issues can significantly affect the distribution of your eBook, or the lack thereof. Check the *Smashwords Style Guide* for common AutoVetter errors.

14. Track sales of your eBooks in the Dashboard section of your Smashwords account.
15. If you have problems, issues, questions, concerns, or just want to meet fellow Smashwords authors, see Sec. 4.2.12.

4.2.11 Publishing with Other eReader Companies

If you opted not to participate in the KDP Select program (described in Sec. 4.2.7), I recommend maximizing the visibility of your eBook by publishing your eBook with several eReaders. Once you've published your eBook with a couple of different eReaders, you should find that the process becomes easier and that the steps are very similar.

Not every eBook publishing service has a strong reputation among authors or readers. The big three – i.e. Kindle, Nook, and Sony – have built strong reputations both among many authors and readers. Before you publish with other eBook companies, I recommend talking with other authors and/or readers about their experiences with those companies. While many of these companies do have good reputations, there are some common complaints with a few eBook publishing services – so it would be wise to learn what these are from your fellow authors before you publish your eBook with them.

There are more eBook publishing services than the couple that I'm listing below. I just selected a couple to help you get started; you can find many other brands at Smashwords. If you would like to find more eBook publishing services, try using your favorite internet search engine.

➤ You can publish with Kobo, Inc. by visiting www.kobobooks.com, scrolling down to the bottom of the page, clicking the Authors & Publishers link, and then clicking Kobo Writing Life.
➤ Check out www.apple.com/itunes/sellcontent, which has information related to publishing iBooks for the iPad or iPhone. Click the Online Application link under Sell Your Books. Click the Learn More link to see important details. Note that Smashwords (Sec. 4.2.10) is an Apple-approved aggregator. Return to the previous webpage (if you clicked the Learn More link) and explore the iAuthor tool, which includes a lot of cool features exclusively for designing a book for the iPad.

4.2.12 Get Additional Help, Meet Fellow Authors, or Find Support for Your eBook

If you come across problems and can't find the solution in this book (such as needing more help with picture formatting), remember that you can discuss your publishing experiences with other self-published authors at the following community help forums. There is a good chance that other authors have had the same problem and figured out a solution, and someone will likely to be happy to help you. These forums are also a good place to go if you have questions, concerns, or would like to meet fellow self-published authors. In addition to community help forums, eBook publishing services also have support pages with instructions for how to publishing your eBook, frequently asked questions, and a method of contacting a representative with help. There is also a good chance that you will find the answer to your problem/question/concern/issue if you type your issue into the search field of your favorite internet search engine. The important thing to remember is that you are not alone. There are thousands of other self-published authors who are encountering similar problems when they self-publish their eBooks. Many authors have valuable advice that they could share – often, wisdom that they have gained from their mistakes – if only someone would ask for help.

The community help forum for Kindle eBooks can be found at:

https://kdp.amazon.com/community/index.jspa

Also try searching Kindle's self-publishing help pages:

https://kdp.amazon.com/self-publishing/help

If you need to submit revisions, look for the heading "Updating Your Published Book" on the left-hand side of the webpage – if there are significant changes, click on the Notifying Customers of Book Updates link. Two other useful links are Conversion Resources and the Frequently Asked Questions. Also explore the "Featured Guides" for more help. It is possible to delete a title from your dashboard, which will make it impossible for a customer to purchase your eBook, but it may not completely remove all trace of your eBook from the internet.

The Nook Press community help forum for Nook eBooks is available at:

http://bookclubs.barnesandnoble.com/t5/NOOK-Press-Help-Board/bd-p/NOOKpress

To access Nook Press's help and support pages, simply click the Support tab at the top of your Nook Press dashboard.

Smashwords provides a wealth of help directly on their website – such as self-publishing style and marketing guides (see Sec. 4.2.10), support pages (click the Comments/questions/customer support link at the top of the page), and a FAQ link and a How to Publish on Smashwords link at the top of their homepage (you can see both of these when you're *not* logged in to your account). On their homepage, scroll down and look on the left to find useful links under "Publish on Smashwords." Just below that, you can find "Socialbuzz," with links to FaceBook and Twitter if you're interested in meeting other authors who have self-published eBooks with Smashwords.

Remember, you can also contact the eBook publisher directly – try looking for "contact us" options in their support and help pages.

Note: Writing and publishing your book is only half the battle. Almost all highly successful books derive their success from effective marketing strategies.

Volume 2 is scheduled for release in April, 2013.

Learn what to look for when you proof your paperback book and preview your eBook, how to create an author page at Amazon and your own author website, useful tips about Amazon's website, and free and low-cost marketing strategies.

Volume 2 Contents

5 Editing Your Proof
     Proofing Your Paperback   Proofing Your eBook
6 Creating Author Pages
     Creating an Author Page at Amazon   Creating Your Own Websites
7 Useful Tips about Amazon and Other Booksellers
     Understanding Amazon's Website   Exploring Other Online Booksellers
8 Marketing Strategies
     Low-Cost Marketing Ideas   Other Marketing Options

RESOURCES

Here you will find a collection of handy resources, all of which are conveniently and freely available on the web. My intention was <u>not</u> to compile a comprehensive list of every possible resource, as I didn't think it would be as useful if you had to sort through a long list to discover a few helpful resources. Instead, I limited this collection to resources which I believed would be very handy to most readers. Also, by limiting the list to popular resources, this list is much less likely to become quickly outdated. You can easily find more resources – as most of the following websites provide several links to yet other resources.

Let's begin with a few major online booksellers of physical books – namely, paperback and hardcover – books:

www.amazon.com
www.barnesandnoble.com
www.booksamillion.com

Following are the websites for some major online bookstores that sell eBooks (these are the bookstores where the eBooks are sold – <u>not</u> the same as where you publish the eBook):

www.amazon.com/kindlestore
www.barnesandnoble.com/nook
www.ebookstore.sony.com (now closed; use Kobo books)
www.kobobooks.com
www.apple.com/apps/ibooks
www.smashwords.com

If instead you want a few major websites for where you can publish your eBook, look here:

kdp.amazon.com
www.nookpress.com
www.kobobooks.com/kobowritinglife
www.smashwords.com

Here is CreateSpace's website, where you can publish a paperback book:

www.createspace.com

If you need help formatting or publishing your eBook, try searching these help pages:

kdp.amazon.com/self-publishing/help

For Smashwords, click the link at the top of their homepage. For Nook, login to Nook Press and click Support. For Kobo, login to Kobo Writing Life and click Learning Center.

Another way to get help is to use the community help forums. You can also meet fellow self-published authors and share ideas. CreateSpace even allows you to post a preview of a portion of your book and solicit opinions and advice. Who knows, some people you meet here may even buy your book. ☺ But don't explicitly promote your work here. Your best chance of selling books this way is when someone gets interested in your work and clicks on your profile – every post you write is a sample of your writing style, personality, and character. Here are the links to community help forums for Kindle and Nook Press. At CreateSpace, click Community. For Smashwords, look for "Socialbuzz" on their homepage.

https://kdp.amazon.com/community/index.jspa

http://bookclubs.barnesandnoble.com/t5/NOOK-Press-Help-Board/bd-p/NOOKpress

Following are a few publishing or marketing guides that are both free and very useful. All of these are available for free from Amazon (if you don't have a Kindle, you can download the free Kindle for PC software). The Kindle guide is also available in PDF format from the KDP self-publishing help pages (see the previous page). The second Kindle guide below is also available in a few other languages, and there is also an English guide for Mac users. The Smashwords guides are also available directly from their website in a variety of formats.

Publish on Amazon Kindle with Kindle Direct Publishing

Building Your Book for Kindle by Kindle Direct Publishing

Smashwords Style Guide by Mark Coker

Smashwords Book Marketing Guide by Mark Coker

Secrets to Ebook Publishing Success by Mark Coker

If you want to visit Amazon's non-US websites, look here:

www.amazon.co.uk (United Kingdom)

www.amazon.ca (Canada)

www.amazon.es (Spain)

www.amazon.fr (France)

www.amazon.de (Germany)

www.amazon.it (Italy)

www.amazon.cn (China)

www.amazon.co.jp (Japan)

Following are some major social media websites:

www.facebook.com

www.facebook.com/publishedauthors

www.twitter.com

www.myspace.com

Looking for applications that can help you format your Kindle eBook? Click the Tools and Resources link on the left-hand side of the KDP self-publishing help page (see the bottom of the first page of this Resources list) under Preparing Your Book.

Every author should have an Author Page at Amazon's Author Central (as described in detail in Chapter 6). The US Amazon Central website is listed below. For other Amazon websites, visit that country's Amazon page, search for a book that has an Author Page, click on that author's Author Page, and find the link for Author Central (it will sure be handy if you speak the native language, or if you can find a friend or acquaintance who does). Some countries, like Canada, may not have an Author Central feature.

https://authorcentral.amazon.com

Here are a couple of websites where you can posts blogs:

www.twitter.com

www.wordpress.com

www.blogger.com

You can purchase ISBN's directly from Bowker at:

www.myidentifiers.com

The homepage for the Library of Congress is listed below, along with a website that provides more information about LCCN assignment.

www.loc.gov/index.html

www.booksandtales.com/pod/aloc.php

Adobe provides a free reader for viewing PDF files and also sells professional PDF conversion software (but, remember, you can convert to PDF for free using Microsoft Word). Another useful PDF converter is Nuance's PDF Converter Professional.

www.adobe.com

www.nuance.com

Want to learn more about the use of color (which may be relevant when you design your cover, for example)? One place to look is HGTV. Click the Color Guide link at the top of HGTV's homepage:

www.hgtv.com

THE AUTHOR

Chris McMullen has written and self-published over a dozen paperback books with CreateSpace and over a dozen eBooks. He enjoys writing books, drawing illustrations on the computer, editing manuscripts, and especially the feeling of having produced a professional-looking self-published book from cover-to-cover.

Chris McMullen holds a Ph.D. in physics from Oklahoma State University, and presently teaches physics at Northwestern State University of Louisiana. Having published a half-dozen papers on the collider phenomenology of large, extra, superstring-inspired extra dimensions, he first wrote a two-volume book on the geometry and physics of the fourth dimension geared toward a general audience, entitled *The Visual Guide to Extra Dimensions*. When he learned about self-publishing on Amazon through CreateSpace, he wrote a variety of golf and chess log books, and published these to gain some experience as a self-publisher before self-publishing his work on the fourth dimension.

Since then, Chris McMullen has self-published numerous math workbooks, a couple of books on self-publishing, and several word scramble puzzle books. The math workbooks were written in response to his observation, as a teacher, that many students need to develop greater fluency in fundamental techniques in mathematics. He began writing word scramble books along with his coauthor, Carolyn Kivett, when he realized that it was possible to make over a thousand words using only the elements on the periodic table. Chris McMullen and Carolyn Kivett first published a variety of chemical word scrambles using elements from the periodic table, and have since published several 'ordinary' word scrambles using the English alphabet instead of chemical symbols.

Check out the blog with free self-publishing resources:
        http://chrismcmullen.wordpress.com
The author website: https://chrismcmullen.com
Email: chrism@chrismcmullen.com
Facebook author page:
   https://www.facebook.com/pages/Chris-Mcmullen/390266614410127
Twitter: @ChrisDMcMullen

Free marketing opportunity created by Chris McMullen:
        http://readtuesday.com

CATALOG

Self-Publishing

How to Self-Publish a Book on Amazon.com
A Detailed Guide to Self-Publishing with Amazon and Other Online Booksellers, Vol. 1
A Detailed Guide to Self-Publishing with Amazon and Other Online Booksellers, Vol. 2

The Fourth Dimension

The Visual Guide to Extra Dimensions, Vol. 1
The Visual Guide to Extra Dimensions, Vol. 2
Full Color Illustrations of the Fourth Dimension, Vol. 1
Full Color Illustrations of the Fourth Dimension, Vol. 2

Science Books

Understand Basic Chemistry Concepts
Understand Basic Chemistry Concepts (Large Size & Large Print Edition)
An Introduction to Basic Astronomy Concepts (with Space Photos)
An Introduction to Basic Astronomy Concepts (Black-and-white Edition)
Basic Astronomy Concepts Everyone Should Know (with Space Photos)
The Observational Astronomy Skywatcher Notebook
An Advanced Introduction to Calculus-Based Physics (Mechanics)
A Guide to Thermal Physics
Creative Physics Problems, Vol. 1
Creative Physics Problems, Vol. 2
Creative Physics Problems for Physics with Calculus, Vol. 1
Creative Physics Problems for Physics with Calculus, Vol. 2
A Research-Oriented Laboratory Manual for First-Year Physics
Laboratory Notebook for Physics Experiments

Improve Your Math Fluency Series

Addition Facts Practice Book
Subtraction Facts Practice Book
Multiplication Facts Practice Book
Division Facts Practice Book
10,000 Addition Problems Practice Workbook
10,000 Subtraction Problems Practice Workbook
7,000 Multiplication Problems Practice Workbook
4,500 Multiplication Problems with Answers Practice Workbook
Master Long Division Practice Workbook
Addition and Subtraction Applied to Clocks
Practice Adding, Subtracting, Multiplying, and Dividing Fractions Workbook
Practice Adding, Subtracting, Multiplying, and Dividing Mixed Fractions Workbook
Practice Arithmetic with Decimals Workbook
Practice Addition, Subtraction, Multiplication, and Division with Negative Numbers Workbook
Fractions, Decimals, & Percents Math Workbook (Includes Repeating Decimals)
Algebra Essentials Practice Workbook with Answers
Trigonometry Essentials Practice Workbook with Answers

Radial Math Workbooks

Radial Arithmetic Facts Math Workbook (Adding and Subtracting 1-12)
Radial Arithmetic Facts Math Workbook (Multiplying and Dividing 1-12)
Radial Math Arithmetic Workbook (Addition and Subtraction)
Radial Math Arithmetic Workbook (Multiplication and Division)
Radial Math Long Division with Remainders Workbook
Radial Fractions Math Workbook (Addition and Subtraction)
Radial Fractions Math Workbook (Multiplication and Division)

Pyramid Math Workbooks

Pyramid Arithmetic Addition and Subtraction Math Workbook
Pyramid Arithmetic Multiplication Math Workbook
Pyramid Arithmetic Long Division (without Remainders) Math Workbook
Pyramid Arithmetic Long Division Math Workbook
Pyramid Fractions – Fraction Addition and Subtraction Workbook
Pyramid Fractions – Fraction Multiplication and Division Workbook
Pyramid Fractions, Decimals, & Percents – Fraction Basics Math Workbook

Word Scramble Puzzle Books (Coauthored)

Christmas Word Scrambles
Fun Word Scrambles for Kids
Football Word Scrambles
Golf Word Scrambles
Teen Word Scrambles for Girls
Song & Artist Music Word Scrambles
Negative/Positive Antonym Word Scrambles Book
Positive Word Scrambles (A Fun Way to Think Happy Words)
Positive Word Scrambles (Fun Positive Visualization)
English-French Word Scrambles (Level 1 Basic)
English-Spanish Word Scrambles (Level 1 Basic)
Igpay Atinlay Ordway Amblesscray
Word Scrambles that Make You Think
VErBAl ReAcTiONS – Word Scrambles with a Chemical Flavor (Easy)
VErBAl ReAcTiONS – Word Scrambles with a Chemical Flavor (Medium)
VErBAl ReAcTiONS – Word Scrambles with a Chemical Flavor (Hard)
Chemical Word Scrambles Anyone Can Do (Easy)
Chemical Word Scrambles Anyone Can Do (Medium)
Chemical Word Scrambles Anyone Can Do (Hard)
Travel-Size Chemical Word Scrambles (Easy to Medium)

Chess Books

The Chess Match Log Book
Make a Personalized Book of 500 Chess Positions

Golf Books

The Golf Stats Log Book
The Golf Stats Scorecard Book
The End-Of-Round Golf Diary
The Practice Session Golf Diary
A Scorecard Sketchbook for 50 Rounds of Golf

Self-Publishing eBooks

How to Self-Publish a Book on Amazon.com
A Detailed Guide to Self-Publishing with Amazon and Other Online Booksellers, Vol. 1
A Detailed Guide to Self-Publishing with Amazon and Other Online Booksellers, Vol. 2

Math eBooks

Digital Addition Flash Cards in Color (Ordered and Shuffled 1-9)
Digital Subtraction Flash Cards in Color (1-9 Shuffled Twice)
Digital Multiplication Flash Cards in Color (Ordered and Shuffled 1-9)
Digital Division Flash Cards in Color (1-9 Shuffled Twice)
Far Out Addition Flash Cards 1-12 (Decorated with Shuttle, Astronaut, and Satellite Photos)
Far Out Multiplication Flash Cards 1-12 (Decorated with Solar System Photos)
Counting Numbers 1-20 Astronomy (with NASA Space Photos)
Trigonometry Flash Cards: Memorize Values of Trig Functions

Science eBooks

Understand Basic Chemistry Concepts
Understand Basic Chemistry Concepts (in Color)
An Introduction to Basic Astronomy Concepts (with Space Photos)
Basic Astronomy Concepts Everyone Should Know (With Space Photos)

Word Scramble eBooks (Coauthored)

Teen Word Scrambles for Girls
Word Scrambles that Make You Think

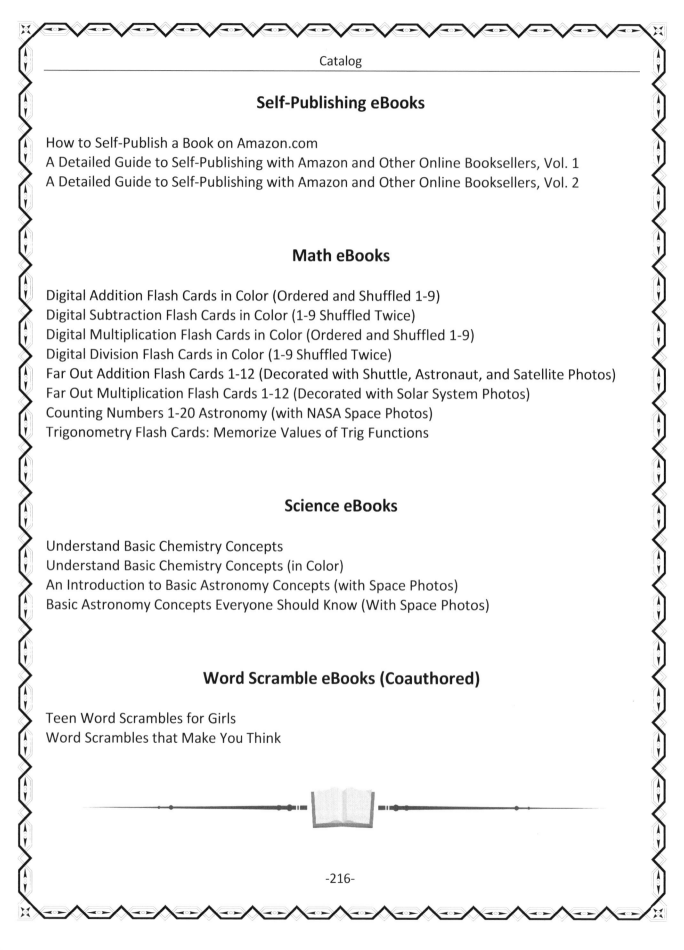

The Visual Guide to Extra Dimensions takes you on a journey into the fourth dimension. It begins with some fascinating features of the second dimension: Intuitively, it might seem like the second dimension should be easier to understand than the third dimension, but it turns out that the second dimension has some surprising features. Most of the book is dedicated toward understanding the fourth dimension – the geometry and physics of a fourth dimension, not spirituality or religion. There are some novel figures of a variety of 4D objects – not just the standard tesseracts and hyperspheres, but other geometric objects like the hecatonicosachoron and spherinder. The book helps you visualize what it would be like to walk on a 4D staircase, for example.

UNdErSTaNd BaSiC Chemistry CoNCePtS focuses on fundamental chemistry concepts, such as understanding the periodic table of the elements and how chemical bonds are formed. No prior knowledge of chemistry is assumed. The mathematical component involves only basic arithmetic. The content is much more conceptual than mathematical. It is geared toward helping anyone – student or not – to understand the main ideas of chemistry. Both students and non-students may find it helpful to be able to focus on understanding the main concepts without the constant emphasis on computations that is generally found in chemistry lectures and textbooks.

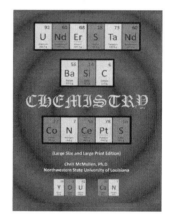

This *Christmas Word Scrambles* book consists of words or phrases that relate to Christmas where the letters have been scrambled. Solve each puzzle by rearranging the letters to form the word or phrase. For example, rearranging the letters T R O F Y S, we can form the word F R O S T Y. Each puzzle consists of a group of related words or phrases, such as common Christmas cookie shapes or images from a Nativity scene. Knowing that the words in each puzzle are related may help you unscramble any words or phrases that you don't see right away. A hints section at the back of the book provides the first letter of each answer, which is handy if you just need a little help; a separate section provides the answers so that you can check your solutions.

CHECK IT OUT

Here are a few cool paperbacks that were published with CreateSpace:[66]

- ❖ *No Naked Numbers* by Christine King and Sequoia Mulgrave. This is a really neat concept and a great way of getting young students engaged in the concept of units (like meters, yards, and inches) – and also to understand it well. It also helps to develop basic problem-solving skills.
- ❖ *Adam's Gluten Free Surprise: Helping Others Understand Gluten Free* by Debbie Simpson. This book features a neat idea – it reads like a nicely illustrated children's book while at the same time spreading awareness of gluten allergies. In almost every classroom there are kids with some type of allergy, so this book is useful for its lesson in social situations even for kids who can't personally relate to the gluten allergy.
- ❖ *Through These Eyes* by Michael Risley and Tom Bradford. I recommend that you take a look at this cover – it's a simple design, yet quite effective. Don't copy the same idea; rather, I hope that this cover will help to inspire a simple, effective design of your own. If you enjoy legal thrillers, you might like the content, too.
- ❖ *Wacky Sentences Handwriting Workbook (Reproducible)* by Julie Harper. If you have children in elementary school and would like a fun way for them to practice their cursive writing skills, this is a neat workbook.
- ❖ *My First Kakuro Book: 200 Puzzles* by DJAPE. If you love math, enjoy puzzles, and like to sit down and figure things out on your own, this is a great way to learn how to solve Kakuro puzzles. The puzzles start out small and grow so that you can learn the technique (without step-by-step instructions – as I implied, this type of puzzle is for people who like to figure things out by themselves). I love it more than Sudoku.
- ❖ *Silly Monsters ABC* by Gerald Hawksley. This book is available both in paperback and on Kindle. This is one of a myriad of self-published kids' ABC books on the market, but is quite well done. Each page features a colorful silly monster, a few words that start with a particular letter, and an interesting sentence.
- ❖ Find more: Search for CreateSpace Independent Publishing Platform on Amazon.

---

[66] Except for Julie Harper (whom I know personally), I have not met any of these authors. I simply found these books on Amazon (except for Julie Harper's workbook, which I discovered in person) and thought that they were cool. The authors did <u>not</u> pay to have their books included here, and they did <u>not</u> contact me to advertise for them. When this book was published, they had <u>no</u> idea that I would be including their books on such a list.

INDEX

A

A-to-Z Guarantee, 159
AbeBooks, 159
about the author, 46, 65, 138-9, 188-9, 202, 211-2
academic institutions, 159, 172
accent characters, 54
acknowledgments, 45
active hyperlinks, 64-5
active table of contents, 62-64, 205
Adobe InDesign, 21
Adobe PDF, 167, 211
Adobe PhotoShop, 105
adult content, 174
affiliate hyperlinks, 64
afterword, 46
Aldiko, 203-6
align tool, 110-1, 122, 124-5
alignment, 32
Amazon
    A-to-Z Guarantee, 159
    about, 6, 132-4
    Advantage, 176
    Associates, 177
    Author Central, 136, 138, 173, 189, 211
    Canada, 162, 175, 210
    categories, 139-43, 173-4, 195
        tip for special categories, 141
    China, 162, 210
    Countdown Deal, 197
    CreateSpace (see CreateSpace)
    Customers Also Bought, 176, 196
    Europe, 103-4, 140, 144-5, 154-5, 159, 161-2, 172, 175, 177, 191, 193
    formatting guides, 210
    four-for-three program, 147, 152, 154
    France, 144, 161-2, 175, 210
    free shipping, 148-50, 154, 160-1, 195-6
    Fulfillment by Amazon, 159
    Germany, 144, 161-2, 175, 210
    Great Britain, 103-4, 144-5, 154-5, 161-2, 172, 175, 177, 191, 193, 210

    guidelines, 179, 199, 210
    India, 197
    Italy, 144, 154, 161-2, 175, 210
    Japan, 162, 210
    keywords, 139-43, 169, 173, 194-5
        tip for special categories, 141
    Kindle (see Kindle)
    Kindlegen, 186, 190
    Last 30 Days/Last 90 Days, 173
    linking multiple formats, 178, 192-3, 198
    Look Inside, 134, 176
    MatchBook, 10, 197
    Mexico, 175
    .mobi, 191, 199
    Mobipocket Creator, 186, 190
    new releases, 173
    Prime, 195-6
    product page, 134-43, 176
    royalty, 143-4, 172, 177-8, 189-94, 200-1
    sales rank, 173, 176, 192, 196
    Search Inside, 45, 134, 176
    search results, 139-43, 169, 173, 176, 192
    second category, 174, 195
    Spain, 144, 154, 161-2, 175, 210
    Special Offers, 148, 154, 160
    Super Saver Shipping, 148-50, 154, 160-1, 195-6
    United Kingdom, 103-4, 144-5, 154-5, 161-2, 172, 175, 177, 191, 193, 210
    website, 209
Amazon Advantage, 176
Amazon Associates, 177
appendix, 46
Apple, 180, 182, 184, 203-6, 209
approve proof, 175-7
arc tool, 109, 113-6
arrow (symbol), 36, 54-5
arrow tool, 108-10, 114-6
artistic effects, 121
aspect ratio, 57-8, 107, 111, 125, 130, 182-7
asterisks, 54, 136
attorney
    commercial use, 34, 118-9
    contracts, 169

copyright, 37-8, 45, 54, 118, 169, 175, 188
    fair use, 37-8
    fictional works, 45
    image use, 118-9
    law, 37-8, 45, 169, 175, 188
    pen name, 169
    trademark, 54, 175, 188, 199
    works for hire, 169
    written permission, 37-8
author biography, 138-9, 173, 179, 188-9, 202,
    211-2
Author Central, 136, 138, 173, 189, 211
author cost, 143-5
author names, 81, 98-104, 168-9, 175-6, 194, 199,
    202
author page, 46, 65, 138-9, 173, 211-2
author photo, 65, 125
autocorrect, 43, 53
autoformat, 53
automated print check, 171
automatic indents, 51
AutoVetter errors, 204-5

B

baby, 174
back matter, 46-7
background, 117-8, 120, 124-5
Baker & Taylor, 159, 203-6
bar code, 82, 93, 103, 157
Barnes & Noble
    in store, 15-6, 165-6
    ISBN, 155, 194, 202
    Nook device, 130, 180-2, 184-5, 187, 191, 201
    Nook Press, 180-2, 184, 187, 191, 193-4, 197,
        201-7, 209-10
    Nook publishing, 180-2, 184, 187, 191, 193-4,
        197, 201-6
    Nook store, 209
    online, 15, 158-9, 209
    pricing, 181, 193, 202
    product page, 134
    PubIt (see Nook Press)
behind text, 59, 117, 124-5
bevel, 96, 108, 122

bibliography, 36-8, 46
biography, 138-9, 173, 179, 188-9, 202
BISAC category, 173-4, 195, 202
    tip for special categories, 141
black-and-white interior, 28-9, 170
blank linespaces
    eBook, 53-4
    paperback, 33
bleed, 26, 88, 93, 171
blog page, 65, 212
Blogger, 211
blurb
    back cover, 81-2, 103, 136
    CreateSpace, 169
    eBook, 187-9, 198, 202
    Kindle, 187-9, 198
    Nook, 202
    paperback, 134-7, 169
    product page, 134-7, 169, 187-9, 198, 202
BMP file, 128
boldface
    cover, 100
    eBook, 48, 53-4
    paperback, 35
book blurb
    back cover, 81-2, 103, 136
    CreateSpace, 169
    eBook, 187-9, 198, 202
    Kindle, 187-9, 198
    Nook, 202
    paperback, 134-7, 169
    product page, 134-7, 169, 187-9, 198, 202
book cost, 143-5
book covers
    author names, 81, 98-104
    back cover, 81-2
    background, 117-8, 120, 124-5
    bar code, 82, 93, 103, 157
    bleed, 88, 93
    book covers, 66-130
    callout, 102-3
    centering, 99-104
    color shift, 84-6, 105
    cover art, 124-5
    cover blurb, 81-2, 103, 136
    cover guide, 87-93, 98-104, 117-8, 125
    design, 82-4, 126-7, 171, 179

eBook, 127-130, 199, 202, 205
file size limits, 189-92, 202
finding sample covers, 67
flattening, 86, 166
front cover, 81
full-cover spreads, 68-80
glossy, 13
help, 126-7
ISBN, 82, 93, 103
live elements, 88
matte, 13
paperback, 67-127
price, 81, 103-4
printing tolerance, 86-7
professional, 171
sample covers, 68-80, 104
services, 126-7, 171, 179
size, 87-8, 130, 189-91, 205
spine text, 14, 81, 87, 102-3
spine width, 87
starburst, 102-3
subtitle, 101
template, 126
temporary edges, 87-93
thumbnail, 82-4, 100, 125, 127-30
title, 81, 98-104
trim size, 87-8, 117
UPC, 82, 93, 103
view, 98, 125, 130
book description
    back cover, 81-2, 103, 136
    CreateSpace, 169
    eBook, 187-9, 198, 202
    Kindle, 187-9, 198
    Nook, 202
    paperback, 134-7, 169
    product page, 134-7, 169, 187-9, 198, 202
book reviews, 136, 196, 198
bookmark hyperlinks, 51, 62-5, 205
Books-A-Million, 158, 209
Books in Print, 157
bookstores
    approaching, 164-6
    chain, 165-6
    distribution channel, 172
    ISBN, 155-6
    local, 164-6

prospects, 15-6, 157-66
borders
    eBook, 47-49
    paperback, 29-30
    pictures, 121
borrows, 193, 195-7
Bowker, R.R.
    description, 12
    ISBN, 156-7, 194, 199, 202, 211
brackets, 37
brand names, 188
bring forward/backward, 111
British English, 161, 175
browse categories, 139-43, 173-4, 195, 202
    tip for special categories, 141
browser, 171, 199
Building Your Book for Kindle, 210
bullets
    eBook, 48, 50
    paperback, 33

C

calculator, 144
callout, 101-2
can tool, 114
Canada, 162, 175, 210
caps, 35, 136
captions, 40, 112, 124
catalog, 46, 65, 213-8
Cataloging in Publication, 163
categories, 139-43, 173-4, 195, 202
    tip for special categories, 141
centered, 32, 54, 99-104, 110, 117
certified wholesalers, 158
character count, 135, 138, 140, 169, 173, 194, 202
character limit, 135, 138, 140, 169, 173, 194, 202
chart, 124
check it out, 218
children's, 174
China, 162, 210
Chris McMullen, 212
CIP, 163
citations, 37-8, 46
clipart, 43-4, 118-9

Index

CMYK, 84-5, 105
coauthor, 169
color adjust, 121
color design, 211
color interior, 28-9, 170
color shift, 84-6, 105
columns
    eBook, 51
    paperback, 30
comments, 43
commercial use, 34, 118-9
community forums, 15, 47-9, 65, 126-7, 134, 171, 197, 199, 206-7, 210
composite images, 110-6
compressing images, 58-9, 120, 123, 190
contact support, 134, 167, 174, 199-200, 204, 206-7, 209-10
content file size limits, 57-8, 181, 186, 189-92, 199-200, 202, 204
content guidelines, 179, 199
contents
    bookmarks (**best method**), 62-4, 205
    eBook, 49, 62-3
    paperback, 45
    Smashwords, 205
    table of contents tool, 62-3
contracts, 169
contributors, 169, 199, 202
conversion services, 47-9, 65, 181
conversion to PDF, 42, 123, 125-7, 166-7, 211
converting currency, 154
copy and paste, 41, 111, 168, 170, 198
copyright
    commercial use, 34, 118-9
    contracts, 169
    fair use, 37-8
    fictional works, 45
    image use, 118-9
    law, 37-8, 45, 169, 175, 188
    notice, 44-5, 163
    page, 44-5, 52, 81, 100, 102, 155, 163, 168, 170, 179, 199, 204-5
    pen name, 169
    symbol, 54
    trademark, 54, 175, 188, 199
    works for hire, 169
    written permission, 37-8

corrections, 200
Countdown Deal, 197
country of publication, 173
coupons, 203
cover art, 124-5
cover blurb, 81-2, 103, 136
cover guide, 87-93, 98-104, 117-8, 125
cover size, 87-8, 130, 189-91, 205
cover template, 126
covers (see book covers)
cream paper, 14, 170
CreateSpace
    about, 6-16, 132-4
    approve proof, 175-7
    benefits, 10
    biography, 138-9, 173, 179
    book description, 134-7, 169, 179
    bookstores, 15-6, 157-66, 172
    categories, 139-43, 173-4
        tip for special categories, 141
    community forum, 15, 47-9, 65, 126-7, 134, 171, 210
    contact, 134, 167, 174, 199
    conversion, 48-9, 181
    Cover Creator, 126, 166, 172
    CreateSpace Direct, 158, 166, 172
    description of, 6
    discount codes, 177
    distribution channels, 172
    eStore, 133-4, 144, 159, 162-4, 172, 177
    Europe, 103-4, 140, 144-5, 154-5, 159, 161-2, 172, 175, 177
    Expanded Distribution (see Expanded Distribution)
    Expert Setup, 168-9, 172
    file review, 172, 174
    glossy covers, 13
    Great Britain, 103-4, 144-5, 154-5, 161-2, 172, 175, 177
    Guided Setup, 167-72
    guidelines, 179
    Interior Reviewer, 171
    ISBN, 12, 82, 93, 103, 155-7, 159, 176
    keywords, 139-43, 169, 173
        tip for special categories, 141
    Kindle, 48-9, 178
    libraries, 159, 162-4, 172

link to Kindle, 178, 192-3, 198
MatchBook, 10, 197
matte covers, 13
Member Dashboard, 168, 170
proof, 175-7
publishing, 132-179
royalties, 143-55, 157, 172, 177-8
royalty reports, 177-8
sales reports, 177
second category, 174
services, 15, 47-9, 65, 126-7, 134, 170-1, 179, 181
step-by-step, 167-179
submit files for review, 174
support, 134, 167, 174, 209, 210
title/subtitle, 81, 98-104, 139-43, 168, 175-6, 179
United Kingdom, 103-4, 144-5, 154-5, 161-2, 172, 175, 177
website, 209
What's This, 168, 174
cropping, 58, 121, 123
cross-references, 36-7, 50, 205
crowdSPRING, 171
cube, 113, 115
curly quotes, 51
currency conversion, 154
curve tool, 108-10, 114, 116
customer reviews, 196, 198, 200
Customers Also Bought, 176, 196
cylinder, 114

D

dash (punctuation), 51
dashboard
    CreateSpace, 168, 170
    Kindle, 198, 201
    Nook, 203
    Smashwords, 204, 206
dashes (drawing), 96
date of publication, 173, 199
dedications, 45
delayed royalties, 161, 178
delivery fee, 58, 189-92

depth, 108, 114
description
    back cover, 81-2, 103
    eBook, 187-9, 198, 202
    Kindle, 187-9, 198
    of CreateSpace, 169
    Nook, 202
    paperback, 134-7, 169, 179
    product page, 134-7, 169, 179, 187-9, 202
Diesel, 203-6
Digital Rights Management, 199, 202
discount codes, 177, 203
display size, 181-7
distribute images, 111
.doc/.docx files, 21-2, 42, 56, 60-1, 105, 111, 171, 190, 199, 202, 204
dot, 110
downloadable previewer, 200
DPI, 167
dragging objects, 94, 107-9, 113
drawing, 105-16
DRM, 199, 202
drop caps
    eBook, 51-3
    paperback, 34

E

eBooks
    Amazon Kindle (see Kindle)
    Apple, 180, 182, 184, 203-6, 209
    Barnes & Noble (see Barnes & Noble)
    book description, 187-9, 198, 202
    concept, 16-8
    conversion services, 48-9, 181
    conversion warning, 181
    delivery fee, 58, 189-92
    Digital Rights Management, 199, 202
    file size limits, 181, 186, 189-92, 199-200, 202, 204
    formatting, 18-9, 47-65, 180-1, 198
    Google Nexus, 182
    guide books, 210
    indents, 48-53
    iPad, 180, 182, 184-5, 200, 203-6

iPhone, 180, 184-5, 200, 203-6
Kindle Direct Publishing (see Kindle)
Kindlegen, 186, 190
Kobo, 182, 184, 194, 197, 203-6, 209
margins, 183, 185
Microsoft Surface, 182, 184-5
.mobi, 191, 199
Mobipocket Creator, 186, 190
non-indents, 52-3
Nook device, 130, 180-2, 184-5, 187, 191, 201
Nook Press, 180-2, 184, 187, 191, 193-4, 197, 201-7, 209-10
pixel count, 57, 130, 184-187, 205
pricing, 17-8, 181, 189-94, 200, 202, 205
Publt (see Nook Press)
publishing, 180-207
royalties, 189-94, 200-1, 204
Samsung Galaxy, 182
Samsung Papyrus, 184
screen size, 183-7
services, 47-9, 65
Smashwords, 180-2, 194, 197, 199, 201-7, 209-10
Sony, 180-2, 184, 194, 197, 203-6, 209
style guide, 204-5, 210
styles, 53-4
tablet, 182, 184-5
economics, 150
edit pictures, 123
edit points, 108, 113, 116
edit shape, 108
editing services, 47, 65, 170, 179
edition number, 198
editions (linking), 178, 188, 192-3, 198
editorial review, 136, 202
effects
    pictures, 122
    shapes, 97, 108
eligibility, 157
em dash, 51
email address hyperlink, 64-5, 212
email resolution, 59, 190
embedding fonts, 167
en dash, 51
endnotes
    eBook, 51
    paperback, 36-7

English/American, 161, 175
enter key problem, 53-4
epub, 199
equations
    equation editor, 22, 38-9
    equations, 38-9, 56, 59-62, 95, 181, 190
    mid-sentence, 59-61
    stand alone, 59-62
eReaders
    Apple, 180, 182, 184, 203-6, 209
    brands, 16, 180-188
    Google Nexus, 182
    iPad, 180, 182, 184-5, 200, 203-6
    iPhone, 180, 184-5, 200, 203-6
    Kindle (see Kindle)
    Kobo, 182, 184, 194, 197, 203-6, 209
    margins, 183, 185
    Microsoft Surface, 182, 184-5
    Nook, 130, 180-2, 184, 187, 191, 197, 201-6
    pixel count, 57, 130, 184-187, 205
    Samsung Galaxy, 182
    Samsung Papyrus, 184
    screen size, 183-7
    Sony, 180-2, 184, 194, 197, 203-6, 209
    tablet, 182, 184-5
eStore, 133-4, 144, 159, 162-4, 172, 177
euro, 103-4, 144-5, 154-5, 172, 175, 191
Europe, 103-4, 140, 144-5, 154-5, 159, 161-2, 172, 175, 177, 191, 193
exclusivity, 195-7
Expanded Distribution
    academic institutions, 159, 172
    Baker & Tayler, 159
    book description, 134, 169, 179
    bookstores, 15-6, 157-66, 172
    Cataloging in Publication, 163
    CIP, 163
    CreateSpace Direct, 158, 166, 172
    distribution, 15, 157-166, 172
    eligibility, 157
    Ingram, 158, 166
    ISBN, 155-7, 159, 176
    LCCN, 162-3, 211
    libraries, 159, 162-4, 172
    Library of Congress, 162-3, 211
    NACSCORP, 158, 166
    PCN, 163

Preassigned Control Number, 163
printing variations, 176
royalties, 143-4, 146, 148-50, 152, 157, 160, 172, 178
selecting channels, 172
third-party sellers, 132, 143, 150, 158-60, 176
trim size, 24-5, 170
wholesalers, 158
Expert Setup, 168-9, 172
external hyperlinks, 64-5

F

Facebook page, 65, 210, 212
fair use, 37-8
fictional works, 45
figures (see pictures)
file corruption, 42, 106
file review, 172, 174
file saving, 41-2, 106, 166-8, 170, 200
file size, 57-8, 181, 186-8, 189-92, 199-200, 202, 204
Firefox, 171, 199
first line indent, 52-3
flattening, 86, 166
floating images, 59
flowchart, 124
follow path, 96-7
font sizes
    cover, 100
    eBook, 48
    paperback, 34
font styles
    eBook, 48, 50, 54-5
    embedding, 167
    paperback, 34-6
footers
    eBook, 47-9
    paperback, 31
footnotes
    eBook, 48, 51
    paperback, 36-7
foreign languages, 154, 162, 173, 175, 199, 202
foreword, 45
formatting
    alignment, 32

bleed, 26, 88, 93, 171
bullets, 33, 48, 50
columns, 30, 51
covers (see book covers)
drawing, 105-16
drop caps, 34, 51-3
eBooks, 18-9, 47-65, 180-1
equations, 38-9, 56, 59-62, 95, 181, 190
footers, 31, 47-9
guide books, 210
guidelines, 199, 210
headers, 31, 47-9
headings, 35, 53-4
indents, 32, 48, 50-4
interior, 20-65
layout, 29-30, 47-9, 130, 167
lists, 33
margins, 27
marks, 50
page numbering, 31, 47-9
paperback, 21-47
paragraphs, 32-3
pictures (see pictures)
section breaks, 30, 54
services, 47, 65, 126-7, 170-1, 179
shapes (see shapes)
Smashwords Style Guide, 204-5, 210
symbols, 35, 48, 50, 54-5, 136
table of contents, 45, 49, 62-3, 205
tables, 39-40, 48, 51, 181, 190, 201
textboxes (see textboxes)
styles, 36, 53-4
unpublished, 198
WordArt (see WordArt)
formulas, 38-9
four-for-three program, 147, 152, 154
France, 144, 154, 161-2, 175, 210
free promotion, 195-7
free shipping, 148-50, 154, 160-1, 195-6
freeform tool, 110
front matter, 44-5
Fulfillment by Amazon, 159
full-color, 28-9, 170
full-justified, 32

G

Galaxy, 182
Germany, 144, 154, 161-2, 175, 210
glossary, 46
glossy covers, 13
glow 35, 48, 55, 96, 108, 122
glyphs, 54
Google Nexus, 182
gradient, 95-6, 106, 114
grammar, 43, 135, 138, 170
graph, 124
grayscale, 28-9
Great Britain, 103-4, 144-5, 154-5, 161-2, 172, 175,
    177, 191, 193, 210
gridlines, 110-1, 113
group, 111, 115, 122, 125, 166
guide rectangles, 87-93, 98-104, 125
Guided Setup, 167-72
guidelines, 179, 199, 210
gutter, 27

H

hardcover, 11, 13, 147, 176
headers
    eBook, 47-9
    paperback, 31
headings
    eBook, 53-4
    paperback, 35
HGTV, 211
highlighting, 35
.htm, 199
HTML, 169, 190, 199, 202
http (see hyperlinks)
hyperlink bookmarks, 51, 62-5, 205
hyperlinks
    active, 64-5, 205
    affiliate, 64
    bookmarks, 51, 62-5, 205
    cover, 205
    email, 65

external, 64-5
internal, 64
mail:to, 65

I

iBooks, 180, 182, 184, 203-6, 209
illustrations (see pictures)
illustrator, 169, 199
image compression, 58-9, 120, 123, 167, 190
image resolution, 57, 167, 186-7, 190, 201, 205
image size, 57, 130, 167, 182-7, 191-2, 202, 205
image use guidelines, 118-9
image wrap, 59, 112, 117, 122, 124-5
images (see pictures)
imprint, 155-6, 199, 202
in front of text, 59, 97, 112, 124-5
in line with text, 59, 97, 112
indents
    automatic, 51
    book description, 136, 189
    eBook, 48, 50-3
    first line, 52-3
    non-indents, 52-3
    normal style (**best method**), 53-4
    paperback, 32
    problem with tab key, 32, 50-3, 136, 189
    spacebar problem, 51
    tab key, 32, 50-3, 136, 189
InDesign, 21
index
    eBook, 49, 62-4
    paperback, 42, 46
India, 197
Ingram (distribution), 158, 166
Ingram Spark, 12
insert chart, 124
insert equation, 22, 38-9, 56, 59-62, 95
insert picture, 117-8, 120-4, 124-5
insert shapes, 106-12
insert textboxes, 48, 50-1, 93-104, 130
insert WordArt, 35-6, 44, 50-1, 56, 93-104, 130
interior formatting, 20-65, 180-1, 198
Interior Reviewer, 171
interior type, 170

internal hyperlinks, 64
internal margins, 183, 185
internet browser, 171, 199
Internet Explorer, 171, 199
introduction, 45
iPad, 180, 182, 184-5, 200, 203-6
iPhone, 180, 184-5, 200, 203-6
ISBN
    academic institutions, 159
    Baker & Taylor, 159
    Books in Print, 157
    bookstores, 155-66
    Bowker, 12, 156-7, 194, 199, 202, 211
    cover, 82, 93, 103
    CreateSpace, 12, 155-7, 159, 170, 176
    custom, 156
    custom universal, 156
    direct purchase, 156
    eBook, 194, 199, 202
    free, 156
    imprint, 155-6, 199, 202
    Kindle, 199
    libraries, 159, 162-4
    NACSCORP, 158, 166
    Smashwords, 181, 194, 199, 202-3
    warning, 170, 194, 199
italics
    eBook, 48
    paperback, 35
Italy, 144, 154, 161-2, 175, 210

J

Japan, 162, 210
JPEG conversion, 55-7, 123, 127-30
JPEG files, 55-7, 59-61, 86, 123, 127-30, 191, 199, 202, 205
justified text, 32
juvenile, 174

K

keywords, 139-43, 169, 173, 194-5, 202
    tip for special categories, 141
Kindle borrowing and lending, 193, 195-7, 200
Kindle conversion, 48-9, 65, 181
Kindle device
    6", 184
    DX, 184
    eInk, 130, 180, 184, 200
    file size limits, 57-8, 181, 186, 189-92, 199-200
    Fire, 130, 180, 182-5, 200
    Fire HD, 130, 180, 184-5, 189, 200
    for PC, 182, 185
    Keyboard, 184
    Paperwhite, 184
    Touch, 184
Kindle Direct Publishing
    community forum, 65, 197, 199, 206-7, 210
    corrections, 200
    Countdown Deal, 197
    Cover Creator, 126, 166, 172
    dashboard, 198, 201
    Digital Rights Management, 199
    file size limits, 57-8, 181, 186, 189-92, 199-200
    formatting guides, 210
    guidelines, 199, 210
    help, 65, 197, 199-200, 207, 209-10
    KDP Select, 16-7, 180, 182, 193, 195-8, 201, 206
    keywords, 194-5
        tip for special categories, 141
    Kindlegen, 186, 190
    KOLL, 195-7
    lending and borrowing, 193, 195-7, 200
    link to paperback, 178, 192-3, 198
    MatchBook, 10, 197
    .mobi, 191, 199
    Mobipocket Creator, 186, 190
    previewer, 123-4, 180-1, 187, 190-1, 200
    publishing, 180-201
    reports, 201
    revisions, 200
    step-by-step, 198-201
    support, 199-200, 206-7, 209-10

website, 209
What's This, 199
Kindle Owner's Lending Library, 195-7
Kindle previewer, 123-4, 180-1, 187, 190-1, 200
Kindle Singles, 201
Kindle store, 209
Kindlegen, 186, 190
KOLL, 195-7

L

labels, 112
laminate cover, 14
landscape
eBook, 183, 200
paperback, 26-7
languages, 154, 162, 173, 175, 199, 202
large print, 34, 156, 174, 178
Last 30 Days/Last 90 Days, 173
lawyer
commercial use, 34, 118-9
contracts, 169
copyright, 37-8, 45, 54, 118, 169, 175, 188
fair use, 37-8
fictional works, 45
image use, 118-9
law, 37-8, 45, 169, 175, 188
pen name, 169
trademark, 54, 175, 188, 199
works for hire, 169
written permission, 37-8
layout
eBook, 47-9, 130
paperback, 29-30, 167
LCCN, 162-3, 211
left aligned, 32
legal issues
commercial use, 34, 118-9
contracts, 169
copyright, 37-8, 45, 54, 118, 169, 175, 188
fair use, 37-8
fictional works, 45
image use, 118-9
law, 37-8, 45, 169, 175, 188
pen name, 169

trademark, 54, 175, 188, 199
works for hire, 169
written permission, 37-8
lending, 195-7, 200
libraries, 159, 162-4, 172, 203-6
Library of Congress, 162-3, 211
Lightning Source, 12
line art, 105-16
line breaks, 30, 49
line tool, 108-10, 113-6
linespacing
book description, 189
eBook, 53-4
enter key problem, 53-4
paperback, 33
linking multiple formats, 178, 192-3, 198
list price
eBook, 181, 189-94, 200, 202, 205
paperback, 143-55, 172
live elements, 26, 88
logo, 155
Look Inside, 134, 176
Lulu, 12

M

mail:to, 64
margins
eReader screen, 183, 185
paperback 27, 30
Mark Coker, 204, 210
marketing, 46-7, 65, 176, 178-9, 197, 203-4, 210
MatchBook, 10, 197
mathematical symbols, 36
matte covers, 13
mature content, 174
maximum file size, 57-8, 181, 186, 189-92, 199-200, 202, 204
McMullen, 212
Member Dashboard, 168, 170
memory limits, 57-8, 181, 186, 189-92, 199-200, 202, 204
memory problems, 42-3, 106
memory size, 187-92, 199-200, 202, 204
merge cells, 39

Mexico, 175
Microsoft Paint, 56-7, 105, 120, 123, 186, 191
Microsoft Surface, 182, 184-5
Microsoft Word
    advantages, 21
    alignment, 32
    autocorrect, 43, 53
    borders, 29-30, 47-9
    bullets, 33, 48, 50
    columns, 30, 51
    compress images, 58-9, 120, 123, 190
    cover design, 66-130
    cross-references, 37, 50, 205
    default settings, 33
    different versions, 21-2, 93, 105, 111, 125
    .doc/.docx files, 21-2, 42, 56, 60-1, 105, 111,
        166, 171, 190, 199, 202, 204
    drawing, 105-16
    drop caps, 34, 51-3
    eBook formatting, 47-65, 180-1
    endnotes, 36-7, 51
    equations, 38-9, 56, 59-62, 95
    font styles, 34, 48, 50, 54-5
    footers, 31, 47-9
    footnotes, 36-7, 48, 51
    headers, 31, 47-9
    headings, 35, 53-4
    help, 40
    indents, 32, 48, 50-3
    interior formatting, 20-65, 180-1
    justification, 32
    layout, 29-30, 47-9, 130, 167
    lists, 33
    margins, 27
    note for novices, 40
    page break, 30, 48, 202
    page layout, 29-30, 47-9, 130, 167
    page numbers, 31, 47-9
    page size, 25-7, 47-8, 130
    paperback formatting, 21-47
    paragraph styles, 32-3
    pictures (see pictures)
    shading, 29-30
    shapes (see shapes)
    spellcheck, 43, 135, 138, 141, 161, 170, 173,
        198
    symbols, 35, 48, 50, 54-5, 136
    tables, 39-40, 48, 51
    tabs, 32, 48, 50-3, 136, 189
    templates, 27
    textboxes (see textboxes)
    word count, 43, 135, 188, 198
    WordArt (see WordArt)
.mobi, 191, 199
Mobipocket Creator, 186, 190
moving objects, 94, 108
Mozilla Firefox, 171, 199
MySpace, 210

N

NACSCORP, 158, 166
negative review, 198
new releases, 173
Nexus, 182
Nook device
    file size limits, 57-8, 181, 186, 189-92, 202
    Nook, 130, 180-2, 184, 187, 191, 201
    Nook Classic, 184
    Nook Color, 130, 180-2, 184, 187, 201
    Nook HD, 184-5, 187
    Nook Simple Touch, 184
    Nook Tablet, 184, 187
Nook publishing
    file size limits, 57-8, 181, 186, 189-92, 202
    Nook Press, 180-2, 184, 187, 191, 193-4, 197,
        201-7, 209-10
    PubIt (see Nook Press)
normal style, 53-4
novella, 188, 192
Nuance PDF Converter Professional, 167, 211
numbered lists, 33
numbered pages
    eBook, 47-9
    paperback, 31

O

object, 38
ordered lists, 33
orientation, 183
outline (lists), 33
outline (text formatting), 35

P

page borders
    eBook, 47-9
    paperback, 29-30
page break
    eBook, 30, 48, 202
    page break tip, 30
    paperback, 30
page color, 14, 30, 170
page count, 143, 202
page footers
    eBook, 47-9
    paperback, 31
page headers
    eBook, 47-9
    paperback, 31
page layout
    eBook, 47-9, 130
    paperback, 29-30, 167
page margins
    eBook, 48
    paperback, 27, 30
page numbers
    eBook, 47-9
    paperback, 31
Page Plus, 21
page references, 36-7, 50
page size, 25-7, 130, 187-8
pages in eBooks, 47-8
pagination, 31
Paint, 56-7, 105, 120, 123, 186, 191
paper color, 14, 170
paper weight, 14
paperback formatting, 21-47

paperback quality, 14
Papyrus, 184
paragraph button, 50
paragraph styles, 32-3
paraphrasing, 37-8, 46
paste, 41, 111, 168, 170, 198
pattern, 86
PCN, 163
PDF Converter Professional, 167, 211
PDF file, 42, 123, 125-7, 166-7, 171, 181, 190, 199, 211
pen name, 169
photo viewing tip, 59
photos (see pictures)
PhotoShop, 105
picture border, 121
picture compression, 58-9, 120, 123, 190
picture effects, 122
picture resolution, 57, 186-7, 190, 201, 205
picture size, 57, 130, 182-7, 191-2, 202, 205
picture styles, 122
pictures
    artistic effects, 121
    aspect ratio, 57-8, 107, 111, 125, 130, 182-7
    background, 117-8, 120, 124-5
    bevel, 122
    book covers (see book covers)
    border, 121
    captions, 40, 112, 124
    clipart, 43-4, 118-9
    color adjust, 121
    combining images, 110-6
    compression, 58-9, 120, 123, 190
    copyright/image use, 118-9
    cropping, 121, 123
    DPI, 167
    drawing, 105-16
    eBook, 55-9, 123-4, 181-7, 205
    editing problems, 123, 182
    effects, 122
    eReaders, 181-7
    flattening, 86, 166
    flowchart, 124
    full-screen, 182-7
    glow, 122
    graph, 124
    group, 122, 125, 166

guidelines, 179, 210
insert picture, 117-8, 120-4, 124-5
JPEG conversion, 55-7, 123
Kindlegen, 186, 190
looking sideways, 183
.mobi, 191
Mobipocket Creator, 186, 190
orientation, 183
paperback, 43-4, 66-130
patterns, 86
pixel count, 57, 130, 184-187, 205
reflection, 122
reset picture, 121
resizing, 122, 125, 130, 182-7, 189-92
resolution, 57, 186-7, 190, 205
rotating, 122
sample drawings, 113-6
scan, 123-4
screen size, 183-7
screenshot, 123, 128-9
shadow, 122
shapes (see shapes)
size, 57, 130, 182-7, 191-2, 202, 205
SmartArt, 124
snipping tool, 123, 128-9
soft edges, 122
styles, 122
texture, 86
three-dimensional, 122
tone, 121
transparency, 86, 120
wrap, 59, 112, 117, 122, 124-5
pixel count, 57, 130, 184-187, 205
plagiarism, 37-8
PNG file, 56, 126, 128
POD (see print on demand)
point, 110
portrait mode, 183, 200
positioning objects, 94, 111
pounds, 103-4, 144-5, 154-5, 172, 175, 191
Preassigned Control Number, 163
preview, 123-4, 180-1, 187, 190-1, 200-2, 205
price match, 181, 191
pricing
    black-and-white interior, 28, 143-55
    color interior, 28, 143-55
    cover price, 81, 103-4

eBook, 17-8, 58, 181, 189-94, 200, 202, 205
economics, 150
Europe, 144-5, 154-5, 172, 175, 177, 191, 193
Expanded Distribution (see Expanded
    Distribution)
Great Britain, 144-5, 154-5, 172, 175, 177, 191,
    193
list price, 143-55, 172, 181, 189-94, 200, 202,
    205
paperback, 28, 143-55, 172
price match, 181, 191
royalty calculator, 144, 172
United Kingdom, 144-5, 154-5, 172, 175, 177,
    191, 193
Prime membership, 195-6
print on demand
    about, 6-10, 13-5, 132-4
    advantages, 6-8
    choosing a service, 10-3
    definition, 6
    disadvantages, 8-9
    libraries, 163, 172
    options, 13-5
    printing variations, 86-7, 176
printing tolerance, 86-7
printing variations, 86-7, 176
Professional Design Services, 170, 179
proof, 175-7
PubIt
    note about PubIt's replacement, 201
    PubIt (see Nook Press)
public domain, 38, 191, 202
publication date, 173, 199
Publish on Amazon Kindle, 210
publishing
    Amazon Kindle (see Kindle)
    author biography, 138-9, 173, 179, 188-9, 202,
        211-2
    book blurb, 81-2, 103, 134-7, 169, 187-9, 198,
        202
    book covers (see book covers)
    bookstores, 15-6, 157-66, 172
    categories, 139-43, 173-4, 195, 202
        tip for special categories, 141
    CreateSpace, 6-16, 132-79
    eBook, 180-207
    how to, 131-207

Ingram Spark, 12
interior, 20-65
ISBN, 12, 82, 93, 103, 155-7, 159, 176, 181, 194, 202-3, 211
keywords, 139-43, 169, 173, 194-5, 202
    tip for special categories, 141
Kindle Direct Publishing (see Kindle)
Kobo, 182, 184, 194, 197, 203-6, 209
libraries, 159, 162-4, 172, 203-6
Lightning Source, 12
Lulu, 12
Nook Press, 180-2, 184, 187, 191, 193-4, 197, 201-7, 209-10
options, 13-5
paperback, 132-179
print on demand, 6-10, 13-5, 163
PubIt (see Nook Press)
rights, 199-200, 202
self-publishing, 6-9, 13-5, 131-207
Smashwords, 180-2, 194, 197, 199, 201-7, 209-10
Sony, 180-1, 184, 194, 197, 203-6, 209
title/subtitle, 81, 98-104, 139-43, 168, 175-6, 179, 188, 194, 198, 201-2, 204
traditional, 6-9
vanity, 12
pyramid, 115

Q

quotation marks
    curly, 51
    eBook, 51
    paperback, 37-8
    straight, 51
quotes
    eBook, 51
    paperback, 37-8

R

rank, 173, 176, 192, 196
redo, 41, 108
references, 36-8, 46
reflection, 35, 96, 108, 122
reproducing objects, 111
reset picture, 121
resizing objects, 58, 94-5, 107, 111, 122, 125, 130
resolution, 57, 186-7, 190, 205
resources, 209-11
reveal formatting, 50
review files, 174
review options, 43
reviews, 136, 196, 198, 200
revisions, 200
RGB, 84-6, 105
RGB values, 85
rich text file, 166, 171, 199, 202
right aligned, 32
rotating objects, 95-6, 107, 111, 113-5, 122
royalties
    Amazon, 143-4, 172, 189-94, 200-1
    author cost, 143-5, 172
    black-and-white interior, 28, 143-55, 172
    calculator, 144, 172
    color interior, 28, 143-55, 172
    CreateSpace, 28, 143-55, 172
    delays, 161, 178
    delivery fee, 58, 189-92
    eBook, 58, 189-94, 200-1
    economics, 150
    eStore, 144, 162
    Europe, 144-5, 154-5, 172, 175, 177, 191, 193
    Expanded Distribution, 143-4, 146, 148-50, 152, 157, 160, 172, 176, 178
    Great Britain, 144-5, 154-5, 172, 175, 177, 191, 193
    Kindle (see Kindle)
    list price, 143-55, 172, 181, 189-94, 200, 202, 205
    minimum threshold, 175
    Nook, 201
    paperback, 28, 143-55, 172
    reports, 177-8, 201, 204

Smashwords, 204
United Kingdom, 144-5, 154-5, 172, 175, 177, 191, 193
royalty calculator, 144, 172
royalty delays, 161, 178
royalty reports, 177-8, 201, 204
.rtf file, 166, 171, 199, 202

S

sales rank, 173, 176, 192, 196
sales reports, 177, 201, 203, 206
sample covers, 68-80
sample drawings, 113-6
Samsung
Galaxy, 182
Papyrus, 184
saving your file
backups, 41-2
CreateSpace, 168, 170-1
.doc versus .docx, 21-2, 42, 56, 60-1, 190, 199, 202, 204
embedding fonts, 167
file corruption, 42-3, 106
Kindle, 200
memory problems, 42-3, 106
PDF conversion, 42, 123, 125-7, 166-7, 171, 190, 211
problem with .doc submission, 166-7, 204
save as draft, 200
scan, 123-4
screen size, 183-7
screenshot, 123, 128-9
scribble tool, 110
Search Inside, 45, 134, 176
search keywords, 139-43, 169, 173, 194-5, 202
tip for special categories, 141
second category, 174, 195
section breaks, 30, 54
Select (KDP), 16-7, 180, 182, 193, 195-8, 201, 206
selecting objects, 94, 106, 166
selection pane, 100-1, 125
self-publishing
advantages, 6-8
Amazon Kindle (see Kindle)

author biography, 138-9, 173, 179, 188-9, 202, 211-2
book blurb, 81-2, 103, 134-7, 169, 187-9, 198, 202
book covers (see book covers)
bookstores, 15-6, 157-66, 172
categories, 139-43, 173-4, 195, 202
tip for special categories, 141
concept, 6
CreateSpace, 6-16, 132-79
disadvantages, 8-9
eBook, 180-207
how to, 131-207
Ingram Spark, 12
interior, 20-65
ISBN, 12, 82, 93, 103, 155-7, 159, 176, 181, 194, 202-3, 211
keywords, 139-43, 169, 173, 194-5, 202
tip for special categories, 141
Kindle Direct Publishing (see Kindle)
Kobo, 182, 184, 194, 197, 203-6, 209
libraries, 159, 162-4, 172, 203-6
Lightning Source, 12
Lulu, 12
Nook Press, 180-2, 184, 187, 191, 193-4, 197, 201-7, 209-10
options, 13-5
paperback, 132-79
PubIt (see Nook Press)
Smashwords, 180-2, 194, 197, 199, 201-7, 209-10
Sony, 180-1, 184, 194, 197, 203-6, 209
title/subtitle, 81, 98-104, 139-43, 168, 175-6, 179, 188, 194, 198, 201-2, 204
vanity press, 12
series, 169, 197-8, 202
Serif Page Plus, 21
services,
conversion, 48-9, 65, 181
cover design, 126-7, 171, 179
CreateSpace, 15, 47-9, 65, 126-7, 134, 179, 181
eBook, 48-9, 65
editing, 47, 65, 170, 179
formatting, 47-9, 65, 126-7, 170, 179
marketing, 179
translation, 154, 175

Index

shading, 33
shadow, 35, 96, 108, 114, 122
shape effects, 97, 108
shape fill, 95-7, 105-6, 109, 114-5
shape outline, 95-7, 105-6, 109, 114-5
shapes
    add point, 108
    align, 110-1, 122, 124-5
    arcs, 109, 113-6
    arrows, 108-10, 114-6
    aspect ratio, 107, 111, 125, 130, 182-7
    bevel, 108, 122
    bring forward/backward, 111
    can, 114
    centering, 110
    combining images, 110-6
    cube, 113, 115
    curves, 108-10, 114, 116
    cylinder, 114
    delete point, 108
    depth, 108, 114
    distribute, 111
    dot, 110
    dragging, 107-9, 113
    edit points, 108, 113, 116
    edit shape, 96, 106, 108
    effects, 97
    fill color, 95-7, 105
    freeform, 110
    glow, 108, 122
    gradient, 106, 114
    gridlines, 110-1, 113
    group, 111, 115, 122, 125, 166
    lines, 108-10, 113-6
    middle, 110
    moving, 108
    outline color, 95-7, 105
    point, 110
    positioning, 111
    pyramid, 115
    reflection, 108, 122
    reproducing, 111
    resizing, 107, 109, 111, 122, 125, 130
    rotating, 107-8, 111, 113-5, 122
    sample drawings, 113-6
    scribble, 110
    selecting, 106, 166

    shadow, 108, 114, 122
    shape effects, 108
    shape fill/outline, 106, 109, 114-5
    snap objects, 111
    soft edges, 108, 122
    sphere, 113-4
    three-dimensional, 108, 113-5, 122
    ungroup, 111, 124-5
    wrap text, 112, 117, 122, 124-5
shift enter, 44
short stories, 188
size, 58, 94-5, 107, 130, 182-7, 191-2
SmartArt, 124
Smashwords, 180-2, 194, 197, 199, 201-7, 209-10
snap objects, 111
snipping tool, 123, 128-9
social media, 210-1
social security number, 175
soft edges, 108, 122
Sony Reader, 180-2, 184, 194, 197, 203-6, 209
sources, 37-8, 46
spacing after, 33
Spain, 144, 154, 161-2, 175, 210
special characters
    book description, 136
    eBook, 48, 50, 54-5
    paperback, 36, 110
special edition note, 205
Special Offers, 148, 154, 160
spellcheck, 43, 135, 138, 141, 161, 170, 173, 198
sphere, 113-4
spine text, 14, 81, 87, 102-3
spine width, 87
split cells, 39
square (wrap), 112
stagger, 99
starburst, 101-2
straight quotes, 51
strikethrough
    eBook, 48
    paperback, 35
style guide, 204-5, 210
styles, 36, 53-4
submit files for review, 174
subscript
    eBook, 48, 55, 202
    paperback, 36

subtitle, 101, 139-43, 168, 175-6, 179, 194, 198
Super Saver Shipping, 148-50, 154, 160-1, 195-6
superscript
    eBook, 48, 55
    paperback, 36
support, 134, 167, 174, 199-200, 204, 206-7, 209-10
Surface, 182, 184-5
symbols
    book description, 136
    eBook, 48, 50, 54-5
    paperback, 36, 110

T

table of contents
    bookmarks (**best method**), 62-4
    eBook, 49, 62-3, 205
    paperback, 45
    table of contents tool, 62-3
tables
    captions, 40
    eBook, 48, 51, 181, 190, 201
    formatting, 39-40
tablet, 182, 184-5
tabs
    automatic, 51
    book description, 136, 189
    eBook, 48, 50-3
    first line, 52-3
    non-indents, 52-3
    normal style (**best method**), 53
    paperback, 32
    problem with tab key, 32, 50-3, 136, 189
    spacebar problem, 51
    tab key, 32, 50-3, 136, 189
tax ID number, 165
tax information, 175
teen, 174
templates, 27, 126
territories, 200, 202
text effects, 35, 55, 96-7
text file, 199, 202
text fill, 95-7
text outline, 95-7
text wrap, 50-1, 97-8, 112, 117, 122, 124-5

textboxes
    bevel, 96
    cover, 99-104
    dashes, 96
    dragging, 94
    eBook, 48, 50-1
    follow path, 96-7
    glow, 96
    gradient, 95-6
    labels, 112, 114-5, 122, 130
    moving, 94
    paperback, 93-98
    positioning, 94
    reflection, 96
    resizing, 94-5, 130
    rotating, 95-6
    selecting, 94, 100-1
    shadow, 96
    shape fill/outline, 95-7
    starburst, 101-2
    text effects, 96-7
    text fill/outline, 95-7
    three-dimensional, 96
    warped, 97
    wrap text, 97-8
texture, 86
thank you note, 65
third-party sellers, 132, 143, 150, 158-60, 176
three-dimensional, 96, 108, 113-5, 122
thumbnail, 82-4, 100, 125, 127-30
TIFF file, 128-9, 199
title, 81, 98-104, 139-43, 168, 175-6, 179, 188, 194, 198, 201-2, 204
title page, 44
tone, 121
trademark, 175, 188, 199
trademark symbol, 54
traditional publishing
    advantages, 8-9
    disadvantages, 6-8
    how to, 11
translation, 154, 175
transparency, 86, 120
trim size
    cover, 87-8, 117
    distribution note, 170
    interior, 23-5, 170

Twitter, 210-2
.txt file, 199, 202

U

underline
    eBook, 48, 54
    paperback, 35
undo, 41, 108
ungroup, 111, 124-5
United Kingdom, 103-4, 144-5, 154-5, 161-2, 172,
    175, 177, 191, 193, 210
unordered lists, 33
unpublished, 198
unsupported characters, 54-5
upc, 82, 93, 103
updates, 200
url (see hyperlinks)

V

value-added tax, 161, 191
vanity press, 12
VAT, 161, 191
versions of Word, 21-2, 93, 105, 111, 125
view, 41, 98, 125, 130
volume number, 169, 190, 197-8

W

warped text, 96-7
web browser, 171, 199
Webdings, 36
websites, 209-11
What's This, 168, 174, 199
white paper, 14, 170
wholesalers, 158
Wingdings, 36
word count, 43, 135, 188, 198
Word, Microsoft
    (see Microsoft Word)

WordArt
    bevel, 96
    cover, 99-104
    dashes, 96
    dragging, 94
    eBook, 35-6, 44, 93-98
    follow path, 96-7
    glow, 96
    gradient, 95-6
    labels, 112, 114-5, 122, 130
    moving, 94
    paperback, 50-1, 56
    positioning, 94
    reflection, 96
    resizing, 94-5, 130
    rotating, 95-6
    selecting, 94, 100-1
    shadow, 96
    shape fill/outline, 95-7
    starburst, 101-2
    text effects, 96-7
    text fill/outline, 95-7
    three-dimensional, 96
    warped, 96-7
    wrap text, 97-8
WordPress, 211-2
works for hire, 169
wrap image, 59, 112, 117, 122, 124-5
wrap text, 50-1, 97-8, 112
written permission, 37-8

Z

zip file, 199
zoom, 41, 59, 98, 125, 130

Made in the USA
San Bernardino, CA
06 June 2014